THE
WRITER'S
OPTIONS

THE WRITER'S OPTIONS

Combining to Composing

THIRD EDITION

Donald A. Daiker
Andrew Kerek
Max Morenberg

Miami University
Oxford, Ohio

1817

HARPER & ROW, PUBLISHERS, New York

Cambridge, Philadelphia, San Francisco,
London, Mexico City, São Paulo, Singapore, Sydney

Sponsoring Editor: Phillip Leininger
Project Editor: Eleanor Castellano
Text Design: North 7 Atelier
Cover Design: 20/20 Services Inc.
Text Art: Fineline Illustrations
Production Manager: Jeanie Berke
Compositor: ComCom Division of Haddon Craftsmen, Inc.
Printer and Binder: R. R. Donnelley & Sons Company

THE WRITER'S OPTIONS: Combining to Composing, Third Edition

Library of Congress Cataloging-in-Publication Data

Daiker, Donald A., 1938–
    The writer's options.

    Includes index.
    1. English language—Rhetoric. I. Kerek, Andrew, 1936– .
II. Morenberg, Max, 1940– . III. Title.
PE1408.D13 1986   808'.042   85-17627
ISBN 0-06-041478-2

85 86 87 88 9 8 7 6 5 4 3 2 1

CONTENTS IN BRIEF

CONTENTS IN DETAIL

PREFACE

The third edition of *The Writer's Options: Combining to Composing* continues the movement of the second edition toward greater emphasis on the rhetorical and contextual elements of the combining and composing process.

The three units brand new to this edition—on discovering and generating ideas, on using details, and on revision—all focus on segments of discourse larger than the sentence and thus make clear that the strategies of sentence combining apply to the paragraph and essay as well as to the discrete sentence. *The Writer's Options* is now organized into three distinct but related sections: sentence strategies, paragraph strategies, and discourse strategies. In addition to the three new units and a new structure, the unit introductions have been revised, in some cases extensively, and the exercises themselves—still the heart of the book—have been updated and polished. For many of the whole-discourse exercises, the instructions have been rewritten so as to specify aim and audience. The central purpose of these changes is to give students increased control over the options available to them as writers.

The Writer's Options grows out of work in sentence combining and syntax by Kellogg W. Hunt, Francis Christensen, John C. Mellon, and William Strong, and—even more directly—out of research made possible by the Exxon Education Foundation. This research suggests that sentence combining practiced within a rhetorical context significantly improves the quality of student writing.

Almost 300 Miami University freshmen participated during the fall of 1976 in a controlled research study designed to test the relative effectiveness of two teaching methods in improving writing quality. Half these students, following what has become known as the current-traditional approach, read and analyzed essays from a college reader and worked closely with a standard college rhetoric. The other half approached all aspects of writing, from diction and sentence structure to tone, coherence, and thesis development, exclusively through practice in sentence combining. After 15 weeks, the sentence-combining students wrote original compositions that a panel of 26 experienced college composition teachers judged to be superior in quality—at a statistically significant level—to the compositions of the conventionally trained students.

A follow-up study suggests that the improvement in writing developed through a sentence-combining curriculum is permanent. Two years later, although the difference between the two groups had diminished, the sentence-combining students retained the level of writing quality that they had achieved earlier.

The achievement of students trained in rhetorically based sentence combining encouraged us to write a textbook that would emphasize—through combining exercises that vary in length, format, and focus—the wide range of options open to writers. We accepted Robert M. Gorrell's definition of *rhetoric* as "the art of making choices among available means of discourse," and we tried to create exercises that help students recognize their options and choose wisely from among them. For this reason, *The Writer's Options* includes exercises that help students learn to control structures like participles, appositives, absolutes, and subordinate clauses; to employ strategies of coherence, emphasis, and rearrangement; and even to generate ideas, select and organize material, and develop a clearly defined central idea. Throughout the book, the combining exercises consistently move beyond the sentence to provide the larger context of a paragraph or essay. On the other hand, while the focus is on exploring options, a number of exercises encourage students not to make longer sentences out of shorter ones but to simplify and shorten sentences that have become too long and unwieldy. After all, "not to combine" is one of the writer's major options. Despite their variety, the exercises are alike in providing students with the disciplined writing practice that helps to develop writing skills and to build confidence.

Because any significant element of composition can be taught through sentence-combining exercises that are used along with original student writing, *The Writer's Options* can serve as the sole textbook in a writing course, or it can be used with other texts. *The Instructor's Manual for The Writer's Options,* available from Harper & Row, includes sample syllabi for both arrangements. In either case, the book contains more exercises than can be covered in a term, so teachers have a wide range of options in making assignments.

* * *

In making this book, others have helped considerably. Some of the exercises were written by Nancy Herr, Dennis Herron, Beth Neman, Diane Onken, Susan Russell, Janet Ziegler, and especially Mark Holland, Russ Reising, Mike Shea, and John Streamas. In revising these exercises, we have been guided by advice from our colleagues Paul V. Anderson, Richard D. Erlich, Patricia Harkin, Mary Fuller Hayes, Frank Jordan, Jr., James J. Sosnoski, Edward L. Tomarken, Randolph L. Wadsworth, and Jack E. Wallace. For their insightful comments on our work, we are grateful to Robert L. Brown of the University of Minnesota; John P. Clifford of the University of North Carolina at Wilmington; Richard L. Larson of Herbert H. Lehman College of the City University of New York; Elisabeth McPherson, formerly of Lake Forrest Community College; Jack Selzer of the Pennsylvania State University, and William Stull of the University of Hartford.

We remain indebted to our friend and typist, Betty Marak, and to our friend and editor, Phil Leininger.

Donald A. Daiker
Andrew Kerek
Max Morenberg

INTRODUCTION

The purpose of *The Writer's Options* is to help you become a better writer.

In order to help your writing improve, *The Writer's Options* is organized around a series of combining exercises that provide you with disciplined writing practice. In fact, one of the assumptions that guides this book is that the most direct way to improve writing is to practice writing. Studying grammar, analyzing essays, and reading books about writing—all these may be useful activities, but they are not the most efficient way to become a better writer. *Writing* is. The book's second major assumption is that writing improvement occurs when you learn to recognize the writing options open to you and then to choose, in context, the one that is most appropriate.

The exercises in *The Writer's Options* are designed to extend your control over an increasingly large number of sentence structures, paragraph patterns, and broader writing strategies. But at the same time, most of the exercises provide a specific context for testing the appropriateness of whichever structures, patterns, or strategies you choose. So the exercises work in three direct ways to help improve your writing: they give you actual practice in writing sentences, paragraphs, and essays; they help you master new constructions; and they encourage you to make writing decisions in terms of context and purpose. And because there are usually no right or wrong answers, the exercises invite you to play with words and phrases, to experiment with language, to explore new and exciting ways of expressing your feelings and ideas.

In doing the exercises, as in writing the original compositions that you will submit to your instructor, you will always have choices to make. For example, the first combining exercise in the book asks you to combine the following four sentences as the conclusion of a short descriptive paragraph about hockey:

The referee blew his whistle.
The referee called to the team captains.
The referee dropped the puck.
The referee began the game.

Perhaps the simplest way to combine the four sentences is this:

The referee blew his whistle, called to the team captains, dropped the puck, and began the game.

But you have other options as well:

The referee blew his whistle, called to the team captains, and then dropped the puck to begin the game.
After blowing his whistle and calling to the team captains, the referee dropped the puck and began the game.
The referee blew his whistle and, calling to the team captains, dropped the puck to begin the game.
The game began after the referee blew his whistle, called to the team captains, and dropped the puck.

If you tried, you could probably make several more sentences from the original four. Your ability to create a number of longer, more complex sentences from four shorter ones indicates that you have already learned many important writing skills. It also shows that the English language enables you to express essentially the same information in a variety of different ways. Sentence-combining exercises build upon your writing skills to help you develop new writing options.

But sentence-combining exercises, despite their name, do not always require that you combine shorter sentences into longer ones. Long, complex sentences are often appropriate, but so are short, simple sentences. For example, you can rewrite the four sentences about hockey like this:

> After blowing his whistle, the referee called to the team captains and dropped the puck. The game began.

The sentence "The game began," shorter and less complex than any of the original four, illustrates that you always have the option of not combining. Indeed, your writing is most likely to improve if you consider all your options and if you do the exercises creatively rather than mechanically. Since there is no one correct answer for any exercise, don't worry whether your version is the right one. Instead, try to respond to the exercises as if they were a game in which you occasionally take risks and experiment with different moves. Don't be afraid to substitute words, rearrange sentences, or even add details whenever such changes make your writing clearer or more interesting. To give more excitement to your sentences about hockey, you might rewrite them this way:

> After blowing his whistle and calling to the team captains, the referee dropped the puck between two slashing sticks. The game was on.

If you do the exercises carefully and creatively and then consciously use in your own writing the same structures, patterns, and strategies, you can expect to become a better writer. A research study at Miami University showed that freshman composition students who practiced combining exercises for a semester wrote papers that college instructors graded higher than those written by students who had not practiced sentence combining. This study strongly suggests that the writing skills you develop by working out the exercises, and by comparing your versions to those of your classmates and instructor, will transfer to your actual writing. Constructing exercise sentences with participial or appositive phrases helps you use the same structures effectively in your own compositions. Building well-organized and coherent exercise paragraphs helps the organization and coherence of your own paragraphs. As you can see, doing the exercises is only a means to an end. The end is improved writing. The real test of improvement will come in the original compositions assigned by your instructor. They will demonstrate how fully the writing skills developed through the exercises transfer to the writing that really counts. Few things in a student's life are certain, but if you consciously use in your compositions the writing strategies you practice in the exercises, it's a good bet that you'll become a much better writer. Your instructor will probably think so too.

The Writer's Options is organized into three main parts: "Sentence Strategies," "Paragraph Strategies," and "Discourse Strategies." The units in "Sentence Strategies" give you practice in writing specific kinds of sentences—sentences that illustrate constructions often found in effective prose. But at the same time that you're building sentences that include structures like absolutes and appositives, participial phrases and noun substitutes, you'll also be incorporating such sentences into paragraphs and entire essays. So even when you're dealing with sentence strategies, you will write sentences not in isolation but as part of a larger whole. In "Paragraph Strategies," the second part of the book, the exercises focus on the writer's options in constructing paragraphs, including strategies of coherence, rearrangement, repetition, emphasis, tone, and paragraph patterning. "Discourse Strategies," the book's third part, deals with the processes of writing entire essays, such as generating, selecting, and organizing ideas, adding details, and revising.

Most of the 19 units of *The Writer's Options* consist of an introductory section followed by a series of exercises. The introduction explains a sentence, paragraph, or discourse strategy and illustrates its use. But the essence of each unit—and of the whole book—is the exercises: they give you active practice in composing and revising.

The whole-discourse exercises—those with titles like "Blind Date," "Dracula," and "American Graffiti"—are especially important because they ask you to combine sets of short sentences into paragraphs or essays, and thus they provide a specific context for your combining practice.

The whole-discourse exercises alternate with other types of exercises that help you practice basic sentence patterns, creative patterns, and various constructing or revising strategies. By working out the basic "constructing" exercise before doing the first whole-discourse exercise in any unit, you can test your mastery of that strategy. If you cannot do the basic exercise, this is a good place to stop. Try rereading the introductory section or raising questions in class.

The creating exercises take you one step further. They ask you to complete or to expand sentences by adding facts or ideas of your own, following the construction or strategy practiced in the unit. In this way, the creative pattern exercises help you create constructions on your own and thus encourage you to transfer your selecting and combining skills into actual writing. Additional kinds of exercises both add variety to the book and provide practice with different writing tasks.

Here is a short whole-discourse exercise like those you'll sometimes be given as a homework assignment. The instructions are simply to construct an effective paragraph from the given sentences. The spaces between groups of sentences indicate where one of your sentences may end and another may begin, but you may ignore the spaces whenever you choose.

HYPNOTISM

1. Franz Mesmer was a physician.
2. Franz Mesmer was from Germany.
3. Franz Mesmer invented hypnotism.
4. Hypnotism was invented in the eighteenth century.

5. Hypnotism remained an amusing gimmick.
6. It remained a gimmick for over a century.
7. The gimmick was for nightclub acts.
8. The gimmick was for parlor games.

9. Physicians now use hypnotism.
10. Dentists now use hypnotism.
11. Psychiatrists now use hypnotism.
12. Hypnotism is used to treat various ailments.
13. Hypnotism is used to control chronic pain.
14. Hypnotism is used as a replacement for anesthesia.

In constructing a paragraph from these sentences, you're likely to be most successful if you follow three suggestions. First, go slow. The easiest way to put sentences together is not always the best. Second, experiment with different combinations. See what happens when you rephrase or reorder parts of sentences and when you shift sentences within the paragraph. Only by experimenting will you increase your writing options, and only by increasing your options will you extend your power over language. Third—and this is most important of all—listen to what you have written. As you are writing out different combinations, sound them out as well. Because you've listened to many more sentences than you've read, your ear is often a better judge than your eye.

After you've constructed several versions of "Hypnotism" and then chosen the best of them, your instructor may ask three or four students to write their completed paragraphs on the blackboard or to submit them before class so that they can be duplicated and distributed. The paragraphs may look something like these:

1. Franz Mesmer was a physician from Germany. He invented hypnotism in the eighteenth century. Hypnotism remained an amusing gimmick for over a century. It was used for nightclub acts and parlor games. Physicians, dentists, and psychiatrists now use hypnotism. It is used to treat various ailments, to manage chronic pain, and as a replacement for anesthesia.

2. Franz Mesmer, a German physician, invented hypnotism in the eighteenth century. But for over a century it remained an amusing gimmick for nightclub acts and parlor games. Physicians, dentists, and psychiatrists now use it to treat various ailments, to manage chronic pain, and to replace anesthesia.

3. Hypnotism was invented by the German physician Franz Mesmer in the eighteenth century. Yet for over a hundred years it remained merely an amusing gimmick for nightclub entertainers and party hosts. Now physicians, dentists, and psychiatrists use it not only to replace anesthesia but to manage chronic pain and to treat various ailments.

4. Although hypnotism, which was invented in the eighteenth century by the German physician Franz Mesmer, remained an amusing gimmick for nightclub acts and parlor games for over a century, it is now used by physicians, dentists, and psychiatrists to treat various ailments, control chronic pain, and replace anesthesia.

Once the four paragraphs have been read aloud so that the differences among them can be heard as well as seen, your class can begin discussing those differences. It's likely that discussion will begin with students either praising versions 2 and 3 or voicing reservations about version 1. There is, of course, nothing "wrong" with version 1: it is clear, grammatically correct, and free from common writing errors. But it sounds dull in comparison to the other versions. It is also the longest and most repetitive of the four versions. What accounts for its dullness? For one thing, every sentence in version 1 is approximately the same length. For another, each sentence follows the same order, beginning with the subject, which is immediately followed by the predicate. Although the English language provides writers with many ways of varying sentence length and order, the writer of paragraph 1 has not taken advantage of them.

Now compare the beginnings of paragraphs 1 and 2:

1. Franz Mesmer was a physician from Germany. He invented hypnotism in the eighteenth century.

2. Franz Mesmer, a German physician, invented hypnotism in the eighteenth century.

One difference between the two versions is that 2 is three words shorter than 1, yet at least as clear and informative. How has the writer of version 2 managed to say in 11 words what took 14 words in version 1? First, she made the phrase "from Germany" into the single word "German." Then she combined the two sentences "Franz Mesmer was a German physician" and "Franz Mesmer invented hypnotism in the eighteenth century" into the single sentence "Franz Mesmer, a German physician, invented hypnotism in the eighteenth century." To make this combination, she shortened the full sentence "Franz Mesmer was a German physician" to the phrase "a German physician." Through such changes, the writer of version 2 made her sentence not only more concise but also more focused. That is, her sentence makes clear to the reader that Mesmer's invention of hypnosis is a more important fact than his having been a German physician. By contrast, the sentences in version 1 make those two facts seem equally important. The options you choose will often affect the meaning you convey.

The writer of version 3 made use of still another option. He changed the order of his first sentence to make "hypnotism," instead of "Franz Mesmer," its subject and first word. By doing so, he seems to be indicating to the reader that he regards "hypnotism" as the more important term. Do you think this change is an effective one? As you discuss this question, others will arise. Do the paragraphs become more coherent when their second sentence begins with a connecting word like "but" or "yet"? Why has the writer of version 3 substituted the phrase "over a hundred years" for "over a century"? Why has he added the word "merely" before "an amusing gimmick"? Which of the paragraphs ends most successfully? How effective is version 4, which consists of a single sentence? Why do you find it more or less effective than the other versions? Discussing questions such as these with your classmates and instructor will increase your awareness of the possibilities open to you as a writer. It will also help you become more sensitive to those options that work best in specific contexts.

You are likely to gain most from the combining exercises if you at least occasionally approach them in the spirit of play. Look on the exercises as a kind of game and you'll be more willing to take risks and to try new ways of expressing yourself. See if you don't sometimes have fun in substituting one word for another, in manipulating phrases and clauses, and in changing the position of sentences. But aside from the fun, what you'll find is that the more you play with language, the more you will be able to control it. And that's the ultimate purpose of this book: to help you become a better writer by teaching you to control the vital sentence, paragraph, and discourse strategies of written language.

*part***ONE**

SENTENCE
STRATEGIES

unit*1*
WARM-UPS

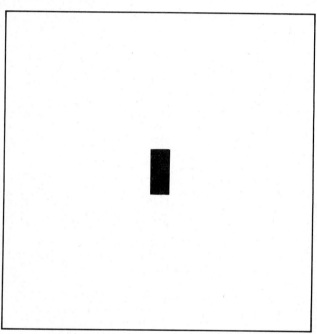

OPENING FACE-OFF

Combine the following sentences into a paragraph that describes the opening of a hockey game. The spaces between the groups of sentences indicate where one of your sentences may end and another may begin. But you may ignore the spaces if you choose in order to make sentences either larger or smaller.

1. The fans leaned forward.
2. The fans were eager.
3. The players leaned forward.
4. The players were eager.

5. The referee skated to center ice.
6. He was going to drop the puck.
7. The colors of the players' uniforms reflected from the surface of the ice.
8. The surface was glassy.
9. The ice was newly made.

10. The referee blew his whistle.
11. The referee called to the team captains.
12. The referee dropped the puck.
13. The referee began the game.

HOW TO GET AHEAD

Combine the sentences below into a story that conveys the humor created when a young man has to think on his feet in order to get out of a sticky situation.

1. A woman shuffled up to Bill.
2. The woman was pudgy.
3. Bill worked as a clerk at a supermarket.

4. The woman asked Bill about the price of lettuce.
5. Bill told the woman that lettuce cost 99¢ a head.

6. The woman complained.
7. She said the lettuce would spoil before she could eat all of it.
8. She said she wanted only half a head.

9. Bill said, "I can't sell you half a head of lettuce."
10. Even after this, she asked again.
11. Then she demanded to see the store manager.

12. Bill rolled his eyes.
13. Bill stalked to the back office to tell his boss.
14. Bill didn't realize something.
15. The woman was following him.

16. "Sorry to bother you, Ms. Hayes," Bill said to his boss.
17. "But some idiot woman wants to buy half a head of lettuce."
18. Bill turned around.
19. Bill pointed to the front of the store.

20. Then Bill saw something.
21. The woman was right behind him.

22. "And this nice lady wants to buy the other half," Bill said.

DELUXE PIZZA

Combine the sentences below into an appetizing description of a pizza. If you choose, you may add details to make the description more vivid.

1. The pizza sits in the middle of the table.
2. It is fresh from the oven.

3. Its crust rises up.
4. The crust is thick.
5. The crust is golden brown.
6. It is like a wall.
7. The wall surrounds the rest of the ingredients.

8. The sauce steams.
9. The sauce bubbles.
10. Its smell fills the room.
11. The smell is slightly sweet.

12. The pizza is covered with pepperoni slices.
13. They are shiny.
14. They are dappled.
15. They contrast with the sauce.
16. The sauce is dull red.

17. Mushroom slices rest in the sauce.
18. The slices are shriveled.

19. The slices are soft.
20. Their edges are slightly curved.

21. Green olives are scattered about.
22. Black olives are scattered about.
23. They dot the surface.

24. Cheese melts over the pizza.
25. The cheese is creamy.
26. It enmeshes everything in its weblike strands.
27. They trap the taste until someone releases them with a bite.

CABLE CAR

Combine the following sentences into a narrative that shows what happens on a cable car trip to Fisherman's Wharf in San Francisco.

1. The cable car approaches.
2. It is empty.
3. It clangs its bell.
4. It sways as though slightly drunk.

5. The brakes grind.
6. The grinding is harsh.
7. The grinding is metallic.
8. The grinding drowns out the babbling of the people.
9. The people are waiting in line.

10. Most of them are tourists.
11. They are adorned with sunglasses.
12. They are adorned with cameras.
13. They press to secure a good view.
14. The pressing is excited.

15. One man refuses to move.
16. He has a good vantage point.
17. He is fatter than the rest.

18. He angers the other passengers.
19. He forces them to squeeze past his hulking frame.

20. The tourists are all crammed inside.
21. Then the cable car lurches from the station.
22. The lurching is awkward.
23. The cable car heads down to Fisherman's Wharf.

24. At Fisherman's Wharf it will pick up another batch of passengers.
25. The passengers will be impatient.
26. It will struggle back up the hill.

THE SUBWAY

Combine the following sentences into a narrative that captures the tension felt by five people forced by circumstance onto a subway car together. You may add details to heighten the tension if you choose.

1. The subway train pulled out of the station.
2. The train hissed and screamed as it entered the darkness of the tunnel.
3. The station was grimy and graffiti covered.

4. The third car held five people.
5. They were forced by circumstance into a tense and intimate situation.
6. The five were an old woman, her granddaughter, a middle-aged man, and two young men.

7. The old woman glanced repeatedly at the young men.
8. The old woman tightly clutched an oversized pocketbook to her body.
9. The old woman only half-listened to her granddaughter talk excitedly of their outing.
10. The young men were leather-clad.
11. The young men looked tough.

12. One of the young men stared out the window into the darkness.
13. He was amused by the girl's animated movements.
14. He tried to avoid her grandmother's glances.

15. The other young man studied the familiar ads above the windows.
16. His head was bobbing to the rhythm of the train.

17. The middle-aged man held a newspaper open to the business section.
18. He concentrated on the small print of the stock-market report.
19. He acted as if he could hide within the paper's comforting folds.

20. The scene outside brightened.
21. This happened when the train came to a halt at the next station.
22. It was screeching with the high-pitched sound of metal resisting metal.

23. Then the train filled with people.
24. This offered the unwilling intimates the safety and privacy of a crowd.

"POLLY WANNA RITZ?"

Combine the sentences below into an explanation of why people use brand names rather than generic terms for popular items.

1. You sneeze.
2. Afterwards, do you ask for a facial tissue?

3. You cut yourself.
4. Then do you call out for a plastic bandage?

5. You burn yourself.
6. After that do you ask for white petroleum jelly?

7. If you do, people may look at you strangely.

8. Most people would ask for Kleenex.
9. Most people would ask for Band-Aids.
10. Most people would ask for Vaseline.
11. Kleenex, Band-Aids, and Vaseline are only brand names.

12. Kleenex, Band-Aids, and Vaseline and other brands are so well-known.
13. Kleenex, Band-Aids, and Vaseline and other brands are so influential.
14. The brand names Kleenex, Band-Aids, and Vaseline have replaced generic names.
15. The generic names are less familiar.
16. The generic names are more awkward.

17. This process has been going on for decades.
18. That is why your grandparents may refer to refrigerators as Frigidaires.
19. That is why your grandparents may refer to men's underwear as B.V.D.'s.

20. So now you know this.
21. Why do people knit their brows when you say you want to buy denim jeans?
22. Why do people knit their brows when you say you want to play table tennis?
23. Why do people knit their brows when you say you want to consume a gelatin dessert?

unit *2*
RELATIVE CLAUSES

An experienced basketball player like Larry Bird or Magic Johnson has a number of moves for any game situation. If he receives the ball near the foul line, for example, his moves include shooting, faking a pass and then shooting, driving left, driving right, passing off, and calling for a time out. Which of these moves the player actually chooses depends on the situation: the score of the game, the time remaining on the game and shot clock, the defensive alignment, the positions of his teammates, the foul situation, and other factors.

Experienced writers have moves, too. Which move or strategy they choose also depends on the situation—primarily on their purpose in writing and their audience. But in any given situation, more experienced writers have more moves or strategies available to them.

They have more options. One major aim of this book is to give you the experience to develop a series of new writing moves or strategies and to suggest ways of choosing among them in specific writing situations.

Constructing a Relative Clause

One useful move is called the RELATIVE CLAUSE. You construct a relative clause by replacing a noun or noun phrase with a pronoun like **which, that, who, whom,** and **whose.** For example, the following two sentences

> The Cro-Magnons developed a spear-throwing device. The spear-throwing device improved the range of their weapons by 30 yards.

can be made into a single sentence with a relative clause. To do so, just replace the repeated noun phrase "spear-throwing device" with the pronoun **which:**

> The Cro-Magnons developed a spear-throwing device **which improved the range of their weapons by 30 yards.**

The new sentence you created by constructing a relative clause is more concise than the original version—it is three words shorter— and more readable because you have eliminated the distracting repetition of the words "spear-throwing device." The move from two separate sentences to a single sentence with a relative clause often enables you to write more economically and more effectively.

Choosing a Relative Pronoun

In creating relative clauses, you sometimes have a choice of pronouns. When a relative pronoun replaces a noun that refers to things and animals, you often have the choice between **that** and **which** to introduce the relative clause:

In dealing with each other, the Indian tribes of the Great Plains used an intricate sign language. The sign language consisted of a series of mutually understood gestures.

↓

In dealing with each other, the Indian tribes of the Great Plains used an intricate sign language **that consisted of a series of mutually understood gestures.**

OR

In dealing with each other, the Indian tribes of the Great Plains used an intricate sign language **which consisted of a series of mutually understood gestures.**

By the same token, when the relative pronoun replaces a noun that refers to people, you frequently have the option of using either **who** or **that:**

The peasant farmers till the Nile Delta. The peasant farmers still work in the ancient ways of their ancestors.

↓

The peasant farmers **who till the Nile Delta** still work in the ancient ways of their ancestors.

OR

The peasant farmers **that till the Nile Delta** still work in the ancient ways of their ancestors.

When the relative pronoun is **whom,** you have even greater choice: you can choose between **whom** and **that,** or you can eliminate the pronoun altogether:

The college honored the students. The students had made the dean's list for the past two semesters.

↓

The students **whom the college honored** had made the dean's list for the past two semesters.

OR

The students **that the college honored** had made the dean's list for the past two semesters.

OR

The students **the college honored** had made the dean's list for the past two semesters.

One difference among these three sentences is that the version with **whom** sounds more formal than the others. So in an informal writing situation you would probably choose either the version with **that** or the version without any relative pronoun.

There are two instances, however, when you have no choice of pronoun. Whenever the pronoun replaces a proper noun that refers to a person or animal, you must use the pronoun **who:**

Miss Piggy did some modeling before she met Kermit. Miss Piggy wants her career and her frog, too.

↓

Miss Piggy, **who did some modeling before she met Kermit,** wants her career and her frog, too.

You also have no choice when replacing a possessive noun, a noun which takes an apostrophe—like "child's" in the next example. A possessive noun can be replaced only by the relative pronoun **whose:**

The officer picked up the child. The child's arm was broken.

↓

The officer picked up the child **whose arm was broken.**

Punctuating Relative Clauses

You often have a choice of whether to use commas to set off a relative clause from the rest of your sentence, but that choice will usually affect meaning. The first sentence below, without commas, differs importantly in meaning from the identically worded sentence with commas:

Governors **who take bribes from construction companies** misuse the public trust.

Governors, **who take bribes from construction companies,** misuse the public trust.

The first sentence, without commas, implies that only *some* governors take bribes from construction companies and thereby misuse the public trust. The second sentence, with commas, states that *all* governors take bribes from construction companies and that all of them misuse the public trust.

Here are two more sentences, one with commas and one without. Can you tell how they differ in meaning?

History books **which ignore the accomplishments of blacks and other minorities** should not be used in the schools.

History books, **which ignore the accomplishments of blacks and other minorities,** should not be used in the schools.

The second sentence states that all history books ignore the accomplishments of blacks and other minorities and, therefore, should not be used in the schools. The first says that only some history books ignore the accomplishments of blacks and other minorities and that only they should not be used in the schools. It implies that there are other history books.

But with singular proper nouns, you do not have a choice. You must always use commas:

New York's Broadway, **which runs from the Tappan Zee Bridge in the north to Battery Park in the south,** is probably the world's most famous thoroughfare.

Jupiter, **which is the largest planet in the solar system,** has 11 moons.

Relative Clauses with Prepositions

You sometimes have the choice of constructing a relative clause to follow a preposition like **to, for, of, with, by,** and **in:**

> Aesop's fables are famous for the moral lessons they teach. In Aesop's fables animals act like human beings.

↓

> In Aesop's fables, **which are famous for the moral lessons they teach,** animals act like human beings.

OR, WITH THE PREPOSITION **IN,**

> Aesop's fables, **in which animals act like human beings,** are famous for the lessons they teach.

Here is another instance where you may choose to introduce a relative clause with a preposition:

> The terrorist bomb was intended for the judge. The judge had already escaped two previous attempts on her life.

↓

> The judge **for whom the terrorist bomb was intended** had already escaped two previous attempts on her life.

For an informal effect, try moving the preposition **for** to the end of the relative clause or, for an even more informal effect, eliminating **whom** completely:

> The judge **whom the terrorist bomb was intended for** had already escaped two previous attempts on her life.

OR, WITH **WHOM** ELIMINATED,

> The judge **the terrorist bomb was intended for** had already escaped two previous attempts on her life.

You can also create a relative clause when one of your sentences begins with a phrase that expresses quantity, like **most of, some of, none of, several of,** or **all of:**

The impressionist painters tried to present objects not as they are in fact but as they appear to the eye. Many of the impressionist painters lived and worked in Paris.

↓

The impressionist painters, **many of whom lived and worked in Paris,** tried to present objects not as they are in fact but as they appear to the eye.

Television viewers must often doubt the intelligence of game-show contestants. Two game-show contestants recently identified James Mason and Napoleon as U.S. presidents.

↓

Television viewers must often doubt the intelligence of game-show contestants, **two of whom recently identified James Mason and Napoleon as U.S. presidents.**

Relative clauses are often especially effective when they follow an opening prepositional phrase:

Without the 500-mile race **that attracts nearly 400,000 spectators every May,** Indianapolis might be just another midwestern city.

Placed at the beginning of a sentence after a prepositional phrase, the relative clause builds toward and helps emphasize the main clause of your sentence:

To the football fans **who rooted for the Baltimore Colts,** the team's move to Indianapolis was nothing less than an act of betrayal.

See if you can combine the following three sentences into a single sentence that begins with a prepositional phrase followed by a relative clause:

> Nearly a thousand Americans die every year in collisions at railroad crossings. This happens despite all the signs and lights and bells. The signs and lights and bells warn of oncoming trains.

Here is one possibility:

> Despite all the signs and lights and bells **which warn of oncoming trains,** nearly a thousand Americans die every year in collisions at railroad crossings.

Using Relative Clauses To Control Emphasis

Relative clauses can help control what you emphasize in your sentences and paragraphs. Two characteristics make relative clauses especially useful for controlling emphasis. First, relative clauses are grammatically "subordinated" to main clauses. In fact, they are often added as if they were in parentheses, as if they provided supplementary and perhaps incidental information. For this reason, relative clauses often receive less emphasis and attract less attention than main clauses. Second, relative clauses are usually tucked away in the middle of a sentence where they call less attention to themselves.

The following sentences can be combined in two different ways, depending on whether you convert the first or second sentence into a relative clause. But the resulting sentences differ significantly in emphasis:

> Burlesque was banned from New York City in the 1930s by Mayor La Guardia. Burlesque is now taught as an academic subject at a city university.

↓

Burlesque, **which was banned from New York City in the 1930s by Mayor La Guardia,** is now taught as an academic subject at a city university.

OR

Burlesque, **which is now taught as an academic subject at a New York City university,** was banned from the city in the 1930s by Mayor La Guardia.

How do these two sentences differ in emphasis? The first sentence places the information about the banning of burlesque in a relative clause and in that way implies that this information carries less weight than the fact that burlesque is now taught at a city university. By contrast, the second sentence implies that the banning, rather than the teaching, is the center of focus: it does so by placing the information about teaching in the less noticed relative clause and the information about banning in the more important main clause. Unless the relative clause occurs at the end of a sentence, it usually makes sense to place more important material in your main clause and less important material in your relative clause. What determines the importance of your material? Your overall purpose in writing.

Given this principle of emphasis, how would you use a relative clause to combine the two sentences below into a single sentence emphasizing the year in which Richard Nixon became president?

Richard Nixon became president in 1968. Richard Nixon was the first president in U.S. history forced to resign from office.

To emphasize the year in which Nixon became president, keep that information within a main clause and place the other information in a relative clause:

Richard Nixon, **who was the first president in U.S. history forced to resign from office,** became president in 1968.

But if you want to emphasize not the date when Nixon assumed the presidency but the fact of his resignation, then place the date within a relative clause and the information about his resignation within a main clause:

> Richard Nixon, **who became president in 1968,** was the first president in U.S. history forced to resign from office.

Even on the paragraph level, the relative clause is a useful means of controlling emphasis. In the following paragraph on the Norway rat, for example, note how the second sentence disrupts the paragraph's continuity by shifting its focus away from the adaptability of the rat to the origin of the rat:

> The Norway rat is regarded by experts as the most destructive mammal on earth and the most adaptive to changing situations and environments. The Norway rat actually reached this country on the ships of many nations. It abounds in the debris of North American cities, resisting all attempts to control it.

But by converting the second sentence into a relative clause and thereby lessening its importance, you can keep the paragraph focused on its central point—the rat's adaptability:

> The Norway rat, **which actually reached this country on the ships of many nations,** is regarded by experts as the most destructive mammal on earth and the most adaptive to changing situations and environments. It abounds in the debris of North American cities, resisting all attempts to control it.

* * *

The exercises that follow give you practice both in constructing relative clauses and in using relative clauses to control emphasis within your sentences and paragraphs. The important point is that the relative clause is a useful strategy not simply for completing these exercises but for the writing that really counts—for research papers, for letters, for job and scholarship applications.

CONSTRUCTING RELATIVE CLAUSES

Make each sequence of sentences below into a single sentence by converting one or more of the original sentences into a relative clause. For several of the exercises, do more than one version.

Example

1. Walden Pond was once praised by Thoreau for its natural beauty.
2. Walden Pond is now the site of many tourist stands.

Walden Pond, **which was once praised by Thoreau for its natural beauty,** is now the site of many tourist stands.

OR

Walden Pond, **which is now the site of many tourist stands,** was once praised by Thoreau for its natural beauty.

A. 1. The Autobahn was built by Hitler to transport tanks and troops to Germany's borders in World War II.
   2. The Autobahn is still one of the world's finest highway systems.

B. 1. Narcolepsy is a neurological disease.
   2. The disease makes victims suddenly fall asleep during the day.

C. 1. Kwanza has taken root as an Afro-American alternative to Christmas.
   2. Kwanza originated as an African harvest festival.

D. 1. Mount St. Helens had been threatening to erupt for several weeks.
   2. Mount St. Helens finally blew its top on May 18, 1980.

E. 1. The Gypsies were once thought to be Egyptian.
   2. The Gypsies are really a nomadic people from India.
   3. The Gypsies migrated from India into Europe.

F. 1. The town of Hannibal, Missouri, is the boyhood home of Mark Twain.

2. Hannibal holds a fence-painting contest each year.
3. The fence-painting contest is part of an annual celebration.
4. The annual celebration is called "Tom Sawyer Days."

G. 1. In the movie *Butch Cassidy and the Sundance Kid,* Hollywood portrayed the Sundance Kid's girl friend as a schoolteacher.
2. The Sundance Kid's girl friend was actually a prostitute in Fanny Porter's Sporting House.

H. 1. Many track stars have become professional football players.
2. Of them all, only Bob Hayes of the Dallas Cowboys became truly outstanding.

I. 1. Record companies are reluctant to finance concert tours of marginally popular rock bands.
2. Many of the marginally popular rock bands will lose money playing to small crowds.

J. 1. Alfred Hitchcock is probably the most influential American movie director of all time.
2. Alfred Hitchcock's films include *Notorious, Vertigo, Psycho,* and *Rear Window.*

WHO NEEDS WHEELS?

Using relative clauses whenever appropriate, create from the sentences below an explanatory paragraph that shows how the wheelless vehicles of science fiction may one day be put to actual, practical use on earth.

1. This occurs in H. G. Wells's novel *War of the Worlds.*
2. The earth is invaded by Martians.
3. The Martians roam about in machines.
4. The machines look like walking water towers.

5. This occurs in the second *Star Wars* film.
6. The second Star Wars film is *The Empire Strikes Back.*
7. Luke Skywalker battles huge walking machines.
8. The machines look like updated versions of Wells's earlier Martian monsters.

9. But the imaginary creations of science fiction writers may soon stroll.
10. The imaginary creations are vehicles.
11. The vehicles move on legs and feet.
12. They may stroll from the world of science fiction.
13. They may stroll into actual, practical use.

14. Jose M. Soto has designed a walking machine.
15. Jose M. Soto is an engineer from Puerto Rico.
16. The machine is controlled by a steering wheel.
17. The machine is controlled by a stick.
18. The machine is controlled by a computer.

19. Soto has constructed only a model of his walking machine.
20. Soto believes this.
21. This type of vehicle could be used for jobs.
22. It will be able to walk over rough terrain.
23. It will be able to walk through water.
24. The jobs are in places.
25. The places are hard to reach.
26. Tracked or wheeled vehicles cannot go to these places.

USING RELATIVE CLAUSES FOR SENTENCE EMPHASIS

Using one or more relative clauses, combine each sequence of sentences below into a single sentence so as to emphasize the material in the sentence marked with three asterisks***.

Example

1. Two astronauts flight-tested the new space shuttle.***
2. The two astronauts someday hope to fly the craft into earth orbit.

↓

The two astronauts **who someday hope to fly the craft into earth orbit** flight-tested the new space shuttle.

OR

1. Two astronauts flight-tested the new space shuttle.
2. The two astronauts someday hope to fly the craft into earth orbit.***

↓

The two astronauts **who flight-tested the new space shuttle** someday hope to fly the craft into earth orbit.

A. 1. The Cro-Magnons lived in southern Europe some 50,000 years ago.
   2. The Cro-Magnons extended the limit of humanity's destructive power.***

B. 1. Sushi, bagels, and other ethnic foods were once available only in restaurants with specialized menus.***
   2. Sushi, bagels, and other ethnic foods can now be found in fast-food eateries.

C. 1. Home computers like the Apple and the Commodore were once baubles for the very rich.
   2. Home computers like the Apple and the Commodore are now toys for the middle class.***

D. 1. Ralph Nader claims the American consumer needs a stronger voice in the decisions of government.
   2. Ralph Nader attacked General Motors in his book *Unsafe at Any Speed.****

E. 1. W. C. Fields starred in such film classics as *My Little Chickadee* and *The Bank Dick.****
   2. W. C. Fields' real name was Claude William Dukenfield.

ROLLER COASTER

Using relative clauses whenever appropriate, create from the sentences below a descriptive essay that communicates the pleasure and excitement of a ride on the roller coaster.

1. The roller coaster is still one of the most exciting rides in an amusement park.
2. The roller coaster made its appearance in 1884.

3. Its cars and inclines combine the simplicity with the plunges and the swirl.
4. Its cars are open.
5. Its inclines are steep.
6. The simplicity is of a railroad.
7. The plunges are of an Alpine ski jump.
8. The plunges are sudden.
9. The plunges are stomach churning.
10. The swirl is winding.
11. The swirl is of a bobsled run.

12. The coaster starts slowly.
13. The coaster starts like a train.
14. The train is pulling away from a station.
15. At the same time the passengers ready themselves for the first hill.
16. The passengers have waited in line for over an hour.

17. The cars jerk as the coaster climbs to the summit.
18. The jerk is hesitant.
19. The cars' wheels are clicking every inch of the way.
20. The passengers are poised at the peak.
21. The passengers brace themselves for the plunge.
22. The plunge is downhill.
23. The passengers have been waiting for this moment.
24. The plunge is exhilarating.

25. The cars dive.
26. The dive whips the passengers into a frenzy of screams and laughter.

27. The coaster sweeps through the first valley in a flow of motion.
28. And the coaster races on to the other dips in a flow of motion.
29. And the coaster races on to the other turns in a flow of motion.
30. The flow of motion is continuous.

31. The flow of motion leaves the thrillseekers hanging in midair.
32. Their knuckles are white from gripping the retaining bars.

33. Then the cars glide onto the last straightaway.
34. The glide is smooth.
35. The brakes stop the ride.
36. The stop is gradual.

37. The passengers step gingerly out of the cars.
38. The passengers' senses are excited not by the minutes on the straightaways and slow climbs.
39. The passengers' senses are excited by the seconds on the plunges and swirls.
40. The seconds on the plunges and swirls make the roller coaster the most exciting ride in the amusement park.

USING RELATIVE CLAUSES TO CONTROL PARAGRAPH EMPHASIS

Strengthen the focus of each paragraph below by (1) deciding which sentence within the paragraph weakens its focus, (2) transforming that sentence into a relative clause, and then (3) attaching the relative clause you have constructed to an appropriate sentence within the paragraph.

Example

> The antiestablishment youth movement of the sixties sowed the seeds of a movement in the seventies to embrace history. The antiestablishment youth movement of the sixties rejected the past and scorned society's roots. The blacks in the movement confronted the establishment with pride in their own origins and thereby began the ethnic-awareness movement of the seventies.

↓

> The antiestablishment youth movement of the sixties, **which rejected the past and scorned society's roots,** sowed

the seeds of a movement in the seventies to embrace history. The blacks in the movement confronted the establishment with pride in their own origins and thereby began the ethnic-awareness movement of the seventies.

A. Most Americans have become accustomed to driving cars with automatic transmissions. Now that the trend is toward small cars, many of us must learn to drive all over again, learning to put in the clutch at just the right time without killing the engine. Small cars save on gas. And they cost less to run.

B. The speech given by arresting officers, beginning "You have the right to remain silent," comes from a landmark Supreme Court decision involving a warehouse worker named Miranda. Miranda had never been informed of his right to counsel and to remain silent. Miranda was convicted of kidnapping and rape on the basis of his confession. As a result of the *Miranda* decision, all suspects must be read their rights.

C. It is popularly but mistakenly assumed that most people who take their own lives are old and near death. The truth is that those under 50 are more suicide-prone than those over 50. Suicide has now become the third leading cause of death among young people between 15 and 25. Suicide is usually the result of severe depression.

D. Andrew Wyeth's painting *Christina's World* has fascinated viewers for years. The painting is on display at the Museum of Modern Art in New York City. Characterized by Wyeth's use of muted colors, the painting depicts a woman lying in a field of grass, her body turned uphill toward a run-down shack on the horizon.

E. Tears are nature's way of keeping our eyes wet, and we "cry" as a reaction to eye irritation, such as when chopping onions. But why do we shed tears when we are happy or sad—in pleasure and pain, over victory and defeat? Emotional tears have long been a mystery. Such tears are unique to human beings. Some scientists now speculate that through tears our body eliminates certain chemicals which build up in response to stress and create a chemical imbalance. Crying is supposed to make us "feel better" because it restores chemical balance in the body.

TERM PAPER

Using relative clauses when appropriate, try to create from the sentences below an entertaining story that also makes a point about human nature. To help make your story amusing while at the same time developing its point, you will probably want to add details and examples of your own; for the same reason you may want to omit any information below that will not help you achieve those goals.

1. A trash can sat in the corner of the room.
2. The trash can was filled with the pages of a term paper.
3. The pages were crumpled.
4. The pages were rejected.
5. The room was in a dorm.

6. The desk was cluttered with more papers.
7. And the desk was cluttered with books.
8. The desk was old.
9. The desk had initials carved in it.
10. The desk had obscene remarks carved in it.
11. The carving was by two generations of students.
12. The books were piled on top of each other.

13. Some of the books were open to pages.
14. The pages were highlighted by marks.
15. The marks were yellow.

16. Other books were closed.
17. They were forgotten.

18. In the middle of the desk sat a portable typewriter.
19. Jonathan's father had given him the typewriter.
20. The typewriter was a present.
21. The present was for high school graduation.

22. The light shone overhead.
23. The light was fluorescent.
24. The light was giving off a buzz.
25. The buzz was soft.
26. The buzz was droning.
27. The buzz was like bees in a hive.
28. The hive was far off.

29. Jonathan lay on the bed.
30. Jonathan was fully clothed.
31. Jonathan was asleep after a night of writing.
32. Jonathan was asleep after a night of rejecting.
33 Jonathan was asleep after a night of revising.
34. The night was frantic.

35. Then the alarm clock sent a ring through the room.
36. The alarm clock had been set for 9 A.M.
37. The ring was shivering.
38. The ring was drowning out the buzz of the light.
39. The buzz was soft.

40. Jonathan stirred.
41. Jonathan was flailing his right arm.
42. Jonathan was flailing to shut off the noise.
43. The noise was annoying.

44. He succeeded only in doing this.
45. He knocked the clock off the stand.

46. "Damn."
47. He mumbled.
48. At the same time he jumped out of bed.
49. He did so to pick up the clock.

50. A taste welled up in his mouth.
51. The taste was foul.

52. He walked over to the desk.
53. And he picked up the ten pages.
54. The ten pages were neatly typed.

55. The ten pages were his night's effort.
56. A box of No-Doz was falling to the floor.

57. There was a knock at the door.
58. And Harry's voice boomed out.

59. "Jon, are you up?"

60. Jonathan opened the door.
61. He didn't want to yell back.

62. Harry asked whether Jonathan had finished the paper.
63. Harry stood in the doorway.
64. Harry was clad only in a towel.

65. "Sure."
66. He answered.

67. "It was easy."
68. "It was just like I said it would be."

unit3
PARTICIPLES

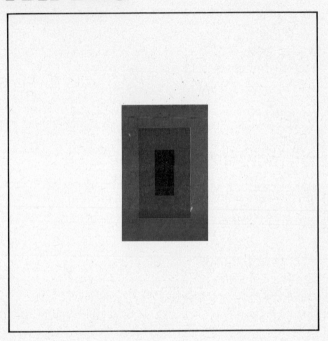

Constructing Participles

When you draft a paper, you are usually more concerned with putting your ideas down in whatever shape you can than with refining your paragraphs and sentences. As a result, you may write some short, choppy, and repetitive sentences, like these from a story about an African warrior:

> The African warrior proved easy prey for the slavers. He was dazed. He was reeling.

When you revise, you can eliminate the repetition and choppiness by making the three sentences into a single sentence, keeping one as a main clause and combining the other two into either a relative or a subordinate clause:

The African warrior, who was dazed and reeling, proved easy prey for the slavers.

Because he was dazed and reeling, the African warrior proved easy prey for the slavers.

But instead of turning the two sentences into clauses, you may reduce them to **dazed and reeling,** which are more simple, direct, and economical modifiers:

The African warrior, **dazed and reeling,** proved easy prey for the slavers.

OR

Dazed and reeling, the African warrior proved easy prey for the slavers.

Dazed and **reeling** are verb forms called PARTICIPLES. **Dazed** is a PAST PARTICIPLE, **reeling** a PRESENT PARTICIPLE. To construct a present participle, you simply add **-ing** to a basic verb form, so that *dance* becomes **dancing,** *read* becomes **reading,** and *preserve* becomes **preserving.** Unlike present participles, past participles do not all have the same form. But for most verbs, those which we call regular verbs, the past participle is the same as the past tense form, so that *disturb* becomes **disturbed,** *caress* becomes **caressed,** and *kick* becomes **kicked.** For some irregular verbs, the past participle ends in **-n,** so that *throw* becomes **thrown** and *blow up* becomes **blown up.** And for a few other irregular verbs, the past participle has individual forms, so that *sing* becomes **sung,** *go* becomes **gone,** and *stand* becomes **stood.** You can usually depend on your intuition to make the correct past participles for irregular verbs.

Participial Phrases

A participle is often supported by additional words built around it and adding details to it. Together, the participle and the additional words form a PARTICIPIAL PHRASE, such as **separated from the guides, cursing anything that caught his eye,**

obviously bored, or **forcefully arguing.** Compare the following sentences:

The African warrior, **dazed and reeling,** proved easy prey for the slavers.

The African warrior, **dazed by a vicious blow to the head and aimlessly reeling like a boxer about to drop to the canvas,** proved easy prey for the slavers.

After reading the first sentence, you might have asked, "how had he been dazed?" and "what did he look like reeling about?" Because it answers those questions, the second sentence, with participial phrases, is more graphic and substantial.

The Function of Participial Phrases

You use participles and participial phrases just as you use other modifiers—to give your writing texture and vitality by adding details to sentences. Notice how the next sentence about Eddie Murphy becomes vivid, recalling some of the comedian's roles, when participial phrases are added to the main clause:

Eddie Murphy changes roles like a chameleon changes colors.

↓

Eddie Murphy changes roles like a chameleon changes colors, **swishing his way past rough gunmen in *Beverly Hills Cop*, donning a cardigan for a Mr. Rogers' takeoff on "Saturday Night Live,"** or **talking tough to a barroom of rednecks in *48 HRS.***

Because they retain the sense of movement associated with verbs, you can best use participles to add lively, animated action to your sentences. This is particularly true for present participles with their **-ing** endings. In the next example, you can almost feel the nervousness of the job applicant because of the present participles **squirming, rolling** and **unrolling,** and **mumbling:**

The applicant waited alone in an outer office for her interview—
squirming on the vinyl chair, rolling and unrolling her resumé, and mumbling answers to imagined questions.

Present participles help you not only to create lively, animated action but also to achieve compactness and variety in your sentences.

Reducing Clauses to Participial Phrases

As we've already seen, you can reduce clauses to more compact participial phrases. By sometimes using full clauses and sometimes phrases, you give your writing more variety. Phrases also allow you to suggest relationships rather than state them openly. In particular, participial phrases imply rather than state cause-and-effect or time relationships.

Since they generally indicate the cause of actions, past participles are good substitutes for clauses beginning with "because" or "since." In the next pair of sentences, for instance, a participial phrase substitutes for a full clause:

Because they were disillusioned by the negative perception of the war in the United States, Vietnam vets often suffered severe mental problems.

↓

Disillusioned by the negative perception of the war in the United States, Vietnam vets often suffered severe mental problems.

In the following pair, a present participle suggests a time relationship without stating it:

We pulled off the interstate. Then we descended the exit ramp to fast-food alley, a long block of deep-fry dens and burgeries stamped out of plastic.

↓

> We pulled off the interstate, **descending the exit ramp to fast-food alley, a long block of deep-fry dens and burgeries stamped out of plastic.**

When a participle follows the main clause, it generally suggests what comes after. When it precedes the main clause, as in the next example, a participle generally suggests what comes before:

> After we tugged off each other's frozen boots, we crawled gratefully into chilly sleeping bags.

↓

> **Tugging off each other's frozen boots,** we crawled gratefully into chilly sleeping bags.

When sentences give no clear indication of time, present participial phrases generally suggest that two actions occur simultaneously.

> I carried the cumbersome bass drum in front of me. I jostled my way through the stubborn crowd to the bandstand.

↓

> **Carrying the cumbersome bass drum in front of me,** I jostled my way through the stubborn crowd to the bandstand.

OR

> I carried the cumbersome bass drum in front of me, **jostling my way through the stubborn crowd to the bandstand.**

When the verbs "carried" and "jostled" appear in separate clauses, they indicate that one thing happened and then the other. But the participles **carrying** and **jostling** imply simultaneous actions.

Sometimes present participles can suggest effects or results, replacing separate clauses that begin with "thus," "therefore," or "as a result":

To play Starman, Jeff Bridges studied how breakdancers and animals move. As a result, he learned to walk with a stiff, flatfooted gait. And he learned to jerk his head like a bird searching for a worm.

↓

To play Starman, Jeff Bridges studied how breakdancers and animals move, **learning to walk with a stiff, flatfooted gait and to jerk his head like a bird after a worm.**

Positioning Participial Phrases

You can often move participial phrases from one position to another in relation to the main clause—before it, after it, or interrupting it. You may vary the placement of participial phrases in order to change sentence rhythm, to shift emphasis, to create sentence variety, or to provide links between sentences. Because it is sometimes difficult to decide just when such movement is possible or effective, it is a good idea to read your versions aloud and listen carefully to the differences among them.

Consider the following possibilities:

Keeping one eye on his professor, Russ quickly scanned the *Playboy* hidden behind his bulky literature anthology.

OR

Russ, **keeping one eye on his professor,** quickly scanned the *Playboy* hidden behind his bulky literature anthology.

OR

Russ quickly scanned the *Playboy* hidden behind his bulky literature anthology, **keeping one eye on his professor.**

Each of these versions affects the reader differently. In the first, the participial phrase initially captures the reader's attention, briefly postponing the action of the main clause and perhaps creating momentary suspense, which in this case heightens the humor of the sentence. In the second, the phrase interrupts the main clause, demanding two pauses, two rhythmic breaks. These interruptions help to make prominent "Russ" and "quickly," the words on either side of the commas. In the third, the participial phrase is so far from its understood subject, "Russ," that the sentence seems a bit awkward.

In sentences with several participial phrases, you have even more options for arrangement. You can keep the participial phrases together or separate them in various ways. Here are just two variations of a sentence with several phrases:

Hagler immediately took control of his opponent, **attacking and driving Hearns against the ropes, bulling him back, hitting him with lefts and rights to the body.**

OR

Attacking and driving Hearns against the ropes, Hagler immediately took control of his opponent, **bulling him back, hitting him with lefts and rights to the body.**

In the first version, the opening clause immediately states the most general fact—Hagler took control. The participial phrases more fully describe that fact, piling action upon action. They capture the initial movement of that classic battle between a boxer and a slugger. We watch Hagler relentlessly attacking and driving, bulling Hearns, finally hitting him with lefts and rights to the body. In the second version, the rhythm of the fight seems to change with the realignment of the phrases. First we see Hagler attacking and driving; then we move to the general statement that he "immediately took control of his opponent"; and finally we return to the bulling and hitting, which now become almost afterthoughts.

Sometimes the ideas within a sentence suggest the best way to arrange participial phrases. For instance, when participial phrases are connected to clauses by either time or cause-effect relationships, ordering them according to the logical sequence of events is the most effective option. Notice how the phrases in the next two sentences are ordered:

Lighting a match, Sharon searched the basement shelves and cupboards for a new fuse.

Depressed by his betting losses, Joey sat alone on the beach.

Since Sharon lit the match *before* she searched the basement and Joey was depressed *because* he had lost money gambling, the participial phrases logically begin these two sentences. The participial phrases in the next two sentences are ordered differently because they have different relationships to the main clauses:

Adam opened the brightly wrapped package, **discovering a small wooden box held shut by a silver clasp.**

A recession makes consumers more hesitant to spend money, **creating financial problems for retail firms.**

Since Adam discovered the box *after* he opened the package and the creation of financial problems *results from* the consumer's hesitancy to spend money, the phrases properly follow the clauses.

The relationship of a sentence with others around it will help you determine the most effective placement of participles. Out of context, the present participial phrase, **dealing with current technology rather than ghosts or goblins,** might occur before or after its subject:

Dealing with current technology rather than ghosts or goblins, contemporary legends preserve the basic structure of classic horror tales.

OR

Contemporary legends, **dealing with current technology rather than ghosts or goblins,** preserve the basic structure of classic horror stories.

But within the context of the following paragraph, you'd be more likely to place the participial phrase at the beginning of its sentence:

Modern life produces its own folktales, called urban legends. **Dealing with current technology rather than ghosts or goblins,** contemporary legends preserve the basic structure of classic horror stories. One such tale concerns an old lady who accidently cooks her dog while trying to dry him in her microwave oven.

When it introduces the second sentence, the participial phrase not only separates the two occurrences of the word "legends," but—more importantly—it also explains the nature of urban legends, thus providing a bridge for the reader between the first sentence and the main clause of the second. A word of caution. Unless you have good reason for beginning a sentence with a participle, as in the urban legend example, it's probably best to place participles in the middle or at the end of your sentences.

Improperly Attached Participles

Be sure that a participial phrase has the same subject as the sentence to which it is attached. The following are properly combined:

The robot's four metal fingers gripped the hexagonal nut.
The robot's four metal fingers clutched it tightly.
The robot's four metal fingers clutched it like a pair of nimble pliers working in tandem.

↓

The robot's four metal fingers gripped the hexagonal nut, **clutching it tightly,** like a pair of nimble pliers working in tandem.

If you ignore this rule, you will end up with an awkward and even confusing sentence that does not say what you mean. In the following sentence, it first seems that the crowd, not the quarterback, limped away from the huddle:

The injured quarterback limped away from the huddle.
The sympathetic crowd cheered the injured quarterback.

↓

Limping away from the huddle, the sympathetic crowd cheered the injured quarterback.

The sentence would be clearer if you made "the quarterback" the subject of the main clause:

Limping away from the huddle, the quarterback was cheered by the sympathetic crowd.

* * *

As you complete the following exercises, keep in mind the characteristics of participial phrases—their economy, their versatility, their ability to indicate action, as well as their ability to indicate cause, effect, and time. You can use participial phrases to suggest relationships instead of stating them explicitly and to create coherence and emphasis within paragraphs.

CONSTRUCTING PARTICIPIAL PHRASES

Combine each sequence of sentences below into a single sentence by converting at least one of the original sentences into a participle or participial phrase.

Example

1. The new storm swept from North Dakota through Ohio.
2. It sent temperatures plummeting.
3. It piled drifts high across roads.

The new storm swept from North Dakota through Ohio, **sending temperatures plummeting and piling drifts high across roads.**

OR

Sweeping from North Dakota through Ohio, the new storm sent temperatures plummeting and piled drifts across roads.

A. 1. Jeff clicked on his calculator with a sigh.
   2. He sat down heavily at his desk.
   3. He opened his calculus book.

B. 1. Prosecutor, judge, and jury were convinced of the defendant's guilt.
   2. They twisted the facts to support their prejudgment.

C. 1. She was born in Atlanta, Georgia.
   2. She now serves as the corporation's legal officer.
   3. She was educated at Duke University.

D. 1. Mandy was mud-covered.
   2. Mandy was shivering.
   3. Mandy sat hunched over a cup of hot chocolate.
   4. Her father had prepared the hot chocolate to drive off the chill.

E. 1. Mark grew more angry.
   2. Mark grew more frustrated.
   3. Mark kicked the Coke machine.
   4. It had just swallowed three of his quarters.

F. 1. Helen was plagued by doubts about her ability.
   2. Helen kept quiet in class.
   3. Helen answered questions only when the teacher called on her.

G. 1. The Argentine soldiers were outmatched.
   2. The Argentine soldiers were outgunned.
   3. The Argentine soldiers quickly surrendered to the British commandos.
   4. The Argentine soldiers threw down their guns.
   5. And the Argentine soldiers raised their arms.

H. 1. Television news people are pawns in the rating game.
   2. They are often hired and fired on the basis of skin tests.
   3. The skin tests are given to viewers to measure their emotional reactions.

I. 1. The locomotive lumbered into Grand Central Station.
   2. It skidded along the tracks.
   3. It splashed sparks onto the passenger platform.
   4. It discharged gray puffs of steam.
   5. It finally screeched to a halt.

J. 1. Dave Parker broke forward with the sound of the bat.
   2. He raced into short right-center field.
   3. He flicked down his sunglasses.
   4. He shouted off the second baseman.
   5. He caught the pop fly to end the game.

A PERFECT TEN

Using participial phrases whenever appropriate, combine the following sentences into a narrative essay. Try to capture the voice and tone of a young woman chiding herself good naturedly because she has put on too much weight to get into her favorite jeans. If you choose, write the exercise from the point of view of a young man. Add details of your own similar to those in sentences 24–26.

1. I reached into my closet.
2. I took out my favorite pair of jeans.
3. It is the pair I always wear.
4. I wear them when I want to feel comfortable.
5. And I began to slip them on.

6. But they didn't slip.
7. They stuck at midthigh.

8. I tugged hard.
9. I finally pulled them over my seat.
10. I was lying in a prone position.
11. My stomach was sucked in.
12. This was in order to zipper the jeans.

13. I was unable to get the jeans zippered.
14. I realized this.
15. I was the first girl on campus to acquire the "freshman ten."
16. The "freshman ten" is ten pounds of flab.

17. I first heard of the freshman ten.
18. Then I was determined.
19. It would not happen to me.

20. I would be disciplined.
22. I would take small portions.
23. I would eat sparingly.

24. My resolve lasted two days.
25. Then a friend ordered a large cheese and sausage pizza.
26. She couldn't possibly eat it by herself.

27. I am always a friend in need.
28. And I remembered what my mother had told me.
29. It was about the starving children in Africa.

30. I aided my friend in devouring the caloric mass in seconds.
31. Gooey cheese was sliding down my greedy chin.

32. Hope was lost.
33. Discipline was cast out the window.

34. I was on the road to acquiring the freshman ten.

35. My battle with midriff bulge was lost to a pizza.

36. Others are beaten by different delights.
37. The delights are gooey.
38. The delights are starchy.
39. The delights are sugary.
40. The delights are cookies.
41. The delights are bagels.
42. The delights are cakes.
43. The delights are candy.
44. The delights are ice cream.
45. The delights are pies.
46. These are from the dining room.
47. And these delights are from student union shops.
48. The delights are especially "care packages."
49. "Care packages" are filled with home-cooked goodies.

50. Most of us consume this junk during evening "pig outs."
51. This leaves our bodies no time to burn off the gorged calories.

52. Thus are excess pounds added to once-slim bodies.

53. My body has been stuffed with sugars and starches.
54. Mine is a formerly svelte cheerleader's body.
55. The sugars and starches have been washed down with beer.
56. The beer is carbohydrate-laden.

57. So here I lie.
58. I am a perfect ten.
59. I am more like a pudgy turtle on its back.
60. I am not like Bo Derek.

CREATING PARTICIPIAL PHRASES

I. To each of the following sentences, add illustrations and details in the form of participles. Add both a past and present participle to at least two of the sentences. Try to make the sentences lively and interesting.

Example

Riley sat at the far end of the bar.

Riley sat at the far end of the bar, **holding his head in his hands.**

OR

Jilted by his fiancée, Riley sat at the far end of the bar, **drinking one highball after another.**

A. Grandma stared at him for a minute.

B. The door creaked open.

C. The coach screamed at the referee.

D. America depends on oil and gas for most of its energy needs.

E. Karen met Jerry during Christmas vacation and a week later agreed to marry him.

II. Choose one of the next five sentences and write a paragraph with it as the controlling idea. Add illustrations and details in the form of participles and other modifiers.

Example

The runner tumbled onto the cinders.

Bumped by a competitor, the runner tumbled onto the cinders, her right leg twisting beneath her. **Raising herself to her knees,** she collapsed again, a crumpled pile of arms and legs. Despite months of arduous training, she could not finish the race. She lay on the gritty track, **softly whimpering, defeated.**

F. The driver buckled her seatbelt.

G. They tentatively reached out their hands toward each other.

H. The pilot managed to pull himself from the wreckage before it burst into flame.

I. Ellen quickened her pace to a trot.

J. The second baseman took the throw from the shortstop and fired to first for a double play.

BLIND DATE

Using participial phrases whenever appropriate, combine the following sentences into a humorous essay that reveals the young man to be more concerned with neatness and appearances than with people. Add details of your own similar to those in sentences 29–31.

1. The young man knocked on the door.
2. The young man was well-dressed.
3. The door was large.
4. The door was a dingy brown.

5. He heard no response.
6. Then he knocked again.
7. He knocked louder.

8. He heard steps on the other side.
9. They were clop, clop, clopping.

10. The door opened.
11. The open door revealed a woman.
12. She was a hippopotamus of a woman.
13. She was in a terry cloth robe.
14. Her hair was in a towel.
15. There was a small puddle of water beneath her.
16. It was where she had dripped.

17. The young man was surprised.
18. He almost stuttered.
19. But he caught himself.
20. And he said this.
21. "I'm Larry Baldwin."
22. "I'm here to pick up Rose Ann."

23. The woman mumbled something.
24. She turned her huge frame.
25. And she pointed toward a couch in the living room.

26. Larry made a place for himself.
27. He picked up the morning paper.
28. The paper lay strewn across the couch.

29. He folded it neatly.
30. Then he placed it atop a pile of magazines.
31. The magazines were next to the coffee table.

32. The woman stared while Larry straightened the pile.
33. He was oblivious to her.

34. He turned only at this time.
35. He heard the clop, clop, clop of wooden-soled clogs.
36. The clop, clop, clop were on the stairs.

37. He thought this to himself.
38. "Good grief. What did I get myself into this time?"

39. "Would Rose Ann be fat like her mother?"
40. "And would she be untidy like this house?"

41. His roommate's girl friend had got him into this mess.
42. She had got him into a mess a month or so ago, too.
43. Then it was with a sorority sister.
44. The sorority sister was too tall.
45. The sorority sister was too thin.
46. And the sorority sister was too ugly.
47. Larry thought this.
48. He lost himself in reverie.

49. But the click of heels startled him into awareness.
50. The click of heels was descending the stairs.

51. He turned quickly.
52. He saw a small, dark girl.
53. She had bright, dancing eyes.
54. She was immaculate.
55. She was in a yellow pinafore.

56. Larry nearly jumped from the couch.
57. He hit his knee on the coffee table.
58. And he stuttered.
59. "Hi, I'm L-L-L-"
60. He was unable to finish his name.

61. Rose Ann replied.
62. "Yes, I know, Larry."
63. "Susan told me about you."
64. She reached over to pick some lint from his jacket.

MAKING PARTICIPLES IN CONTEXT

Reduce the wordiness and sharpen the focus of each passage below by converting at least one of the sentences into a participial phrase.

Example

   Piet Van de Mark, who conducts ocean tours off the coast of Baja California, claims that animals in the wild like people. He notes that grey whales observe his tour boat from afar, then approach and touch the craft with their snouts and refuse to leave until the startled tourists pet them. The tour guide thinks all this means that nature is not necessarily hostile, that if you smile at a whale, it might smile back at you. He doesn't say, though, what might happen if you step on a rattlesnake.

Piet Van de Mark, who conducts ocean tours off the coast of Baja California, claims that animals in the wild like people. He notes that grey whales observe his tour boat from afar, then approach, **touching the craft with their snouts** and **refusing to leave until the startled tourists pet them.** The tour guide thinks this means that nature is not necessarily hostile, that if you smile at a whale, it might smile back at you. He doesn't say, though, what might happen if you step on a rattlesnake.

A. As we entered the main room of the nursing home, I saw my grandfather sitting bent over in his chair. He rummaged through the bag on his walker. And he pulled out one item then another to place on the table before him. These were his remaining possessions—a few photographs, an alarm clock, a book, and a pocketknife that he'd owned since childhood. I had never realized until then just how much his life had diminished—from the unbridled freedom of a child and young man to the protective circumscription of a nursing home.

B. Of all the plants on earth, the poppy has perhaps the most far-reaching potential for good and ill. When it is manufactured legally as codeine and morphine, it provides us with a drug unsurpassed in treating violent pain. When it is manufactured illegally as heroin, it brings addiction and misery to hundreds of thousands. It is at once a blessing and a curse.

C. The underground railroad was no actual railroad of steel and steam. It was a clandestine network of people determined to help fugitive slaves escape from bondage. Its routes led north from the slave states to Canada. As they moved from station to station on foot, the fugitives crossed hundreds of miles of dangerous territory. They slept in barns and churches. And they defied the wrath of slavehunters.

COMRADE STUDENT

Using participial phrases wherever appropriate, combine the following sentences into an explanatory essay about the Soviet school system. You may retain the basically neutral tone of the original sentences or you may change the tone either to criticize or commend the Soviet system of education.

1. He enters the room.
2. Then the 30 pupils rise.
3. They greet their teacher.

5. The students remain standing.
6. Then they are given a sign to take their seats.
7. They are all in uniform.
8. The boys are in blue.
9. The girls are in white.

10. This is the beginning of a fourth-grade class.
11. It is at a Moscow school.
12. It characterizes the Soviet approach to education.

13. The Soviet system has always stressed obedience to authority.
14. It has downplayed creativity.
15. It is not like school systems in the United States.

16. It is a tradition.
17. Schools indoctrinate students with communist ideology.
18. So they are told that the Soviets are striving for peace.
19. At the same time they are told that Americans are deploying more missiles.

20. It is also a tradition.
21. Russian students learn by rote memorization.
22. They learn by constant drill.

23. The Soviet system dampens individual initiative.
24. This has prompted one American educator to comment.
25. "What the Soviet system lacks is the means to develop independent inquisitive attitudes in students."

26. Nevertheless, it has demonstrated its effectiveness.
27. Soviet schools give tenth graders an education.
28. It would take a student through the twelfth grade in the United States.

29. Soviet students study more math and science.

30. Fifty times as many Russian high school students took advanced calculus.
31. This is compared to their American counterparts.
32. This was in the early eighties.

33. The Soviet educational system may have its limitations.
34. But it works well.
35. It produces knowledgeable students.
36. It produces obedient Soviet citizens.
37. It produces them in an efficient manner.

38. Comrade student learns to solve quadratic equations.
39. He does not develop the curiosity.
40. The curiosity might make him question the political system.

unit *4*
APPOSITIVES

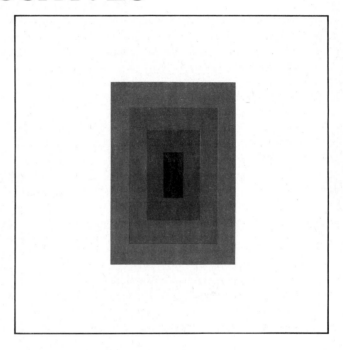

The usual way to define or identify something is by saying what it *is:*

> Mr. Cooper is my favorite zoology professor.
> He is a former trapper from Canada.

Full sentences like these are often appropriate. But sometimes information that defines or identifies—information such as "my favorite zoology professor" and "a former trapper from Canada"—can be more effectively and economically expressed as an APPOSITIVE:

> Mr. Cooper, **a former trapper from Canada,** is my favorite zoology professor.

OR

Mr. Cooper, **my favorite zoology professor,** is a former trapper from Canada.

Although these two sentences contain exactly the same words, they do not have the same meaning: each focuses on a different piece of information about Mr. Cooper. The first version is about the "professor," the second about the "trapper." In each case the appositive simply adds extra information.

Constructing Appositives

You can make an appositive out of just about any sentence in which a noun or nounlike structure is preceded by a form of **be (is, was, are, were).** Omit the noun and this verb, add a comma or dash in its place, and you have an appositive:

Joe Montana was the league's most valuable player.
Joe Montana led the San Francisco Forty-Niners to a second
    Super Bowl championship.

↓

Joe Montana, **the league's most valuable player,** led the San Francisco Forty-Niners to a second Super Bowl championship.

When any of several sentences can be changed to appositives, your choice must depend on your focus. If, in the next example, you want to focus on "Susan is a promising candidate for WOW," keep that sentence as your main clause. Then make the incidental, defining details "an excellent student" and "an international scholarship program for outstanding women" into appositives:

Susan is an excellent student.
Susan is a promising candidate for WOW.
WOW is an international scholarship program for outstanding
    women.

↓

An excellent student, Susan is a promising candidate for WOW—**an international scholarship program for outstanding women.**

Appositives Versus Relative Clauses

If you had chosen, you could have combined the previous three short sentences about Susan into a sentence with two relative clauses instead of two appositives:

> Susan, who is an excellent student, is a promising candidate for WOW, which is an international scholarship program for outstanding women.

Because appositives and relative clauses are very similar, it is often difficult to decide which one to use. Your guiding principles should be clarity and economy: if both versions are equally clear, choose the shorter, more concise one. It is important to be aware of your options: sound them out, listen to them, weigh them. Increasingly, your final choice will be the "right" one.

Test your eyes and ears on the two sentences below to decide which is more effective:

> Even a brief visit to Greece, which is a modern gateway to the past, gives you a profound sense of the roots of our civilization.

> Even a brief visit to Greece, **a modern gateway to the past,** gives you a profound sense of the roots of our civilization.

In the first sentence, the relative "which" and the verb "is" are unnecessary, and they could even cause momentary confusion. As you read "Even a brief visit to Greece, which is . . . ," can you be sure that "which" refers to "Greece" and not to "visit"? Using an appositive instead of the relative "which" helps avoid possible confusion.

Positioning Appositives

Appositive simply means being "positioned" next to something, generally a noun. The noun itself may occur at the beginning, middle, or end of the sentence:

> Joe Pippin, **a free-lance preacher from the West Coast,** has been repeatedly denied a speaking permit by the university.

A speaking permit to Joe Pippin, **a free-lance preacher from the West Coast,** has been repeatedly denied by the university.

The university has repeatedly denied a speaking permit to Joe Pippin, **a free-lance preacher from the West Coast.**

As these three sentences indicate, the most common sentence position for the appositive is immediately *after* the noun that it defines. But the appositive can also be placed at the beginning of a sentence *before* the noun:

A free-lance preacher from the West Coast, Joe Pippin has been repeatedly denied a speaking permit by the university.

By beginning with an interesting detail about Joe Pippin, you heighten the reader's interest in him. Sometimes the larger context will encourage an appositive before the noun. For instance, if you mention Joe Pippin in the preceding sentence, then an initial appositive referring to him can smoothly link your two sentences:

Another addition to the recent list of unwelcome visitors to campus is Joe Pippin. **A free-lance preacher from the West Coast,** he has been repeatedly denied a speaking permit by the university.

Length of Appositives

Just as you have the choice of placing appositives in various sentence positions, so you can construct appositives of different lengths. Short appositives placed at the end of the sentence can be striking and memorable:

Half an hour later, the second diver returned with the same report —**nothing.**

Incorporated in humanistic programs in our schools is one of the most dehumanizing practices in education—**standardized testing.**

Many of America's young people have found new heroes—**themselves.**

While these summarizing appositives consist only of a word or two, other appositives are longer and more detailed. Here is one in the form of a full clause:

The America of the South and West—**what one politician long ago called "the great Baptist subculture of the United States"**—has at last outnumbered and overpowered the America of the long-dominant Northeast.

Even more detail can be packed into a long appositive series:

Most area residents will long remember the winter of '77: **the record temperatures and snowfall, the school closings, the impassable streets, the cold homes and offices, the idle factories.**

It's precisely to keep young runaways from becoming street people—**to house, feed, and protect them and to help them with their problems**—that runaway houses have been established.

Elaborating and Generalizing Appositives

In the last two examples, the appositives provide specifics that elaborate upon a noun or nounlike word: "winter" in the first instance, "to keep" in the second. Appositives are used principally to expand the meaning of nouns by supplying defining details about them. Here are some further illustrations. In the first, the appositive specifies "autumn shot"; in the second, it defines "simple object":

She won the photo contest with the ultimate autumn shot—**golden leaves and a red barn in Vermont.**

"Monopoly" has one simple object: **to bankrupt the other players by buying, selling, and trading real estate and by collecting rents on properties, houses, and hotels.**

But appositives are just as handy for summarizing or generalizing:

To avoid bankruptcy, some major airlines are joining forces with successful regional airlines—**a trend that is likely to continue.**

Negative Appositives

Regardless of their length, appositives can take a negative form. Negative appositives define something by saying what it is not:

Less than 50 feet past the intersection, the Ford started making unusual noises, **not the familiar rattles and knocks.**

Bloodhounds are friendly, gentle creatures, **not the vicious beasts their name would lead you to expect.**

Appositive-like Adjectives

Whether positive or negative, appositives are normally nouns or noun-like structures. But adjectives can function as appositives if they are moved from their usual position in front of the noun they modify. Here is a sentence with adjectives in their usual position before the noun:

My blind date turned out to be an honest, fun-loving, affectionate, wonderful person.

Now here are three of these adjectives shifted to the end of the sentence to function as appositives:

My blind date turned out to be a wonderful person—**honest, fun-loving, and affectionate.**

So long as appositive adjectives are separated by punctuation from what they modify, they can be placed at the beginning, middle, or end of a sentence:

Stark, forbidding, awesome, spectacular—Death Valley is a hauntingly beautiful place to visit, despite its name.

My escort, **tall and bespectacled,** showed me workers who were assembling a 9000-horsepower diesel engine.

The blast that toppled an entire side of Mount St. Helens was simply staggering—**500 times greater than the Hiroshima atomic bomb.**

Special Appositives

Certain appositive constructions have special forms. Some appositives call for the repetition of the noun, others for an appropriate pronoun, and still others for a connective.

Repeated Noun. Whenever several words separate an appositive from the noun it defines, try repeating the noun:

Most Americans depend on **services** over which we have no personal control—**services that we accept unthinkingly from dozens of nameless men and women every day.**

Literally hundreds of heartwarming **stories** unfolded in every corner of the county—**stories of neighbor helping neighbor, of young helping old, of rich helping poor.**

Sometimes this pattern works well even when the two nouns are next to one another, especially when the appositive includes—as in all these instances—a long modifier:

None of the hoopla in recent years about the return of glamour has dealt with *real* **women—women with households to run, jobs to handle, budgets to balance.**

Introductory Pronoun. But when the appositive immediately follows the noun, you may prefer to introduce it not with the repeated noun but with a pronoun like **one, that, the latter, something,** or **the kind:**

None of the hoopla in recent years about the return of glamour has dealt with *real* **women—ones with households to run, jobs to handle, budgets to balance.**

Introductory Connective. Finally, when your appositive provides an example or illustration, you may choose to introduce it with a connective like **namely, in other words, for example, including, especially, particularly, notably,** or **mainly:**

A number of American presidents—**including Lincoln, Roosevelt, and Kennedy**—have died in office.

Some of the world's fastest growing countries, **notably Pakistan and Bangladesh,** are among the world's poorest.

Punctuating Appositives

Whether or not they are introduced by a connective, appositives are set off by punctuation marks such as commas, dashes, and colons.

These punctuation marks may create different effects. Compare the following:

I bought the flowers for my best friend**,** my mother.

I bought the flowers for my best friend**—**my mother.

I bought the flowers for my best friend**:** my mother.

Of these three versions, the first is perhaps the most matter-of-fact statement, giving the feeling that it should not be particularly surprising for the writer's mother to be his or her best friend. In the second sentence, the dash suggests a bit longer pause, which allows a somewhat greater emphasis on **my mother.** The colon in the last sentence creates an even longer pause, lending the appositive a more formal and more serious quality.

* * *

First in the exercises that follow and then in your assigned compositions, try using appositives whenever your goal is to identify or define.

CONSTRUCTING APPOSITIVES

Combine each sequence of sentences below into a single sentence by converting one of the original sentences into an appositive. Eliminate unnecessary words.

Example

1. One of the most controversial public school issues is "mainstreaming."
2. "Mainstreaming" is the practice of integrating physically and mentally handicapped children into regular classes.

↓

One of the most controversial public school issues is "mainstreaming," **the practice of integrating physically and mentally handicapped children into regular classes.**

OR

"Mainstreaming," **one of the most controversial public school issues,** is the practice of integrating physically and mentally handicapped children into regular classes.

A. 1. Pet owners upset by soaring veterinary costs can now register for Medipet.
   2. Medipet is a prepaid insurance plan for dogs and cats.

B. 1. A psychological autopsy is the attempt to describe a person's state of mind during the period leading up to death.
   2. A psychological autopsy is usually performed to determine whether death occurred by suicide or accident.

C. 1. According to the National Safety Council, 1 out of 50 cars coming at you on the highway has a drunk driver behind the wheel.
   2. A driver with at least a 0.10 percent blood/alcohol level is considered drunk.

D. 1. The first ready-made clothes were crude, shapeless, and cheap.
   2. They were scorned by the American public when they appeared in the early 1800s.

E. 1. Shanghai is different from other Chinese cities.
   2. Shanghai is more European.
   3. Shanghai is more cosmopolitan.

F. 1. Jewelers usually consider four factors in determining the price of a diamond.
   2. The four factors are "the four C's."
   3. One factor is color.
   4. Another factor is clarity.
   5. Another factor is cut.
   6. Another factor is carat weight.

G. 1. Whoever goes to Atlantic City expecting to make a fortune is a dreamer.
   2. That person is not an optimist.

H. 1. Just when economy cars are reintroducing the standard transmission, look what happens.
   2. One French-designed bicycle offers a new feature.
   3. The new feature is the automatic transmission.

I. 1. Leonardo da Vinci was a Renaissance master.
   2. He is best known for such incomparable works of art as the *Mona Lisa* and *The Last Supper.*
   3. Da Vinci was also an engineering genius.
   4. He first visualized humans flying.
   5. He first visualized tanks fighting battles.
   6. He first visualized boats driven by paddle wheels.
   7. These visions put da Vinci centuries ahead of his time.

J. 1. The ancient Chinese were a people of inventors and discoverers.
   2. The ancient Chinese were a people of philosophers and soldiers.

3. The ancient Chinese were a people of poets and craftsmen.
4. The ancient Chinese gave the world many of its most useful things.
5. Its most useful things are the compass and the mechanical clock.
6. Its most useful things are paper and poetry.
7. Its most useful things are gunpowder and the wheelbarrow.

STREET MUSICIAN

Using appositives whenever appropriate, combine the sentences below into a descriptive essay that captures the writer's interest in the blind banjo player. At your option, invent and add further details.

1. I saw street musicians in Boston last summer.
2. The most moving was a banjo player.
3. He was blind.
4. He was a young man.
5. He was about my age.

6. He sat in front of Woolworth's.
7. His blank eyes were looking at no one.
8. His hair was sticking out from under a headband.
9. His hair was damp.
10. The headband was red.

11. He was an adept musician.
12. He entertained the passersby until this.
13. His fingers slipped on the strings.
14. His fingers were slick with sweat in the city heat.
15. The slipping made it too difficult for him to play.

16. He wiped his hands on a large white handkerchief.
17. He leaned back against Woolworth's front window.
18. The banjo was across his lap.
19. And he sang ballads.
20. They were soft and low intervals of melancholy on a bright Boston day.

CREATING APPOSITIVES

I. Add to each of the following sentences at least one fact or detail in the form of an appositive. Where possible, add a series of appositives.

Example

Some 2000 companies have produced cars in America.

↓

Some 2000 companies have produced cars in America—**a number that is no longer likely to grow.**

OR

Some 2000 companies have produced cars in America, **companies such as Hudson, Nash, Packard, and of course General Motors.**

OR

Hallmarks of a revolutionary industry that created an industrial giant and world leader, some 2000 companies have produced cars in America—**a number that has now shrunk to less than a few dozen.**

A. College life is a series of shocks.

B. Bare-handed rock climbing is a dangerous and grueling sport.

C. She remembered how thoughts of the dark cellar had always filled her with numb excitement.

D. These are the characteristics of an effective teacher.

E. Some women feel threatened by the feminist movement.

II. Select one of the five sentences below. Then, with that sentence as your controlling idea, write a brief paragraph that includes several details in the form of appositives.

Example

> Humans aren't the only creatures that perform romantic antics to attract a mate.

↓

> Humans aren't the only creatures that perform romantic antics to attract a mate. Animals have courtship rituals too. The great horned owl woos his lady love with a gourmet meal—**a freshly killed mouse or rabbit.** And the female cardinal provocatively lounges around near the local birdbath, **a favorite spot for flirting and courting.** But the real Cupid is the humble snail, who shoots tiny calcium darts at the object of his desire.

A. The old rocker hardly looked like the valuable antique it really was.

B. To be a champion bubble blower, you have to use the right kind of gum.

C. Some people believe that honeybee pollen is God's gift to the health-minded.

D. As the speaker stepped to the microphone and began to talk, her self-assurance and sense of humor set the tone for the entire lecture.

E. Twins, and especially identical twins, often show similar interests and talents.

SOME STATE BIRD

Using appositives when appropriate, combine the sentences below into an essay that explains why the mosquito is a pest. Introduce additional details from your own experience.

1. It is a warm summer evening.
2. The sun is just about to set.
3. You are having a lakeside picnic with your friends.

4. Suddenly you hear a familiar buzz.
5. Then you feel a sharp bite on your skin.
6. You swat.
7. But it is too late.

8. A hungry mosquito has had a snack.
9. Your blood was the snack.

10. Mosquitoes have caused misery.
11. Mosquitoes have caused illness.
12. Mosquitoes have caused loss of life.
13. They have caused more of these than rats and lice.
14. I mean the world's rats and lice combined.
15. This has happened throughout human history.

16. The mosquito is not just a tropical pest.
17. It is busily at work in cooler climates as well.
18. North America has cooler climates.

19. In fact, Ohio records the most cases each year.
20. The cases are of mosquito-related diseases.
21. Ohio is hardly a tropical state.

22. Mosquito species number in the thousands.
23. Four to five hundred species carry diseases.
24. The diseases are carried to humans.

25. Mosquitoes can thrive any place.
26. It is a place where water collects.

27. For example, they infest tree boles.
28. The tree boles are filled with rain.
29. They infest swamps.
30. They infest pools.
31. They infest even small puddles.
32. The small puddles are in the bottoms of abandoned tires.

33. And mosquitoes grow big.

34. Some people refer to these giant mosquitoes as their state bird.
35. These people reside in Minneapolis–St. Paul.
36. The mosquitoes rule Minnesota's lakes and rivers.

37. DDT succeeded only in this:
38. It produced insects.
39. The insects were highly resistant to DDT.
40. DDT is a deadly chemical.
41. This chemical was widely used in some areas.
42. It was used after World War II.
43. It was used to combat mosquitoes.

44. So the pesky little birds live on and multiply.
45. They are likely to use you for a snack.
46. This will happen at your next picnic.

APPOSITIVES IN CONTEXT

Reduce the wordiness and sharpen the focus of each passage below by converting several sentences or clauses into appositives. Feel free to add details of your own, some of them in the form of appositives.

Example

> Ancient garbage dumps are turning out to be modern treasure chests for archeologists. In the dry air and protective sands of Egypt, scientists have found delicate remnants of the common citizen's life millennia ago. These remnants would have crumbled away long before now in another climate. Two-thousand-year-old papyrus letters are especially revealing. Roughly translated, some of the letters written by youth away from home read thus: "Dear Mom and Dad. Please send money."

> Ancient garbage dumps are turning out to be modern treasure chests for archeologists. In the dry air and protective sands of Egypt, scientists have found delicate remnants of the lives of common citizens millennia ago—**remnants that would have crumbled away in another climate long before now.** Especially revealing are 2000-year-old papyrus letters, **forerunners of collect phone calls from today's sons and daughters off to college.** Roughly translated, some of

the letters written by youth away from home carry this blunt message: "Dear Mom and Dad. Please send money."

A. Calligraphy is the art of elegant, beautiful handwriting. It is a cinch to learn even when you use a simple, inexpensive kit. Calligraphy is handy for designing your own party invitations, memorable notes, and attractive posters. It is a valuable skill that can save you money—and turn up friends you didn't know you had.

B. Editors of a leading business magazine tried to write a story about the corporate world's ten toughest bosses. But when they did this they immediately ran into a problem. This problem was fear. Subordinates who managed to overcome their apprehensions of their bosses' vindictiveness and—for a little inducement —granted secret interviews helped the editors pinpoint one key quality of the "tough ten" right away. It was the bosses' ability to inspire respect tinged with terror.

C. Why are babies twice as likely to be born at midnight as at noon? Or why do rejection rates for organ transplant patients jump sharply on the 7th, 14th, 21st, and 28th days after surgery? The reason is, according to one chronobiologist, the clockwork of internal rhythms in the human body. This clockwork consists of mysterious but predictable and synchronized cycles that last minutes, days, months, and even years.

POOH-POOH ON DING-DONG

Using appositives whenever appropriate, combine the sentences below into a humorous explanatory essay that makes fun of early theories on the origin of language. Invent and add appropriate details of your own similar to those given in lines 22–27.

1. How did the first humans learn to communicate with language?
2. We do not know.

3. Linguists know too little about prehistoric people.
4. Linguists study the matter seriously.
5. They are specialists of language.

6. But linguists have not kept others from doing this:
7. Others speculate on the origin of language.

8. Some defend the "bow wow" theory.
9. This theory states that our ancestors began speaking in the following way.
10. They imitated the sounds of animals.

11. According to the bow wow theorists, it happened like this.
12. Humans walked out of the primordial mist.
13. And humans began barking like dogs.
14. Humans began howling like wolves.
15. Humans began chirping like birds.
16. Humans began clucking like chickens.

17. Others put their faith in the "pooh pooh" theory.
18. They believed this.
19. Language derived from instinctive cries.
20. Instinctive cries expressed pain.
21. Or they expressed pleasure.

22. That is, old grandfather Og walked into the cave one day.
23. He was tired from a hunt.
24. He stubbed his toe on a rock.
25. And he cried out "ooh!"

26. But grandmother Ig comforted him.
27. And he cried out "aah!"

28. The "ding dong" theorists had no use for cries of pain and pleasure.
29. They had a different hypothesis about the origin of language.
30. There is a mystic harmony between sound and sense.

31. Here is what they thought.

32. Primitive humans had a peculiar gift to know this.
33. A rock should be called a *rock*.

34. After all, rocks give off "rockness."
35. In the same way bells ring.

36. Yet others believed this.
37. They were the "yo heave ho" theorists.
38. Language derived from sounds.
39. The sounds were emitted during labor.

40. Supposedly, prehistoric people began speaking.
41. They did this while they grunted.
42. And they did this while they groaned.
43. They were doing their daily tasks.

44. There is a basic fallacy in all these theories.
45. They fail to recognize this.
46. Humans remained mute.
47. They began to speak only when they "invented" language.

48. In other words, they had organs for speech before.
49. Now they found a new use for them.

50. But biologists know this.
51. Organs are not yet perfected at their first use.
52. It only happens during the evolution of the species.

53. How did humans learn to speak?
54. We may never know this.

55. But we can be sure of this.
56. Humans didn't learn to speak by saying "bow wow."
57. Humans didn't learn to speak by saying "pooh pooh."
58. Humans didn't learn to speak by saying "ding dong."
59. Humans didn't learn to speak by saying "yo heave ho."

unit*5*
ABSOLUTES

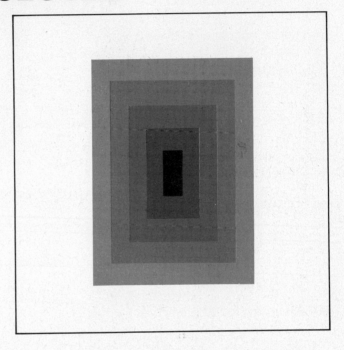

Suppose in a paper describing your roommate as she studies late one night, you begin by writing:

Marie was sitting at her desk. Her head was slightly lowered over a pile of chemistry notes.

When you revise, you decide to connect Marie's sitting at her desk more closely to the detail of her lowered head. So you join the two sentences with a comma and then "and":

Marie was sitting at her desk, and her head was slightly lowered over a pile of chemistry notes.

But you're not altogether happy with this version, so you try again. Eventually you may write something like this:

> Marie was sitting at her desk, **her head slightly lowered over a pile of chemistry notes.**

You may like this version best, both because it is concise and because it closely links Marie's sitting at her desk to her lowered head. What you've done is turn the original second sentence into an ABSOLUTE —a phrase that is almost but not quite a complete sentence. An absolute has a full subject, in this case "her head." But it has only part of a predicate, often only a participial phrase like "slightly lowered over a pile of chemistry notes."

Adding Details

Like other modifiers—relative clauses, participles, and appositives— absolutes are useful for adding narrative and descriptive details to your sentences. Because they have their own subjects, absolutes allow you to shift from a description of a whole to a description of its parts. In the next sentence, for instance, the absolute enables you to shift from the tree as a whole to its branches:

> The sickly tree struggled to grow, **its scrawny branches stretching up through the shadows toward the sunlight.**

In the same way, the series of absolutes in the next example moves from the generalization that "the prisoner stood alone on the wooden platform" to specific details about the prisoner:

> The prisoner stood alone on the wooden platform.
> His hands were tied behind his back.
> His face was covered by a small cotton bag.
> And his neck was fixed securely in a noose.

↓

The prisoner stood alone on the wooden platform, **his hands tied behind his back, his face covered by a small cotton bag,** and **his neck fixed securely in a noose.**

Constructing Absolutes

There are two ways to construct absolutes from full sentences. One way is by removing a form of the verb "be"—such as "is," "are," "was," or "were." Thus by removing the word "was" from the sentence "Her head was slightly lowered over a pile of chemistry notes," we created the absolute "her head slightly lowered over a pile of chemistry notes." The second way to construct an absolute is by changing the main verb into its *-ing* form. In the following sentences about an ominous evening, for example, the verbs "became" and "gave" can be changed into "becoming" and "giving" to produce a pair of absolutes:

The evening grew more ominous. The breeze became gustier. Whitecaps gave the lake a frothy, sinister appearance.

↓

The evening grew more ominous, **the breeze becoming gustier, whitecaps giving the lake a frothy, sinister appearance.**

Now see if you can construct a single sentence with an absolute from these two sentences:

The accountant sat in the office. His eyes were closed.

You can construct the absolute here by removing the word "were" from "His eyes were closed":

The accountant sat quietly in his office, **his eyes closed.**

If you choose, you may eliminate the word "his":

The accountant sat quietly in his office, **eyes closed.**

Indicating Cause and Effect

Aside from carrying details, absolutes can indicate that one event is the cause of another. Suppose, for example, that you wanted to combine the sentences below in order to indicate that the sinking of the battleship was caused by the torpedoes which tore apart its stern:

> The stern of the battleship was torn apart by torpedoes.
> The battleship slowly sank into the Pacific.

Your first impulse may be to write:

> Because its stern was torn apart by torpedoes, the battleship slowly sank into the Pacific.

This sentence is perfectly acceptable, but you can suggest the same cause-effect relationship, more concisely and more subtly, with an absolute:

> **Its stern torn apart by torpedoes,** the battleship slowly sank into the Pacific.

You can most clearly suggest a cause-effect relationship when you place the absolute at the beginning of its sentence. Notice that if the battleship sentence is rewritten with the absolute at its conclusion, the cause-effect relationship is blurred because the reader cannot be sure whether the tearing apart took place at the same time the ship sank or before it sank:

> The battleship slowly sank into the Pacific, **its stern torn apart by torpedoes.**

Positioning Absolutes

An absolute that refers to an earlier event normally appears before the main clause. Notice that sometimes absolutes that begin sentences sound better when they are introduced by the preposition "with":

Her Melville paper was typed and ready to turn in. Cori walked uptown to meet her friends.

↓

With her Melville paper typed and ready to turn in, Cori walked uptown to meet her friends.

An absolute that refers to an event occurring later than the event in the main clause should follow the clause:

The Argentine planes screamed low over the British fleet, **one jet fighter barely clearing a destroyer's mast.**

But when an absolute does not indicate cause or a time relationship, you can position it either at the beginning or end of its sentence:

Their faces lined with exhaustion, the fire fighters trudged back to the truck.

OR

The fire fighters trudged back to the truck, **their faces lined with exhaustion.**

You may even place an absolute in the middle of its sentence, between the subject and the verb:

The fire fighters, **their faces lined with exhaustion,** trudged back to the truck.

The huge combine, **its blade churning,** cut its way steadily through the winter wheat.

Cause-effect or time relationships will sometimes determine whether an absolute can work at the beginning, middle, or end of a sentence. But sometimes you will want to move an absolute from one sentence position to another for the sake of variety or sound.

Other things being equal, though, absolutes work best at the end of sentences. And that is where writers most often put them:

> The speeding car missed the turn and now lay on its back, **wheels spinning.**

> Sally Ride walked down the corridor with her astronaut crewmates, **a shiny helmet in her right hand, an air of confidence in her brisk step.**

Absolutes in a Series

Like other modifiers, absolutes may be used in a series. Using absolutes in a series can be particularly forceful when you want to build the ideas in a sentence toward a climax:

> The arrested woman was slammed against a wall, **her wrists handcuffed, her body frisked, her dignity destroyed.**

The absolute "her dignity destroyed" is probably the most important item of the series, and therefore it should occur as the final series item. The sentence would lose impact if "her dignity destroyed" did not occur as the final series item. To hear the difference, try reading the sentence aloud with "her dignity destroyed" as either the first or second item.

Knowing that a series of absolutes gains power when its items are placed in order of increasing importance, how would you combine these sentences?

> The room was in chaos. Soiled clothes were strewn on the floor. Everything was in disorder. Cosmetics were scattered over the dresser.

Since the sentence "Everything was in disorder" essentially summarizes the chaos in the room, you should probably place it at the end of the series:

The room was in chaos—**soiled clothes strewn on the floor, cosmetics scattered over the dresser, everything in disorder.**

Using Absolutes with Other Structures

Absolutes are especially useful because they combine with other structures to give your sentences variety and texture. Notice how the next three sentences can be rewritten as one sentence with an absolute followed by an appositive:

The first Chinese soft-drink factory was a tribute to American enterprise.
Pepsi Cola provided the capital, the machines, and the expertise.
These three commodities are in short supply on the communist mainland.

↓

The first Chinese soft-drink factory was a tribute to American enterprise—**with Pepsi Cola providing the capital, the machines, and the expertise,** three commodities in short supply on the communist mainland.

Because such combinations of structures are compact and rhythmically interesting, they provide you with useful stylistic options. As another example, the next three sentences can be improved by combining them into a single one with an absolute and a present participial phrase:

The 10:00 P.M. showing of *Beverly Hills Cop* sold out before 9. Ticket holders stood two abreast around the block. They waited restlessly to enter the theater.

↓

The 10:00 P.M. showing of *Beverly Hills Cop* sold out before 9, **with ticket holders standing two abreast around the block, waiting restlessly to enter the theater.**

Punctuating Absolutes

You generally separate an absolute from other sentence parts with a comma:

John McEnroe turned toward the line judge, **a mixture of anger and frustration distorting his face.**

But if you want to emphasize the details in the absolute, you may use a dash:

John McEnroe turned toward the line judge—**a mixture of anger and frustration distorting his face.**

A dash can be especially effective when you have to separate a series of modifiers from a main clause. Here is the sentence about *Beverly Hills Cop,* with a dash replacing the first comma:

The 10:00 P.M. showing of *Beverly Hills Cop* sold out before 9 **—with ticket holders standing two abreast around the block,** waiting restlessly to enter the theater.

*　　*　　*

The exercises which follow give you practice in constructing absolutes as one way of adding details to your own writing.

CONSTRUCTING ABSOLUTES

Combine each group of sentences below into a single sentence by converting at least one of the original sentences into an absolute.

Example

> When I walked in, grandpa was sitting at the kitchen table. The newspaper was spread before him.
>
> ↓
>
> When I walked in, grandpa was sitting at the kitchen table, **the newspaper spread before him.**

A. 1. Jimmy walked slowly to the corner of the playground.
    2. His face was streaked with tears.

B. 1. Alice could see Tom at the other end of the office.
    2. Tom's head was bowed before the angry manager.

C. 1. The station wagon sped away.
    2. The taillights disappeared into the distance.

D. 1. Every night we could hear her singing.
    2. Her high-pitched voice leaped and soared.
    3. Her high-pitched voice was unrestrained by any sense of melody or timing.

E. 1. His opponent had gained a lead of almost 100,000 votes.
    2. The senator publicly conceded that she had lost her reelection bid.

F. 1. The bodies of the two wrestlers were glistening with sweat.
    2. The two wrestlers struggled together.
    3. Each of the two wrestlers was intent on victory.

G. 1. The photographer sits on the 30-yard line.
    2. One knee is folded under his body.
    3. The other knee is upright to support his elbow.

H. 1. A few minutes later I made my way to the Chevy pickup.
   2. Packages were under my arm.
   3. Crudely drawn maps were in my hand.
   4. The pickup was parked in front of the store.

I. 1. The professor rested against the blackboard.
   2. Chalk was in one hand.
   3. A look of profound discouragement was in her eyes.
   4. A textbook was in the other hand.

J. 1. Economic conditions are creating an automotive United Nations.
   2. General Motors is building cars with Toyota.
   3. Ford is investing with Mazda.
   4. Chrysler is in partnership with Mitsubishi and Peugot.

THE GOOD OLD SUMMERTIME

Using absolutes when appropriate, combine the following sentences into an essay that tries to capture the freedom and magic of summertime. Feel free to add details in order to make your essay more personal.

1. Summer is a special season.
2. This is true for teenagers.

3. School is out.
4. There is no reason to stay home at night.
5. There is no history homework.
6. There are only reruns on TV.
7. There is daylight until nine or ten o'clock.

8. Yet there is plenty to do.
9. This is the case after you leave the house.

10. Tennis courts have lights for impromptu night matches.
11. Ball diamonds have lights for impromptu night matches.

12. Film companies release blockbusters.
13. *The Return of the Jedi* is a blockbuster.
14. *Flashdance* is a blockbuster.
15. *Raiders of the Lost Ark* is a blockbuster.

16. Outdoor arenas offer attractions like Bob Seeger.
17. Outdoor arenas offer attractions like Fleetwood Mac.

18. There are moonlight parties at the beach.
19. Hibachis are loaded with hamburgers and steaks.
20. Your friends are dancing barefoot in the sand.
21. They are dancing to music from portable radios.

22. You drive around in an old Mustang.
23. The windows are down.
24. The kids are laughing.
25. The tape player is shouting Springsteen's "Thunder Road."
26. The noise and music are part of the magic.
27. The freedom and friends are part of the magic.
28. The magic makes summer the most special season.

CREATING ABSOLUTES

I. To each of the following sentences add at least one fact or detail in the form of an absolute. Add a series of absolutes to any two sentences. Try to make the sentences vivid and lively.

Example

Diane stood motionless at the end of the diving board.

↓

Diane stood motionless at the end of diving board, **tears streaming down her cheeks.**

OR

Diane stood motionless at the end of the diving board, **hands at her side, heels slightly raised, every muscle anticipating action.**

A. Johnny tumbled down the grassy slope.

B. From across the street the house looked deserted.

C. The freight train stretched out through the valley.

D. A full color ad featuring a beautiful woman is likely to sell more exercise machines than one listing the health benefits of repetitive exercise.

E. By the time the rescue squad arrived, fire fighters had already stretched a ladder from the street to the fourth-floor window.

II. Choose one of the next five sentences and write a paragraph with it as the controlling idea. Add illustrations and details in the form of absolutes and other modifiers.

Example

We had never seen Jennifer so messy.

We had never seen Jennifer so messy. She wore old, faded jeans smeared with dirt. Her sweatshirt, musty and torn, hung on her like an oversized rag. Filthy sneakers barely clung to her feet, **their tongues and laces missing.** Her uncombed hair was wild, sticking together in sweaty clumps. She looked as if she hadn't changed or washed in days.

F. The passengers waited inside the bus terminal.

G. He spoke to her, gently, soothingly.

H. The cheerleader sat alone on the basement floor.

I. It was a typical student apartment.

J. For a full hour the plumber stood in front of the Picasso painting.

PADDLE WHEEL FESTIVAL

Using absolutes whenever appropriate, combine the following sentences into a letter that captures a young woman's joy at witnessing a small river town celebration.

Dear Sarah,

1. Do you remember this?
2. I told you about my friend Amy.
3. Amy is from this little river town downstate.
4. It is called Titusville.

5. Well, the girls in the dorm warned me about this.
6. There isn't much to do in Titusville.
7. All you can do is sit on the bank.
8. And you can watch the coal barges float by.

9. So Amy invited me down to the annual Riverboat Festival last week.
10. I said yes.
11. But I said so only to be polite.

12. And I expected this.
13. The trip would be a dull experience.

14. I couldn't have been more wrong.

15. The sternwheel riverboat is a magnificent old boat.
16. It was built in the nineteenth century.

17. The decks gleam beside the paddle wheels.
18. The decks are whitewashed.
19. The paddle wheels are bright red.
20. The tall smokestacks stand like sentinels above.
21. The sentinels are coal black.

22. The townspeople held a ball on the riverboat.
23. They dressed in nineteenth-century splendor.

24. The women were in white gowns.
25. The men were in black tuxedos.
26. The men wore tall hats.
27. This all happened the first night of the festival.

28. The dance was held in a huge ballroom on the boat.
29. The ballroom was lined with gilded mirrors.

30. The whole thing was like stepping back in time.
31. It was an elegant ballroom scene from *Gone With the Wind.*
32. It was with Rhett Butler and Scarlett O'Hara.

33. The blaring music of a steam calliope announced this.
34. A second boat arrived.
35. And the annual race was beginning.
36. This was on the next day.

37. The two boats were beautiful.
38. Smoke was belching from their stacks.
39. Sternwheels were churning.
40. At this time they moved slowly upriver.

41. It was like the things I had read about in Mark Twain.
42. It was the river.
43. It was the town.
44. It was the people.

45. The sky was lit by fireworks.
46. And local school bands paraded through the streets.
47. They played songs like "My Old Kentucky Home."
48. They played songs like "Swanee River."
49. And they played songs like "America the Beautiful."
50. This happened that night.

51. Sarah, I never thought this.
52. I'd be moved by old time songs like those.
53. But I was.

54. Boy, were those other girls in the dorm wrong.

55. Titusville may be dull most of the year.
56. But during the festival it's great.
57. It's colorful.
58. And it's exciting.

59. I'm glad of this.
60. Amy asked me to come.

Your friend,
Kate

MAKING ABSOLUTES IN CONTEXT

Reduce the wordiness and sharpen the focus of each passage below by converting at least one of the sentences into an absolute.

Example

Banks used to be staid, conservative places of business. Tellers were behind cages. Officers were aloof and available only to the wealthy. But banks are changing their image. The junior officers are situated right out among their customers. Their desks are across from the tellers' booths. The tellers are encouraged to talk to customers about the weather and local gossip and to give out lollipops and balloons to children. If bankers were once thought of as fat cat capitalists interested more in profits than in people, they certainly are working hard to become friendly neighborhood business people.

Banks used to be staid, conservative places of business, **with tellers behind cages, officers aloof and available only to the wealthy.** But banks are changing their image. The junior officers are situated right out among their customers, **their desks across from the tellers' booths.** The tellers are encouraged to talk to customers about the weather and local gossip and to give out lollipops and balloons to children. If bankers were once thought of as fat cat capitalists interested more in profits than in people, they certainly are

working hard to become friendly neighborhood business people.

A. The two boys leaned against the willow tree beside the stream.
Their fishing poles were resting on sticks. Their eyes were gazing
at the bobbers floating on the ripples. The fish didn't take the
lines but periodically teased the boys, nibbling at the bait and
jumping within arm's reach of the bank. The boys tried changing
bait and rods and places. Nothing worked. One tiny bluegill did
strike late in the afternoon but fell off just as it was drawn near
the bank. Because their stomachs were crying for food, because
their backs were burning from too much sun, and because their
legs were stiff from sitting, both boys gathered their gear and
headed for home.

B. Europeans had no accurate way to find directions before the
discovery that magnets pointed north. But the Chinese had developed mechanical pointing devices, called south-pointing
chariots, as long ago as 3000 B.C. These machines depended on
the fact that a chariot's wheels rotate at different speeds through
a curve in the road. So they were equipped with gears to translate
these differences into the orientation of a figure mounted on a
vertical shaft. The gears compensated for twists and turns in the
road. And therefore the figure always pointed south.

C. Winter was approaching. So the Humane Society reminded pet
owners that severe cold weather kills thousands of domestic
animals. One society officer noted that "people tend to forget
animals when the weather's bad." Local veterinarians warned of
dogs and cats freezing to death from being left outside or locked
in uninsulated shelters. All of those involved agreed that there's
nothing worse than finding a dead animal when its paws and legs
are burst open by the cold.

THE BIG SELL

Using absolutes whenever appropriate, combine the sentences
below into an essay that explains how ad writers use alluring images

to sell products. If you wish, include examples of your own that help to substantiate that controlling idea.

1. Modern ads in print rely mainly on alluring images.
2. Modern ads on TV rely mainly on alluring images.
3. They do this for the big sell.

4. For example, the pages of *Newsweek* and other magazines are dominated by the picture of a cowboy.
5. He is tanned.
6. He is rugged.
7. His face expresses calmness and confidence.
8. His hair is dark and curly.
9. One weather-worn hand grasps a pack of Marlboro cigarettes.

10. Marlboro is creating a macho image.
11. The macho image is for their cigarettes.
12. Macho sells.

13. So do sex and romance sell.

14. A large, clumsy Ford pickup becomes more attractive.
15. This happens when a gorgeous woman is draped across its hood.
16. Her hair is windblown.
17. Her mouth is open in awe.
18. Her body is clad in a bikini.

19. Ad makers place a voluptuous blonde on the front seat of a sedan.
20. The sedan is ordinary.
21. They hope to entice viewers to buy a Chevrolet.

22. And Johnny Walker's Scotch seems to become more desirable if this happens.
23. Two young lovers linger over a drink.
24. The two are in romantic surroundings.

25. Even Midas Mufflers are made provocative when this happens.
26. They are surrounded by lustrous hair.
27. They are surrounded by the latest fashions.
28. They are surrounded by Vic Tanny physiques.

29. Sensuous details can also entice us to buy.
30. The sensuous details are in an ad's setting.

31. A cozy fireside scene makes us yearn for Harvey's Bristol Cream Sherry.
32. Snow is gently falling outside.
33. A happy couple is lounging inside.

34. A ski lodge convinces us to buy a new pair of jeans.
35. The ski lodge has a "winter wonderland" appeal.
36. The ski lodge is jammed with students.
37. The students are wearing Levis.

38. Ads satisfy our fondest dreams.

39. They offer warm summer scenes to those of us who long for warmth and sunshine.
41. This is in the brutal cold of winter.

42. The announcer for the Florida Tourist Office says this.
43. "When you've got it bad, we've got it good."
44. "Come to Florida."

45. The background shows this.
46. People are swimming in a tropical ocean.
47. People are waterskiing.
48. And people are frolicking on sandy beaches.

49. Those who want winter sports are offered scenes.
50. They are scenes of skiers swooshing down snowy mountain trails.
51. These are in resorts in Colorado and Utah.

52. Ad writers tempt us with pleasures.
53. Only their products can provide the pleasures.

54. Even Wheaties and Coca-Cola can fulfill our fondest fantasies.
55. This is true in the dreamland.
56. The dreamland is created by ad writers.

unit *6*
SUBORDINATION

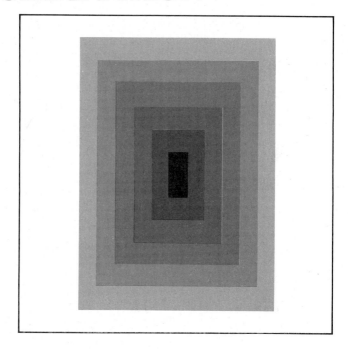

Choosing Subordinate Clauses

The same two sentences combined differently can make different points. Suppose you want to make these two observations:

Some species of whales are nearing extinction.
Many countries refuse to accept even a partial ban on whale hunting.

To suggest that these two sentences are logically related but that neither has more weight than the other, you can combine them with a connective such as **so** or **and yet**:

Some species of whales are nearing extinction, **and yet** many countries refuse to accept even a partial ban on whale hunting.

OR

Many countries refuse to accept even a partial ban on whale hunting, **so** some species of whales are nearing extinction.

If, on the other hand, you want to suggest that one sentence is more important, you can use a subordinator such as **although** or **because** to make the less important sentence into a SUBORDINATE CLAUSE:

Although some species of whales are nearing extinction, many countries refuse to accept even a partial ban on whale hunting.

OR

Because many countries refuse to accept even a partial ban on whale hunting, some species of whales are nearing extinction.

In each version above, the opening subordinate clause creates anticipation and in this way helps emphasize the main clause that follows.

In principle, you can make a subordinate clause out of any simple sentence, as long as you can link its meaning in some logical way to the meaning of another sentence. Since either one of the two given sentences can be subordinated, the sentence you choose for your main clause and the one you choose for your subordinate clause will depend on their relative importance.

Although there are exceptions, especially when a subordinate clause occupies the emphatic position at the end of a sentence, main points normally go into main clauses, and subordinate points normally go into subordinate clauses.

Subordinators

A subordinate clause is introduced by a SUBORDINATOR, an adverb that relates the meaning of the subordinate clause to the meaning of the main clause. Contrast and cause, illustrated by "although" and "because" above, are two of the basic adverbial relationships that subordinators can indicate. Other subordinators specify condition, degree, time, and place:

Contrast:	**Although**
	Even though
	While
Cause:	**Because**
	Since
	As
Condition:	**If**
	When
	Provided that
	In case
	Assuming that
Negative Condition:	**Unless**
Alternative Condition:	**Whether or not**
Degree:	**Inasmuch as**
	Insofar as
	To the extent that
Time:	**When**
	Whenever
	While
	Once
	Before
	After
	Since
	Until
	As long as
	As soon as
Place:	**Where**
	Wherever

As this partial list suggests, you can often choose among several subordinators to express a particular adverbial relationship. To indicate a time relationship between the following two clauses, for instance, you can use **until, before,** or **just when:**

The Mongol hordes threatened to conquer all Europe.
Genghis Khan's death forced them to return to Asia.

↓

The Mongol hordes threatened to conquer all Europe **until Genghis Khan's death forced them to return to Asia.**

OR

Before Genghis Khan's death forced them to return to Asia, the Mongol hordes threatened to conquer all Europe.

OR

Just when the Mongol hordes threatened to conquer all Europe, Genghis Khan's death forced them to return to Asia.

Even when the meaning commits you to subordinating one sentence and not the other, you may still have a choice among subordinators:

Michelangelo's *Pieta* was damaged by a madman.
Michelangelo's *Pieta* is displayed only behind a protective glass shield.

↓

Because
Since } **it was damaged by a madman,** Michelangelo's
After *Pieta* is displayed only behind a protective glass shield.

Any one of these subordinators is appropriate in this sentence, because each logically links the step taken to protect the sculpture (the effect) to the madman's act (the cause). But there is a difference between the subordinators. **Because,** for example, suggests only the cause, whereas both **after** and **since** imply the time sequence as well: first the damage, then the protection.

Positions for Subordinate Clauses

In the sentences about Michelangelo's *Pieta,* the subordinate clauses come before the main clause. But subordinate clauses occur at the end and even in the middle of sentences as well. Varying the position of your subordinate clause helps to control emphasis and to communicate your feelings. Read the next two sentences to see if repositioning a subordinate clause makes a difference:

> **If local residents are willing to put up with them,** nuclear plants are a clean and economical way of producing vast amounts of much-needed energy.
>
> OR
>
> Nuclear plants are a clean and economical way of producing vast amounts of much-needed energy, **if local residents are willing to put up with them.**

The reader of the first sentence is likely to respond to nuclear plants as something desirable, despite the suggestion that residents may have reason to be uneasy about them. But the second version implies a grimmer view, directing attention more to the residents' concern about safety than to the plants' economic advantages. A sentence tends to impress on the reader what it says toward the end, where the stress naturally falls; in the second version the emphasis is further increased by the slight pause at the comma before the subordinate clause. A dash, instead of a comma, lengthens the pause and places greater emphasis on "if," adding to the reader's uneasiness:

> Nuclear plants are a clean and economical way of producing vast amounts of much-needed energy—**if local residents are willing to put up with them.**

Subordination in Context

Where you position a subordinate clause within your sentence also depends in part on the surrounding sentences. For example, the if-clause at the end of the sentence about nuclear plants anticipates a sentence that further focuses on the disadvantages of such plants. Thus the version

> Nuclear plants are a clean and economical way of producing vast amounts of much-needed energy, if local residents are willing to put up with them.

is much more likely to be followed by something like

> In fact, many residents aren't.

than by the sentence

> Diminishing oil supplies make plans for a number of such plants
> especially urgent.

This last sentence, in contrast, would fit well after a statement that
implies the advantages of nuclear plants:

> If local residents are willing to put up with them, nuclear plants
> are a clean and economical way of producing vast amounts of
> much-needed energy. Diminishing oil supplies make plans for
> a number of such plants especially urgent.

Since main points normally go into main clauses and subordinate
points into subordinate clauses, which of two sentences you subordinate—as well as where you position the subordinate clause—affects
the developing context of your writing. For example, in writing an
essay on American music, you might have the following two sentences:

> Other composers have been more inventive or more profound.
> None have captured the American spirit like Aaron Copland.

Suppose you subordinate the first sentence to the second:

> Although other composers have been more inventive or more
> profound, none have captured the American spirit like Aaron
> Copland.

In this case, your reader will expect the rest of the paragraph to
expand the idea that no other composers have captured the American spirit like Aaron Copland:

Although other composers have been more inventive or more profound, none have captured the American spirit like Aaron Copland. This Brooklyn-born son of Russian immigrants created a distinctive American concert music out of a mixture of jazz and folk tunes. His most famous works, the classic American ballets "Rodeo" and "Billy the Kid," mix brash, brassy jazz rhythms with cowboy tunes that swagger in syncopated time.

On the other hand, you may choose to subordinate the second sentence to the first:

Although no composers have captured the American spirit like Aaron Copland, others have been more inventive or more profound.

In this instance, your reader will expect the rest of the paragraph to develop the idea that other composers have been more inventive or profound than Copland:

Although no composers have captured the American spirit like Aaron Copland, others have been more inventive or more profound. Charles Ives, with his experiments in atonal music, produced clamorous though ingenious works. Leonard Bernstein explored the relationship of God to humanity in such works as "Mass" and "Kaddish."

Simplifying Subordinate Clauses

Writing is often a process of building up and then cutting down. One way to cut down, especially as you revise, is to eliminate unnecessary words. A subordinate clause with the same subject as the main clause can sometimes be simplified to a more concise phrase. When you spot a word like "is," "are," "was," and "were" in a subordinate clause, take it as an invitation to simplify:

When you are in doubt about deductions on your tax return, call the IRS collect.

↓

When in doubt about deductions on your tax return, call the IRS collect.

Although they were common a hundred years ago, red wolves are now increasingly rare.

↓

Although common a hundred years ago, red wolves are now increasingly rare.

See if you can simplify the subordinate clause in each of the following two sentences:

Vitamin C tablets, if they are taken regularly, may reduce your chances of getting a cold.

While it was cruising at 33,000 feet, the plane suddenly fell apart.

Each sentence can be made more concise by reducing its subordinate clause to a phrase:

Vitamin C tablets, **if taken regularly,** may reduce your chances of getting a cold.

While cruising at 33,000 feet, the plane suddenly fell apart.

*   *   *

Making one of two sentences into a subordinate clause is a way of emphasizing the relationship between the two sentences. At the same time, subordinating one clause to another usually indicates that the material relegated to the subordinate clause is not as important as the material placed in the main clause. The exercises that follow are designed to help you create subordinate clauses, to choose among patterns of subordination, and, when appropriate, to reduce subordinate clauses to more concise phrases.

CONSTRUCTING SUBORDINATE CLAUSES

Make each sequence of sentences below into a single sentence by converting one or more of the original sentences into a subordinate clause. For several of the sequences, do more than one version. You might want to review the list of subordinators in the introduction to this unit.

Example

> 1. The murderer admitted his guilt.
> 2. The innocent man was executed.

The murderer admitted his guilt **after the innocent man was executed.**

OR

Although the murderer admitted his guilt, the innocent man was executed.

OR

The innocent man was executed **just before the murderer admitted his guilt.**

A. 1. The professor began his lecture.
   2. The student fell asleep.

B. 1. The humps of camels do not in fact store water.
   2. Camels may survive more than a month without a drink anyway.

C. 1. The Kinks perform.
   2. The audience demands to hear "Lola."

D. 1. Men may deny it.
   2. Women may soon be able to compete with men in most sporting events.

E. 1. Columbus spotted chewing gum in the mouths of his Indian hosts.
   2. Long before this time chewing gum had been used to soothe people's nerves and to strengthen their jaws.

F. 1. Many liberal arts graduates will have difficulty finding employment.
   2. They are willing to accept work outside their major subjects.
   3. The economic situation becomes more favorable.

G. 1. The Warren Report has been accepted by most Americans.
   2. The Warren Report left many questions unanswered about the assassination of President Kennedy.

H. 1. Evangelical movements seem to be attracting thousands of American youth.
   2. Traditional churches and synagogues are at the same time losing members.

I. 1. TV soap operas have the potential to tackle tough questions like the changing role of women in American society.
   2. TV soap operas may distort the viewer's perception of reality.

J. 1. The Western world continues to regard acupuncture with suspicion.
   2. Perhaps the reason is that acupuncture is so alien to our own concept of medical treatment.

MOTIVES FOR MARTYRS

Using subordinate clauses whenever appropriate, combine the sentences below into a paragraph that clearly explains Kenneth B. Clark's belief that martyrs act in behalf of others because they are compelled by inner forces to do so.

1. Kenneth B. Clark is a psychologist.
2. Kenneth B. Clark may be right.
3. If so, martyrs are not motivated by their own free will.

4. If so, martyrs are motivated by their physiology.
5. Joan of Arc is an example of a martyr.
6. Mahatma Gandhi is an example of a martyr.
7. Martin Luther King is an example of a martyr.

8. Clark accepts this traditional idea.
9. The traditional idea is that martyrs are distinguished by a highly developed empathy.
10. Empathy is an extreme sensitivity to the needs of other people.
11. Empathy is an extreme sensitivity to the aspirations of other people.
12. Empathy is an extreme sensitivity to the frustration of other people.
13. Empathy is an extreme sensitivity to the pain of other people.

14. But Clark claims this.
15. Empathy has a physiological source.

16. Clark links the capacity for empathy to the development of the cortical base of the brain's anterior frontal lobes.
17. Clark notes that psychiatric patients lose their capacity for empathy.
18. This loss occurs when psychiatric patients are lobotomized.

19. Martyrs are empathetic because they have a highly developed cortical base.
20. This is Clark's conclusion.

21. So martyrs act in behalf of other people.
22. So martyrs act in behalf of moral causes.
23. When they do, they are responding to a need.
24. The need is compulsive.
25. The need is physiological.
26. The need is to identify with those people.
27. The need is to identify with those causes.

28. Clark believes that the martyrs' conduct is no less admirable.
29. Although this is so, Clark's point is this.
30. Martyrs really have no choice.
31. Martyrs must act as they do.

SIMPLIFYING SUBORDINATE CLAUSES

Make each sequence of sentences below into a single sentence by converting one of the original sentences into a subordinate clause. Then, if possible, reduce the subordinate clause to a phrase.

Example

1. You are traveling in Scotland.
2. Then you surely want to visit the city of St. Andrews and its famous golf course.

When you are traveling in Scotland, you surely want to visit the city of St. Andrews and its famous golf course.

When traveling in Scotland, you surely want to visit the city of St. Andrews and its famous golf course.

A. 1. You are denied credit.
   2. Then you are entitled to an explanation.

B. 1. They were just a handful of men and women.
   2. Still, the American transcendentalists exerted a powerful influence in the nineteenth century.

C. 1. He was unable to tell the difference between true love and false love.
   2. For this reason, King Lear lost his kingdom and eventually his life.

D. 1. The mayor was attending a conference on prison reform.
   2. At the same time her house was ransacked by a juvenile gang.

E. 1. They were once deserted during the summer months.
   2. Now ski resorts have created attractions like the Alpine Slide to entice visitors even when there is no snow.

NO MORE BURGERS?

Using subordinate clauses whenever appropriate, create from the sentences below an essay that persuades the reader of the need for shifting to a vegetarian diet. Use reasons and examples of your own whenever you choose. Finally, decide whether to end your essay with sentence 47 below or to create a conclusion of your own.

1. This is usually the case.
2. Meat eaters have regarded vegetarians as fanatics.
3. The fanatics are emaciated.
4. The fanatics pick at a few nuts and berries.

5. These leaf lovers may know something.
6. The leaf lovers are fastidious.
7. Most steak lovers don't want to know it.

8. Populations continue to grow.
9. Available land dwindles.
10. The dwindling is rapid.
11. As these occur, there will be less and less food for the world's hungry mouths.

12. We should shift to basically vegetarian diets.
13. Vegetarian diets encourage wiser use of our land.
14. Vegetarian diets encourage wiser use of our animal resources.
15. Unless we do, we face hunger.
16. The hunger is massive.
17. The hunger is global.

18. This is an example.
19. A steer weighs 1100 pounds.
20. The steer devours almost 3 tons of nutrients.
21. The devouring occurs during the lifetime of the steer.
22. The steer yields only 460 pounds of edible meat.
23. This means that the steer must gobble up over 12 pounds of food.
24. This gobbling is for every pound of its own edible meat.

25. This becomes clear, then.
26. We can feed more people with corn than with sirloins.
27. We can feed more people with lentils than with T-bones.
28. We can feed more people with soybeans than with rib-eyes.

29. This is in addition to the points above.
30. We don't need all that meat for nutrition.
31. Even the World Health Organization acknowledges the fact below.
32. The World Health Organization is a conservative organization.
33. Properly combined meatless meals supply all the nutrients essential to the human diet.

34. Cool fruit salads are meatless meals.
35. Ocean-fresh halibut is a meatless meal.
36. Hot vegetable soups are meatless meals.
37. Swiss cheese fondue is a meatless meal.

38. All indications point to this.
39. Meatless meals provide plenty of nutrition.
40. They do so at lower cost.
41. They do so with more economic use of the land.

42. It may be some time before famines force us to do something.
43. We may have to sacrifice burgers for broccoli.
44. We may have to serve spaghetti without meatballs.
45. While this is true, it's not too soon to start something.
46. We should retrain our taste buds right now.

47. Anyone for eggplant casserole?

USING SUBORDINATION TO STRENGTHEN PARAGRAPHS

Strengthen each paragraph that follows—try to make it clearer, more concise, or more sharply focused—by converting one or more of the original sentences into a subordinate clause.

Example

It will take a while for electric cars to replace the old, reliable internal combustion engine. But some day such cars may become a popular means of commuter transportation. Their future depends on two things. First, they have to be mass-produced. Second, they need to be equipped with batteries that will travel 100 to 150 miles on one charge.

↓

It will take a while for electric cars to replace the old, reliable internal combustion engine. **Before such cars can become a popular means of commuter transportation,** they will have to be mass-produced and equipped with batteries that can travel 100 to 150 miles on one charge.

OR

Although it will take a while for electric cars to replace the old, reliable internal combustion engine, such cars may become a popular means of commuter transportation some day, **provided they are mass-produced and equipped with batteries that will travel 100 to 150 miles on one charge.**

A. The Chinese are taking desperate measures to curb their population explosion. Women in China may have babies. But first they must get permission from their local planning committee. Such committees take their authority seriously. Parents of unapproved babies face rough treatment—in one recent case a $200 fine, public scolding, and denial of a grain ration for the child.

B. John Murphy of Haddon Heights, New Jersey, invented a new "Murphy's Law": he claims that taxes are unconstitutional and refuses to pay them. He does file a tax return every year. But in the small boxes on the form where Americans reveal their most intimate secrets, Murphy evokes the Fifth Amendment. He refuses to "incriminate" himself. Apparently the trick is perfectly legal. No one in the United States has ever gone to jail for refusing to pay taxes on constitutional grounds. The IRS would prefer to keep this bit of news to itself.

C. Apparently music can have strange effects on humans. We know that rock music can cause loss of hearing. Now a doctor has discovered that a certain rock tempo, which he describes as dit-dit-da, dit-dit-da, goes opposite to the heartbeat. As a result, it can throw the heart out of synchronization, and this in turn creates the effect of stoppage. The resulting increase in stress weakens the body and makes it more vulnerable to disease. So the next time you listen to the Supremes or to the Bee Gees or to Mick Jagger and his Rolling Stones—watch your heart!

D. 6079 Smith W.! 2713 Bumstead J.! Do you remember these characters from George Orwell's eerie world of *1984?* Now, it seems, numbers may be coming into use to refer to real people, not just fictional ones. Recently a Minnesota citizen named Michael Herbert Dengler applied to the court to change his legal name to the number 1069. The court admitted that society should respect an individual's right to be known by four digits of his choosing rather than by the name given him by his parents. But the court argued that a decision in Dengler's favor would speed the process of dehumanization that has already gone too far. What do you think?

E. Modern advertising agencies perpetuate a medieval conception of romance. Poets no longer sing about "courtly love"; they did that in the Middle Ages, in the days of the troubadours. But the male is still the active suitor, and the woman is the passive object of his worship. She is portrayed as decorative and precious and innocent, waiting for her knight to return on his "white horse"— his Corvette. Such ads exclude anyone who does not fit the rich, beautiful, heterosexual stereotype. Thus they are almost pernicious. They limit women to passive and exploitive roles.

DRACULA

Read over the following sentences in order to decide whether the material there better supports the thesis that (1) the appeal of the Dracula legend lies in its implied sexuality or that (2) the appeal of the Dracula legend stems from its veiled promise of eternal life.

Then, using subordinate clauses whenever appropriate, construct an explanatory essay that develops the thesis you have chosen. Be sure to exclude from your essay any facts or details that do not help develop its thesis.

1. "Good evening. I am Count Dracula."

2. Bela Lugosi's voice chilled theatergoers.
3. His voice is now famous.
4. Then it ushered in the modern Dracula era.
5. It did this 50 years ago.

6. The blood-sucking count has walked the night.
7. He has walked since the days of ancient Egypt.
8. He has walked since the days of ancient Greece.

9. And now he lurks in the rock group Kiss.
10. And now he lurks in the Vampire Research Society of America.

11. Some of this interest is devoted to the historical Vlad the Impaler.
12. Vlad was a fifteenth-century Romanian prince.
13. He was nicknamed Dracula.
14. Dracula means "son of the devil."

15. Vlad was famous for torturing to death 30,000 Turks.
16. He did this in one day.
17. Dracula's appeal transcends a mere historical interest.
18. The interest is in one otherwise obscure prince.

19. What makes the infamous Prince of Evil so potent a monster?

20. What explains the endurance of the count?
21. The endurance is from one generation to the next.

22. He endures for this reason.
23. We see in him the hope for immortality.

24. He endures for this reason.
25. His sexual appeal fascinates us.
26. His sexual appeal is latent.

27. A vampire's existence may not appeal to many people.
28. The appeal is conscious.
29. But the all-important promise of life after death strikes a chord.
30. The chord is deep in our unconscious.
31. The chord is the powerful will to live.
32. This is despite the cost.

33. It is this sexual magnetism of Dracula.
34. The sexual magnetism makes the count the ultimate sexual partner.
35. It is his lurid machismo.

36. He is so polite.
37. He is so aristocratic.

38. Death has traditionally been a metaphor.
39. The metaphor is for the moment of sexual ecstasy.
40. Who but Count Dracula can make one "die" so thoroughly?
41. Dracula roams only at night.

42. The horror of seeing Dracula's victims collapse in death is offset.
43. The vision of their resurrection offsets it.
44. Their resurrection is in a new existence.

45. His awful bite holds the promise of a ghoulish paradise.
46. It is a paradise of perpetual youth.

47. Dracula's own immortality in myths reinforces his appeal.
48. Dracula's own immortality in history books reinforces his appeal.
49. Dracula's own immortality in novels reinforces his appeal.
50. And Dracula's own immortality in movies reinforces his appeal.

51. Movie heroines and devotees have never been able to resist.
52. They can't resist his bedroom voice.
53. He seduces them with his kiss.

54. The count's passion for virgins contributes to his reputation.
55. He devours them with his steady gaze.
56. He evokes their deepest passion.

57. The most engrossing moments are always the ultimate moments of passion.
58. The moments are in Dracula stories.
59. The young, innocent woman submits to the count's charm.

60. She collapses with him.
61. They are in a passionate embrace.
62. Her desire and blood are drained together.

63. Audiences grow quiet.
64. Dracula wins another convert.
65. They don't grow quiet for the horror.
66. They grow quiet for the passion of the moment.

67. Bela Lugosi stays young in the old movies.
68. The old movies are on TV.
69. And the character Dracula is given a new resurrection.
70. Christopher Lee resurrected the character.

71. Suppose we look hard enough.
72. Then we can always find Dracula alive.
73. And we can always find Dracula ageless.

74. The phallic image is an appropriate symbolic end.
75. The image is of a stake.
76. The stake is driven deep into the vampire's heart.
77. It is the appropriate symbolic end for a creature.
78. The creature's fangs have drained the blood.
79. The blood is from many a virgin.

80. We find him.
81. Then we can submit to his bite.
82. We submit to it in our minds.
83. And we can hope to live on.
84. We will live on as one of his disciples.

85. One of his disciples is able to enjoy the immortality forever.
86. Only a vampire's bite can grant the immortality.

87. We may not realize the sexual passion on one level.
88. The passion is latent in Dracula's character.
89. But the next time you meet him in a book, see this.
90. The next time you meet him on the screen, see this.
91. The next time you meet him around the corner, see this.
92. What wins Dracula a place in your heart?
93. Is it the castle and bats?
94. Is it the lurid seduction?

unit*7*
COORDINATION

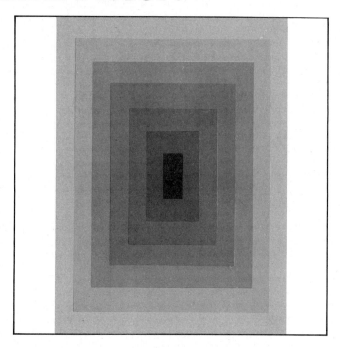

Simple Coordination

In everyday talking and writing, in ordering lunch at the Pizza Hut, or in sending off a postcard, we use coordination more frequently than any other pattern. Coordination is so simple and so basic that all of us were coordinating almost as soon as we began to talk. Since you already use coordination in your writing—you may even over-use it—you obviously don't need instruction in how to coordinate or encouragement to coordinate more frequently. What may be helpful, however, and what this unit offers is practice with various patterns of coordination.

The simplest sort of coordination occurs when a word called a COORDINATOR—a word like **or, and,** or **but**—connects one element in a sentence to another. The elements joined by a coordinator may be single words

students **and** teachers
happy **but** tired
walking **or** running

or phrases

students from Stanford **and** teachers from Berkeley
happy with her achievement **but** tired from the struggle
walking down the street **or** running through an alley

or clauses

if the students are from Stanford **and** the teachers are from Berkeley
since she is happy **but** he is tired
boys who are walking down the street **or** who are running through an alley

Interrupted Coordination

Simple coordination is surely the most common and often the most effective way of joining two similar elements within a sentence. But occasionally you may prefer a somewhat more subtle pattern of coordination. One such pattern involves the deliberate interruption of coordinated elements with a modifying word, phrase, or clause:

The conference on nuclear energy was attended by students from Stanford and, **predictably,** teachers from Berkeley.

Beth was happy with her achievement but, **after three days of intense competition,** tired from the struggle.

Ernie spends Saturday nights walking down the street or, **when the cops are after him,** running through an alley.

The interrupting word, phrase, or clause normally comes right after the coordinator **and, or,** or **but,** and it is usually set off from the rest of the sentence by commas or dashes. Interrupted coordination is a way of adding details smoothly and concisely while at the same time varying the structure and sound of your sentences.

Paired Coordinators

A second pattern of coordination makes use of paired coordinators to strengthen the connection between two words, two phrases, or two clauses. There are six common pairs of coordinators:

1. both . . . and
2. either . . . or
3. neither . . . nor
4. whether . . . or
5. not . . . but (only)
6. not only . . . but (also)

Because each pair includes two coordinators, its connecting power is greater than that of a single coordinator. Paired coordinators therefore help both to emphasize the relatedness of the elements they join and to make writing tighter and more coherent:

1. Methodists set out for the Oregon Territory in the 1830s **both** to convert the Indians **and** to support American government claims to the area.

2. We now dispose of nuclear waste **either** by burying it in the earth **or** by dumping it into the sea.

3. According to the first law of thermodynamics, energy can be **neither** created **nor** destroyed.

4. **Whether** measured in terms of dollars spent **or** people in-volved, education is the largest "industry" in the nation.

5. Women make less money than men **not** because they're less qualified **but** because they're women.

6. Subsidiaries of Pepsico, Inc. include **not only** fast-food restaurants like Taco Bell **but also** transportation firms like North American Van Lines.

As with simple coordination, sentences with paired coordinators may be interrupted by a modifier that adds details or that helps define the writer's attitude. The interruption usually occurs just after the second of the paired coordinators:

Methodists set out for the Oregon Territory in the 1830s both to convert the Indians and, **though most of them didn't know it,** to support American government claims to the area.

We now dispose of nuclear waste either by burying it in the earth or—**more commonly**—by dumping it into the sea.

Women make less money than men not because they're less qualified but—**you guessed it!**— because they're women.

A great deal of simple coordination will tend to make your writing seem relaxed and casual, sometimes even innocent and childlike. By contrast, paired coordinators and interrupted coordination will tend to make your writing seem more formal, serious, and sophisticated. For any writing situation, then, you have choices to make. Do you want to sound offhanded in asking Mom and Dad to send extra money for your Christmas skiing vacation at Squaw Valley? Then use lots of simple coordination in your letter, and you will come across as just an innocent and lovable kid. But if you want to impress either a prospective employer or a distant lover with both your maturity and sophistication, then your letter should include not only paired coordinators but, when appropriate, coordinated elements interrupted by modifiers.

Series Variation

A third pattern of coordination involves the SERIES, a list of three or more items. A series is usually written with commas following each item except the last, and with a coordinator—**and** or **or**—connecting the final two items:

The Triple Crown of thoroughbred racing consists of **the Kentucky Derby, the Preakness, and the Belmont Stakes.**

There are five types of discharge from military service: **honorable, general, undesirable, bad conduct, and dishonorable.**

But the series, like other constructions, offers a number of options. To make the series move slowly and seem lengthy and drawn out and perhaps even tired, try omitting the commas and repeating the coordinator:

At weekend tournaments in California, skateboarding contestants demonstrate all sorts of feats—wheelies **and** kick flips **and** revolutions **and** handstands.

Raising vegetables presents endless opportunities for weeding **and** thinning **and** hoeing **and** watering.

To make the series more rapid, to create a suggestion of urgency, excitement, anger, fear, try eliminating all coordinators:

Individuals are less troubled by feelings of guilt when they share responsibility for killings with a group**—a street gang, lynch mob, terrorist organization.**

Vietnam differed from all earlier American wars in **the elusiveness of the enemy, the widespread use of drugs, the American soldier's sense of outrage.**

It is even possible to combine in a single sentence a series that repeats coordinators with one that eliminates them completely:

There is **no pattern, no meaning, no larger significance** in last week's outbreak of crime except what is weary **and** obvious **and** painful: ours is an era of ugly violence.

Here, the opening series with coordinators eliminated suggests a sense of frustration, even anger, but the repeated coordinators of the second series indicate that the initial anger has given way to fatigue and resignation. In the sentence below, the eliminated coordinators of the opening series contrast with the repeated coordinators of the second to help emphasize the differences between city and country life.

> In the country there are **no honking horns, no diesel trucks, no pollution**—just the sounds of wind rustling the tree leaves **and** red squirrels chattering in the distant oaks **and** cool creek water rushing down its endless course.

Just as two coordinated elements may be interrupted by a modifier in a sentence like "Willie Mays played for the Giants and, **during his final years,** the Mets," so may the three or more items of a series:

> Raising vegetables presents endless opportunities for weeding, thinning, hoeing, watering, and, **one always hopes,** harvesting and eating.

> The filming of *Black Sunday,* a movie in which an Israeli agent chases a Goodyear blimp into the Orange Bowl, required permission from the city of Miami, the Orange Bowl, and, **most importantly,** Goodyear.

When the series contains over three items, there are more options than just repeating or eliminating coordinators and interrupting the coordinated items. Instead of items listed one after the other, such as in

> Only a few cities are known as "good baseball towns"—Boston, Chicago, Cincinnati, Detroit, Los Angeles, and New York.

they can be grouped into pairs:

Only a few cities are known as "good baseball towns"—Boston **and** Chicago, Cincinnati **and** Detroit, Los Angeles **and** New York.

And rather than write

Black American writers like Frederick Douglass, W. E. B. DuBois, Malcolm X, and Eldridge Cleaver have found autobiography an especially congenial form.

you can pair the items:

Black American writers **from** Frederick Douglass and W. E. B. DuBois **to** Malcolm X and Eldridge Cleaver have found autobiography an especially congenial form.

However the series is coordinated and arranged, try to order it so that the most important item, if there is one, comes last.

Coordinating Full Sentences

As well as joining words, phrases, and clauses, coordination also functions to connect full sentences. There are four major patterns of coordination for connecting one full sentence to another. The most common pattern uses a comma and then a coordinator—**and, or, but, for, so, yet**— between the two sentences:

A small percentage of the Mexican population is comfortably rich, **and** a large portion is distressingly poor.

There are over 3000 baseball players in the minor leagues, **but** only about 600 of them will ever reach the majors.

A second, more formal way of coordinating full sentences is by replacing the comma, and usually the coordinator as well, with a semicolon:

A small percentage of the Mexican population is comfortably rich; and large portion is distressingly poor.

There are over 3000 baseball players in the minor leagues; only about 600 of them will ever reach the majors.

When the second full sentence either defines or illustrates the generalization of the first, there is a third way of coordinating them: the colon. So long as the colon comes after a full sentence—not after a phrase or subordinate clause—it is especially appropriate for introducing an explanation or series:

There is one golden rule for dressing socially: if you are wearing the right clothing and everyone else is wearing the wrong clothing, change.

As a boy, Watergate burglar Gordon Liddy tried hard to overcome his numerous fears: he climbed high-tension towers, he strapped himself in a tree during an electrical storm, and he even forced himself to eat the haunch of a dead rat.

A final way of coordinating full sentences involves the paired coordinators such as **either . . . or** or **not (only) . . . but (also):**

Either you register to vote before election day **or** you lose the right to vote.

Not only do Americans now consume more soda than milk or fruit juice **but** they soon will drink more soda than water.

Sentence coordination is usually most appropriate when the two coordinated sentences are equal or nearly equal in importance:

The Columbia Phonograph Broadcasting Company sold for $400,000 in 1928, **and** now its annual sales approach $1 billion.

But even in a coordinated sentence the parts may *not* be equal. In the next example, the clause introduced by "but" clearly commands the attention:

> The Columbia Phonograph Broadcasting Company sold for $400,000 in 1928, **but** its annual sales now approach $1 billion.

Should you want to make it even clearer that the second part of the sentence is more important for the direction of your paper, you would probably reduce the first part to a subordinate clause or a phrase:

> Although the Columbia Phonograph Broadcasting Company sold for $400,000 in 1928, its annual sales now approach $1 billion.

OR

> The Columbia Phonograph Broadcasting Company, which sold for $400,000 in 1928, now has annual sales approaching $1 billion.

OR

> Sold for $400,000 in 1928, the Columbia Phonograph Broadcasting Company now has annual sales approaching $1 billion.

Like coordinated words, phrases, or clauses, coordinated sentences lend themselves to interrupting modifiers:

> The Columbia Phonograph Broadcasting Company sold for $400,000 in 1928, but **—known as CBS—**it now has annual sales that approach $1 billion.

Without interrupters, coordinated sentences are particularly effective for reinforcing a sense of informality and spontaneity:

Toss a pop bottle out of any college dorm, **and** it will probably hit somebody struggling to get into law school.

Coordination becomes more informal as the coordinated sentences become shorter and more numerous and if commas are omitted. Here is an umpire explaining why players have more fun:

A player can strike out twice **and** make three errors **and** then hit a single in the ninth **and** win a ball game **and** he's a hero. **But** an ump can get ten plays right in a row **and** nobody says anything **and** then miss one **and** everybody's mad.

*　　　*　　　*

Interrupted coordination, paired coordinators, series variation, and the patterns of coordinating full sentences can make your writing more varied in sound and structure as well as more specific and more coherent. Try to use these patterns in your compositions.

USING PATTERNS OF COORDINATION

Combine each of the following groups of sentences into a single sentence by using one or more of the patterns of coordination—interrupted coordination, paired coordinators, series variation, or sentence coordination.

Example

    1. New Hampshire does not have a general sales tax.
    2. New Hampshire does not have an income tax.
    3. New Hampshire is the only state that doesn't have at least one of the two taxes.

↓

New Hampshire is the only state without **either** a general sales **or** an income tax.

OR

New Hampshire is the only state that has **neither** a general sales **nor** an income tax.

A. 1. For the first time I saw my father not as the giant of my childhood.
    2. I saw my father simply as a lonely man.

B. 1. More and more universities are creating loan plans to aid middle-income families.
    2. Middle-income families are not rich enough to pay rising college costs.
    3. Middle-income families are not poor enough to qualify for scholarships.

C. 1. Lawyers should be committed to their clients.
    2. Lawyers should also be committed to the judicial process.
    3. Above all, lawyers should be committed to the operation of justice.

D. 1. You can usually recognize the villains of cartoon adventure programs in two ways.

2. The villains laugh fiendishly.
3. The villains speak with a foreign accent.

E. 1. Cave diving is an incredibly complex sport.
2. It is a risky sport.
3. It is an exhilarating sport.
4. It requires a wealth of diving skills.
5. It requires the best of underwater technology.

F. 1. Aging and neglected, America's infrastructure is heading toward collapse.
2. The infrastructure is a vast, vital network.
3. It is a network of roads.
4. It is a network of bridges.
5. It is a network of sewers.
6. It is a network of railroads and mass transit systems.

G. 1. Opponents of gun control cite several proper uses of handguns.
2. One proper use is law enforcement.
3. Another proper use is target practice.
4. Yet another proper use is self-defense.
5. Self-defense is a proper use especially for those tired of being robbed.

H. 1. Male chauvinists find Gloria Steinem a formidable opponent.
2. Gloria Steinem's facts are accurate.
3. Gloria Steinem's opinions are significant.
4. Gloria Steinem's arguments are convincing.

I. 1. The four largest hotel companies in the United States are Hilton, Sheraton, Hyatt, and Western International.
2. Western International is the fastest growing hotel company.

J. 1. The viewers of pantomime are unhampered by stage properties.
2. The viewers of pantomime are aided by the supple mind of the actor.
3. The viewers of pantomime are aided by the supple body of the actor.

4. The viewers of pantomime can see what is not there.
5. The viewers of pantomime can hear what is not said.
6. The viewers of pantomime can believe the impossible.
7. They believe it for a short while at least.

NOT MY CHILDREN

Using, where appropriate, patterns of coordination such as interrupted coordination, paired coordinators, series variation, and sentence coordination, combine the sentences below into an explanatory paragraph. From your own experience add examples to support the thesis that some married women prefer not to have children.

1. There have always been married women without children.
2. It used to be thought that there was something wrong with such women.
3. There was something wrong with them physically.
4. Or there was something wrong with them emotionally.

5. But the facts below come from a recent psychological study.
6. There are married women today who plan to have no children.
7. These women are not raving maniacs.
8. These women are not frustrated neurotics.
9. These women are as well-adjusted as women who plan to be mothers.

10. Married women who plan to have no children are happy in their marriages.
11. Married women who plan to have no children are successful in their careers.

12. Three-fourths of the women who plan to have no children have earned a college degree.
13. Even more than three-fourths of these women have found a good job.

14. Some of the women who plan to have no children have entered business.

15. Others are in education.
16. Still others are in law.
17. Still others are in medicine.
18. And still others are in sciences like chemistry and physics.

19. Women who plan to have no children are typically middle-class people.
20. They are well-educated.
21. They are settled in responsible jobs in professional fields.
22. They are happy to be living without children.

REVISING PATTERNS OF COORDINATION

Make each of the following sentences more effective by changing the patterns of coordination. Use patterns like interrupted coordination, series variation, paired coordinators, and sentence coordination.

Example

For decades FBI agents wiretapped the phones of American citizens with the attorney general's approval, and they didn't have warrants.

For decades FBI agents wiretapped the phones of American citizens **with** the attorney general's approval and **without** warrants.

A. More people live by themselves and more women work and more money is available, and for these reasons one of every three American food dollars now goes to restaurants or fast-food shops.

B. Television has been called a source of information, a means of entertainment, and a "plug-in" drug; especially its severest critics call it a "plug-in" drug.

C. Marijuana smuggling has become a multibillion-dollar industry, and the American government does not collect any taxes from it; neither does any other government.

D. Rugby is played with no substitutions, no regard for life and limb, and no pads.

E. Although he has long been retired from boxing, Muhammed Ali remains one of the best-known personalities in the world, and he is also the best boxer in history—at least in the eyes of many he is the best boxer in history.

F. Stories that appear on local television newscasts are usually not selected by journalists; instead, they are usually selected by "consultants" who search for stories the public will find least objectionable.

G. James Bond is a refined gentleman, a witty conversationalist, a ruthless killer, and a charming companion; that James Bond is a ruthless killer many agents of SPECTRE have learned.

H. Some of the German immigrants in America crossed the Atlantic as virtual slaves while others came as free men, but in either case they established an early reputation for hard work, thoroughness, and thriftiness.

I. In Frisbee golf, the "tee" is likely to be a small rock, and the "hole" will probably be a drinking fountain, or it might be a lamp post.

J. New York City is the art capital of the world; not only that, New York City is a cheap place to live—by the standards of any other major cultural center.

LAST CALL

Using several patterns of coordination as appropriate, combine the following sentences into an essay that persuades either (1) high school students or (2) parents of high school students that drinking by the young has become a serious social problem. Make whatever changes are necessary—including the addition of details of your own—so that your essay is especially persuasive for the audience you have chosen.

1. A 9-year-old arrested for drunken driving in a stolen MG?

2. It sounds incredible.
3. Nearly 200 children were arrested for drunken driving in one part of the country alone.
4. This occurred in 1983.
5. The children were under age 11.

6. Police files record thousands of other crimes.
7. Vandalism is one of those crimes.
8. Theft is one of those crimes.
9. Even rape is one of those crimes.
10. These crimes were committed by children who were drunk.

11. Arrests are made.
12. But drunkenness among teens and preteens continues to spread.
13. And alcoholism among teens and preteens continues to spread.

14. Here is an example.
15. This occurs in Boston.
16. This occurs in New York.
17. Eleven- and 12-year-olds frequently come to school drunk.
18. Sometimes they even bring their bottle of Canadian Club along.

19. Young drunks crash local dances.
20. Teenage gangs clash in Burger King parking lots.
21. This occurs nationwide.

22. Students gather at Friday night drinking blasts.
23. These are high school students.
24. And these are junior high school students.
25. Even respected students gather.

26. But it's not always party time.

27. Teenage drinking has increased so much.
28. There are now close to one million alcoholics under age 21.
29. One million is an estimate.
30. In addition, there are now over 25 special Alcoholics Anonymous chapters.
31. Their activities are geared solely to teens and preteens.

32. Alcohol abuse accounts for the majority of young suicides.
33. Not only that, at least 15,000 traffic deaths are attributed to teenage drinking each year.
34. And 75,000 serious injuries are attributed to teenage drinking each year.

35. This is despite these sobering facts.
36. Most parents condone drinking at home.
37. Most parents condone drinking at social gatherings.

38. Most parents are thankful that their kids are not experimenting with pot.
39. Most parents are thankful that their kids are not experimenting with cocaine.
40. Most parents are thankful that their kids are only trying booze.
41. Booze is the same drug the parents themselves enjoy.

42. Young people are coaxed by their peers.
43. Young people are encouraged by their parents.
44. Young people often resort to drinking like adults.
45. Young people often resort to committing crimes like adults.
46. Young people often resort to dying like adults.
47. Dying like adults is saddest of all.

COORDINATING IN CONTEXT

Strengthen each paragraph below by using, where appropriate, one or more patterns of coordination—interrupted coordination, paired coordinators, series variation, or sentence coordination. Make other changes that will improve the paragraph.

Example

Although Volkswagen Beetles have been hopelessly left behind by advances in automotive technology, they can still be seen bugging around on America's streets and highways. Beetles are sluggish, and they are uncomfortable. And don't they make a lot of noise! Besides, Beetles are hardly pretty. So why the appeal? Perhaps Beetles are popular because they can be easily remodeled to reflect the personality of their owner.

Although Volkswagen Beetles have been hopelessly left behind by advances in automotive technology, they can still be seen bugging around on America's streets and highways. **Not only** are Beetles sluggish but they are **also** noisy, ugly, and—**above all** —uncomfortable. So why do they have such continuing appeal? Perhaps because they can be easily remodeled to reflect the personality of their owner.

A. More and more teachers moonlight because they cannot make it on their regular income. They are victims of declining payscales and the lack of public support for their efforts. According to one expert, teachers have only two choices. One choice is that they can leave teaching. The other is that they can find second jobs to supplement their income. Unfortunately, many teachers have found their other job so lucrative and enjoyable that they are taking the first alternative and resigning their jobs. And those who leave the teaching profession are often the best. They are the type it can least afford to lose.

B. Hershey's is—according to a popular advertising jingle—the "Great American Chocolate Bar." And Hershey, Pennsylvania, may just be the Great American Small Town. It has clean, tree-lined streets. It has magnificent gardens. You can also find museums and a 76-acre amusement park, not to mention a school for underprivileged children. Founded by candy magnate Milton Snavely Hershey, the little paradise reportedly has no jail. It does not have poverty. It has no shortage of chocolate. For sure.

C. A Soviet magazine editor has predicted that people in his country will eventually live 150 or even 200 years, as some in the Caucasus apparently already do. Imagine what such routine longevity would do to American society! Midlife would begin at 110 or so; by the onset of old age, retirees would have fished every lake, and they would have hunted all wildlife to extinction. All golf courses would have been reduced to stubble, and they would have drawn Social Security for 100 years. You and I may live that long—but will American society?

TATTOOING

Using, where appropriate, patterns of coordination such as interrupted coordination, paired coordinators, series variation, and sentence coordination, combine the following sentences into an explanatory essay which develops the thesis that in our society tattooing is associated with violence and crime. Omit details that weaken your thesis and add details that strengthen it.

1. The arm of a seaman is decorated with a cobra.
2. The arm is sweaty and muscular.
3. The arm glistens with salt spray.
4. The cobra is red and green.
5. The cobra is coiled.
6. The cobra is ready to strike.

7. A well-dressed gentleman slyly raises his pant cuff.
8. He is in a smoke-filled bar.
9. A sleazy trumpet moans in the background.
10. He reveals a blue infinity sign.
11. The sign identifies him as a member of a secret gang.

12. Three high school students gawk at the design book.
13. They decide on the naked bust of a sultry brunette.
14. The bust will be emblazoned on their upper leg.
15. The bust will be safely hidden from their parents' gaze.

16. The practice of tattooing has appealed to various people.
17. It has appealed for various reasons.
18. It apparently derives much of its appeal from an aura.
19. It has an aura of mystery.
20. It has an aura of evil.

21. In primitive societies tattooing was used as magic.
22. A tattoo of a snake supposedly protected a warrior from his enemies.
23. A tattoo of a cat supposedly increased a warrior's cunning and agility.

24. In modern societies, however, tattooing has usually been associated with evil.
25. Tattooing has usually not been associated with magic.

26. In modern societies, the practice of tattooing has always been frowned upon.
27. The practice of tattooing has sometimes been banned.

28. Tattooing was forbidden in Europe.
29. It was forbidden after the introduction of Christianity.
30. But it maintained its popularity in underworld circles.

31. Convicts in prison were identified by tattoos.
32. This occurred as late as the nineteenth and early twentieth centuries.
33. The tattoos were in conspicuous places.
34. Conspicuous places are the back of the hand and the cheek.

35. Today, tattoos are most common among military personnel, motorcycle gangs, and criminals.
36. The criminals now use tattoos to identify themselves as gang members.
37. The criminals now use tattoos to indicate their rank within the gang.

38. It is with these values that most people associate the innocent practice of tattooing.
39. These values are a life of violence or a life of crime.

40. Most recently, tattooing's shadowy aura of evil and mystery has been amplified.
41. Tattoo parlors have been banned in major cities.
42. One such city is New York.
43. Health authorities fear that tattooing may lead to hepatitis and cancer.

44. But even today young people are fond of tattoos.
45. The young people are of both sexes.
46. Perhaps their fondness is because there is glamour in being marked.

47. The most popular style for women is a finely sketched flower.
48. The flower is tattooed on a shoulder, thigh, or breast.

49. The most popular style for men is a large dragon.
50. The body of the dragon is wrapped around the arm.
51. Or the most popular style for men is a heart.
52. A woman's name is enclosed within the heart.

53. Tattooing may one day shed its associations with the underworld.
54. This may occur if there are more talented artists.
55. This may occur if there are safer methods.
56. This may occur if there are less painful methods.

57. Tattooing may even become a legitimate art form.
58. Tattooing may not be just a means of identifying criminals.
59. Tattooing may not be just a means of identifying members of secret gangs.

60. Tattooing may gain acceptance by society at large.
61. If so, it will have lost its special aura of mystery and evil.

unit 8
PREPOSITIONAL PHRASES AND INFINITIVES

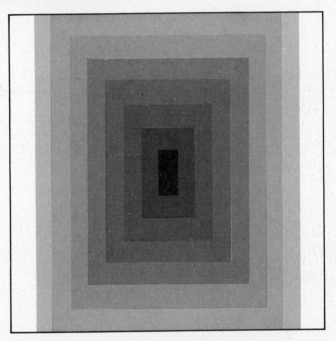

Prepositional Phrases

You probably can't speak or write beyond a sentence or two without using a PREPOSITION. When you tell **about** your trip **to** Greece **with** some friends **during** the summer, argue **for** or **against** prayer **in** the schools, brag that your new computer can play chess **like** a master, or explain how scientists turn salt water **into** fuel **by** a new chemical process—you're using prepositions. Prepositions not only make relationships more specific between and among sentence parts but they also establish points of reference for readers, like information signs on highways.

The most common prepositions are **at, by, for, from, like, of, on, to,** and **with;** others include **after, before, between, despite, over, through, under, until,** and **without.** Some prepositions consist of more than one word, such as **according to, as far back as, because of, contrary to, except for, in addition to, in compliance with, in the absence of, rather than,** and **thanks to.**

A preposition never occurs by itself. As its name implies, it is a *pre-*position: it is positioned before a noun or noun phrase, which serves as its object. A preposition together with its object forms a PREPOSITIONAL PHRASE, such as **with us, against the B-1 bomber, because of her favorable experience with co-educational dorms,** and **thanks to the high voter turnout.**

The Role of Prepositional Phrases

Prepositional phrases occur so frequently that it's easy to forget how important they are in constructing clear, expressive sentences. They function in two important ways in sentences: they can either clarify statements by indicating such concepts as manner, reason, likeness, cause, and condition, or they can provide the context for statements by indicating such concepts as place and time. In other words, they help to amplify ideas and to direct readers through your prose. Notice that in the next sentence prepositional phrases indicate place:

> I crossed the U.S. 36 bridge and drove **past Elwood, Kansas, across the Missouri's rich farmland, through bustling Troy, up wooded valleys to the West's high rolling plains.**

But they do more as well. Because of those prepositional phrases, readers can almost feel the movement **past, across, through,** and **up,** until—along with the writer—they get **to** the West's high rolling plains. In the next example, the prepositional phrase **After the television series "The Winds of War"** provides the time context for the statement that Americans showed a renewed interest in World War II history:

> **After the television series "The Winds of War,"** Americans showed a renewed interest in World War II history.

Besides place and time, prepositional phrases can also indicate adverbial concepts such as manner, reason, likeness, and condition.

> Manner: **With the bright architects and engineers he gathered around him,** Henry Ford learned to produce cars efficiently, quickly, and profitably.

> Reason: **For their work in genetics,** two Americans and a Frenchman received the Nobel Prize in medicine.

> Likeness: **Like Swiss army knives,** some stone-age tools served multiple purposes—scraping, cutting, and drilling.

> Condition: Vegetarians get plenty of protein from nuts and dairy products, whole grains, and beans, **despite the common belief that only meat provides adequate amounts of protein.**

Reducing Clauses to Prepositional Phrases

Prepositional phrases can sometimes substitute for full clauses. As you revise your early drafts, you may find that a full clause either makes a particular sentence wordy or does not convey precisely the relationship you intend between two ideas. In such cases, prepositional phrases provide you handy options for making your sentences more concise and often more clear as well:

> Although they have a menacing appearance, most reptiles aren't really vicious if you leave them alone.

↓

Despite their menacing appearance, most reptiles aren't really vicious if you leave them alone.

Because gasoline prices have increased and because the public has become interested in fitness, bicycles have become a popular means of urban transportation.

↓

With the increase in gasoline prices and the public's interest in fitness, bicycles have become a popular means of urban transportation.

OR

Thanks to the increase in gasoline prices and the public's interest in fitness, bicycles have become a popular means of urban transportation.

Not only will the museum purchase the Renoir paintings, but it will also purchase two Monet sketches.

↓

In addition to the Renoir paintings, the museum will also purchase two Monet sketches.

Sometimes you can reduce a full clause to a phrase containing a preposition and an **-ing** noun:

Before she drowned herself, Virginia Woolf wrote a lovely suicide note to her husband.

↓

Before drowning herself, Virginia Woolf wrote a lovely suicide note to her husband.

After they bury the nuclear waste in steel and concrete casks, the Department of Energy will erect markers to warn future generations of the radiation danger.

↓

After burying the nuclear waste in steel and concrete casks, the Department of Energy will erect markers to warn future generations of the radiation danger.

Arranging Prepositional Phrases

You can sometimes move a prepositional phrase from one sentence position to another. Whether or not you can move a phrase depends on the individual characteristics of its preposition, the meaning of the phrase, and its role in the sentence. You can usually depend on your intuition to tell you whether you can move a phrase. In the sentence about bicycles above, the phrase beginning with **thanks to** can be moved to the end, but the phrase introduced by **with** cannot:

Bicycles have become a popular means of urban transportation, **thanks to the increase in gasoline prices and the public's interest in fitness.**

BUT NOT

Bicycles have become a popular means of urban transportation, **with the increase in gasoline prices and the public's interest in fitness.**

When the prepositional phrase modifies a short subject noun, then the phrase can usually occur on either side of the noun:

For all its quiet simplicity, Calder's art represents a complex fusion of many elements.

OR

Calder's art, **for all its quiet simplicity,** represents a complex fusion of many elements.

Despite their increased numbers in the work force, women still earn less than men.

OR

Women, **despite their increased numbers in the work force,** still earn less than men.

Balanced Phrases

You can use prepositions to create balanced phrases, either in pairs or by repetition in a series. The use of paired prepositions such as **from-to, with-without,** or **for-against** creates the effect of balancing opposites or suggests that a subject has been completely covered:

The mad dancing epidemics of southern Europe in the Middle Ages have been blamed on just about everything, for example on mildew in the rye meal and religious fanaticism.

↓

The mad dancing epidemics of southern Europe in the Middle Ages have been blamed on everything **from** mildew in the rye meal **to** religious fanaticism.

Glamorous couples have always lured audiences to movie theaters, as John Barrymore and Greta Garbo did it in the past and Robert De Niro and Meryl Streep do now.

↓

Glamorous couples—**from** John Barrymore and Greta Garbo **to** Robert De Niro and Meryl Streep—have always lured audiences to movie theaters.

A series, on the other hand, enumerates parallel points, linking them in a tight chain:

The Chinese have built a society **with** an educational system radically different from ours, **with** aspirations challenging some of our most cherished values, and **with** a strong sense of mission at times enviable, at times frightening.

The election dramatized the confrontation **between** liberals and conservatives, **between** Democrats and Republicans, **be-**

tween the smokestack North and East and the sunbelt South and West.

Just as they can link phrases within sentences, paired prepositions can link sentences within paragraphs:

Mail to California took up to six long weeks by ship. But then the Pony Express was started and the same mail took only ten days.

↓

Before the Pony Express, mail to California took up to six long weeks by ship. **After** the Pony Express, the same mail took only ten days.

In fact, linking sentences either with pairs of prepositions or with series of prepositions is one way you can achieve coherence and emphasis within your paragraphs. Notice that by repeating the preposition **under** in the next pair of sentences, the writer not only links the sentences tightly but also emphasizes the seriousness of the new situation:

While Carter was in office, one embassy was seized. But since Reagan's first term, several embassies have been blown to smithereens.

↓

Under Carter, one embassy was seized. **Under** Reagan, several embassies have been blown to smithereens.

Infinitive Phrases

Similar in appearance to prepositional phrases are adverbial INFINITIVES. Such infinitives are always introduced by the word **to** or the phrase **in order to,** followed by a simple verb form as their object: **to see, to write, to daydream, in order to make as much profit as possible.** Unlike infinitives used as noun substitutes, which are discussed in Unit 9, an adverbial infinitive generally implies an intention, goal, or purpose, something that a person might "want" to do:

Do you want to prevent animals from eating your garden?
Then you can spray the vegetables with a solution of garlic and
pepper.

↓

To prevent animals from eating your garden, you can
spray the vegetables with a solution of garlic and pepper.

Cowpunchers want to soften a new rope.
Cowpunchers will spend hours pulling it, stretching it, and twisting it.

↓

To soften a new rope, cowpunchers will spend hours pulling
it, stretching it, and twisting it.

Ordinarily, we understand an infinitive to have the same subject as
the rest of its sentence—"you" and "cowpunchers" in the last two
examples. For this reason, when you begin a sentence with an infinitive phrase, you should usually put the subject immediately after it:

The sociology department wanted to attract new majors.
The sociology department made imaginative curriculum changes.

↓

To attract new majors, the sociology department made imaginative curriculum changes.

RATHER THAN

To attract new majors, imaginative curriculum changes were
made by the sociology department.

Adverbial infinitives may occur at the end as well as at the beginning of a sentence:

Medical students serve an internship **in order to gain
firsthand experience before they officially begin
their careers.**

Kaplan's book closely examines Mark Twain's image, **to get at all the mischief, pathos, and creative energy of the man himself.**

Adverbial infinitives may also occur in the middle of the sentence, either to create the effect of an important afterthought, as in

Repeaters are given study materials designed especially for them and, **to avoid the stigma of studying with younger children,** placed in classes with children their own age.

or to highlight the infinitive phrase:

EPA researchers, **in order to measure the damage done to forests by air pollution,** are exposing trees to auto emissions, then spraying them with "homemade" acid rain.

You can use either commas or dashes to separate infinitives from main clauses. Because dashes create longer pauses than commas, they give added emphasis to infinitives, especially in the middle or end of a sentence:

Kaplan's book closely examines Mark Twain's image—**to get at all the mischief, pathos, and creative energy of the man himself.**

EPA researchers—**in order to measure the damage done to forests by air pollution**—are exposing trees to auto emissions, then spraying them with "homemade" acid rain.

Infinitives, like prepositions and other modifiers, can occur in a series, either preceding or following a main clause:

To meet our energy needs, to compete with foreign industry, to build a projected 30 million new homes,

and to maintain our standard of living, we need staggering amounts of new capital.

For variation, you may omit the word **to** after the first infinitive in a series:

To meet our energy needs, compete with foreign industry, build a projected 30 million new homes, and maintain our standard of living, we need staggering amounts of new capital.

Like other phrase-length modifiers, adverbial infinitives can often replace whole clauses, as in the following examples:

Because she wants to erase the traditional image of God as a man, the Reverend Elisabeth Jans refers to God as a woman.

↓

To erase the traditional image of God as a man, the Reverend Elisabeth Jans refers to God as a woman.

If you want to avoid auto maintenance rip-offs, ask your friends to recommend repair shops that have given them good service.

↓

To avoid auto maintenance rip-offs, ask your friends to recommend repair shops that have given them good service.

*   *   *

You can use both prepositional phrases and infinitive phrases to convey details. Because they express such adverbial relationships as place, time, manner, and reason, prepositional phrases give readers the background information and orientation necessary to understand the other ideas in your sentences. With infinitive phrases you can suggest intention or purpose. You can move both these structures from one sentence position to another and use them to replace long clauses in order to make your writing more concise, more varied, and more interesting.

CONSTRUCTING PREPOSITIONAL PHRASES AND INFINITIVES

Combine each set of sentences below into a single sentence using one or more prepositional phrases (Example I) or infinitives (Example II).

Example I: Prepositional Phrases

1. The principal lined up the offenders.
2. And, one by one, he swatted them on the rear.
3. He did this in front of their classmates and teachers.

In front of their classmates and teachers, the principal lined up the offenders and, one by one, swatted them on the rear.

A. 1. Woody Guthrie's songs are a national treasure.
   2. Woody Guthrie's songs are like Yellowstone or the Grand Canyon.

B. 1. Some 50 million Americans have become the legal owners of one-third of corporate America.
   2. Pension funds have made this possible.

C. 1. There are traffic jams.
   2. The administration has banned all cars.
   3. You can no longer drive into the central campus area.

D. 1. Pygmies do not grow to full adult height.
   2. Pygmies inherit their stunted stature.
   3. Pygmies are not like children born to dwarf parents.
   4. Children born to dwarf parents almost always grow to full adult height.

E. 1. Student dress is a mixture of styles.
   2. The styles range from the rag-tag to the impeccable.

3. The styles range from wrinkled surgical greens to permanent press Izod shirts.

Example II: Infinitives

1. The auditorium management wanted to prevent crowd-control problems.
2. The auditorium management initiated reserved seating for rock concerts.

↓

To prevent crowd-control problems, the auditorium management initiated reserved seating for rock concerts.

F. 1. The reporters wanted to uncover local welfare fraud.
   2. The reporters interviewed bureaucrats and welfare recipients alike.

G. 1. The hijackers wanted to attract the attention of the American public.
   2. The hijackers tried to force a major network to do this:
   3. The network was to broadcast the hijackers' political demands.

H. 1. The aim of the school was helping students understand death as the natural end of a life cycle.
   2. The school introduced a noncredit course.
   3. The title of the course was Death.

I. 1. Many Americans want to overcome their fear of unknown assailants.
   2. The unknown assailants stalk city streets.
   3. Many Americans take instruction.
   4. They are instructed in some sort of Oriental self-defense.

J. 1. Do you want to produce a really well-written paper?
   2. You should write several drafts.
   3. You should revise as you go.

4. You should tighten as you go.
5. You should reorganize as you go.

MAIDENS OF THE SEA

Using prepositional phrases and infinitives whenever appropriate, combine the following sentences into an explanatory essay about the mermaids who abound in our folklore. At your option, add details that make the essay more informative. You might, for instance, include some information about Andersen's fairy tale or details from the movie *Splash!*

1. The mermaid is probably the best known of all the creatures.
2. The mermaid is probably the least understood of all the creatures.
3. She is one of the creatures that inhabit folklore.

4. Mermaids have been reported.
5. The reports have been from the frozen northland.
6. The reports have been from the tropical seas.
7. The reports have been from ancient Greece.
8. The reports have been from modern America.

9. They abound in poetry.
10. They abound in art.
11. And they even abound in advertising.
12. One mermaid became the symbol for a brand of tuna.

13. But most mermaids are unlike that innocent fish woman.
14. Americans find that innocent fish woman on their tuna cans.
15. Most mermaids are sultry.
16. Most mermaids are mysterious.

17. They can even be provocative.
18. They can even be dangerous.

19. Some sing offshore.
20. They are like the Sirens of the *Odyssey*.
21. They lure sailors to shipwreck in rocky shallows.

22. Other mermaids beguile men.
23. The beguiling is with their beauty.
24. Their beauty is incredible.

25. They have a comb in one hand.
26. They have a mirror in the other.
27. They float among the waves.
28. They tempt mariners to watery deaths.

29. They lure men into the sea.
30. Even though they do this, they often desire to live on shore.

31. A lovely young fish woman gives up her life for this.
32. It is the love of a handsome prince.
33. This happens in Hans Christian Andersen's "The Littlest Mermaid."

34. Hollywood adds to the legend of half-human ocean creatures.
35. They learn to live on dry land.
36. Hollywood does this in old movies like *Mr. Peabody and the Mermaid.*
37. Hollywood does this in new movies like *Splash!*

38. Psychologists suggest this.
39. Mermaids must satisfy a basic psychological need.
40. They do this to have survived as folklore.

41. Perhaps they personify forbidden desires.
42. Or perhaps they simply do this.
43. They allay our fears about the impersonality of nature.

44. Mermaids have sung to humans for centuries.
45. And even today they tantalize us with their elusive mystique.
46. These are true whatever the reason for their existence.

REDUCING CLAUSES

Make each of the following sentences more concise by reducing one or more of the full clauses to a prepositional phrase or an infinitive. Rearrange parts of the sentence when necessary.

Example

> Because some countries have strong religious laws, women are not allowed in the streets except when they have a male chaperone.

↓

Because of strong religious laws, women in some countries are not allowed in the streets **without a male chaperone.**

OR

In some countries **with strong religious laws,** women must have a male chaperone **to be allowed** in the streets.

A. A French meal is incomplete if there is no cheese between salad and dessert.

B. Cattle farmers shot dozens of calves in front of network TV cameras, because they wanted to dramatize their serious economic problems and hoped to make you choke on your steak dinner while watching the six o'clock news.

C. The late nineteenth century saw the advent of the railroad and the telegraph, and, as a result of this, our world shrank more in a single generation than in the preceding 5000 years.

D. The Bermuda Triangle mystery is not reinforced by eyewitness reports, but similar mysteries, like UFOs, Bigfoot, the Loch Ness Monster, and the Abominable Snowman, are.

E. The aim of the editors was learning how college students feel about clothing, so they interviewed over 1000 students on 50 campuses across the country.

F. When Laverne is at the dinner table, the deficiencies of her upbringing become glaringly apparent.

G. Howard Hughes invested millions of his own money because he was interested in keeping the flying boat project alive after the government discontinued its support.

H. The young bus driver kept a baseball bat beside her seat for the purpose of discouraging any trouble that developed on her route.

I. The United States and the Soviet Union wanted to contain the war in the Middle East, so they declared their neutrality and urged other nations to do likewise.

J. Because they hope that it will ease the telephone traffic problem, telephone companies are converting from copper wire to optical fibers.

AMERICAN GRAFFITI

Using prepositional phrases and infinitives whenever appropriate, combine the following sentences into an essay which explains that graffiti has become less personal and more political. Add to your essay at least two other examples of graffiti that you have seen on campus or elsewhere.

1. Graffiti has been around since the stone age.
2. America has recently witnessed a renaissance of these comments.
3. These comments are provocative.
4. These comments are witty.

5. Some students of the subject claim this.
6. The protest movements during the sixties fostered the trend.
7. The trend was away from the old "Pete loves Kathy" graffiti.
8. The trend was toward a more articulate wall writing.
9. The trend was toward a more socially conscious wall writing.

10. This claim may be true or not.
11. The movement against the war in Vietnam gave us pithy antiwar comments like this.

12. "War is good business—invest your sons."
13. And "How many Vietnamese fought in our civil war?"

14. The drug culture produced such witticisms as this.
15. "LSD melts in your mind, not in your hand."

16. But it was the women's lib movement.
17. The women's lib movement came up with the most creative wall statements.
18. The women's lib movement came up with the most acerbic wall statements.

19. One lady wrote the following.
20. It is a spoof of a traditional message.
21. "Remember, girls, the way to a man's heart is through the left ventricle."

22. It is in the age of electronic media.
23. It is in the age of big, impersonal government.
24. Graffiti may be the only outlet for articulate, personal protest.

25. Certainly it's not going away.
26. This is much to the chagrin of the bar owner.
27. The bar owner neatly printed this sign in his bathroom.
28. "Do not write on walls."

29. One customer retorted.
30. The retort was written on the wall in purple crayon.
31. The retort was wise.
32. "You want we should type maybe?"

MAKING PREPOSITIONAL PHRASES AND INFINITIVES IN CONTEXT

The paragraphs below lack focus and coherence because some sentences are wordy and others are not clearly related to one another. Strengthen each paragraph by using prepositional phrases and infinitives to revise those weak sentences. Make whatever other changes you think might strengthen the paragraph. Be sure to write out the complete paragraph.

Example

> Bach's life differs little from the lives of other musicians in the seventeenth century, unless you consider the fact that he wrote better musical compositions. When he was alive, Bach was an obscure musician, trudging from court to court for jobs as choirmaster or organist. He remained obscure for over a hundred years. But his music was "discovered" in the nineteenth century. Our own century considers Bach's work impervious to time and the composer himself a living presence to whom almost everything in music is somehow indebted. We consider the Beetles indebted to him and Beethoven as well.

↓

> **Except for the quality of his musical compositions,** Bach's life differs little from the lives of other musicians in the seventeenth century. **During his lifetime,** Bach was an obscure court musician, trudging from court to court for jobs as choirmaster or organist. He remained obscure for over a hundred years, until his music was "discovered" in the nineteenth century. Our own century considers Bach's work impervious to time and the composer himself a living presence to whom almost everything in music, **from Beethoven to the Beatles,** is somehow indebted.

A. Sometimes avid crossword puzzle fans or Scrabble players know the names for certain common things around us that few of us know. Do you know, for instance, that the plastic tip of your shoelace is called an *aglet?* That the plastic shield over a restaurant salad bar is a *sneeze guard?* Or that the indentation between your nose and lip is called a *philtrum?* Most people do not. You probably just call such items *thingamajigs* or *whatchamacallits.*

B. Because we now have compact audiodisc players, which use a laser beam to read music encoded on a small, silvery disc, the turntable and tapedeck are becoming obsolete. Since no needles touch the disc's surface, the CD player delivers sound free from scratches, hisses, wows, and flutters. Just as important to the success of the new technology, record companies are marketing thousands of discs. These discs have music for every taste, Mozart as well as the Talking Heads.

C. Suicide seems to have its roots in the childhood fantasy of "disappearing." Disappearing allows children to escape from unpleasantness or to punish others for hurts. Little kids pack their bags and leave home, "to show momma." Suicides, too, are running away from reality. By the time people decide to commit suicide, though, they see themselves as disconnected from family and friends and see their lives as meaningless. They conclude that life is empty. Then potential suicides become convinced that disappearing from the world is the only solution.

D. Hawthorne's tale of the aftermath of Hester Prynne's adultery, *The Scarlet Letter,* created controversy when it was first published in the 1850s. Though it is tame by modern standards, the story is again stirring up controversy. A toxicologist claims that Hester's husband, who passed himself off as a doctor named Chillingworth, poisoned Hester's lover, Dimmesdale. He used atropine obtained from local plants. The toxicologist gives evidence—the fact that Hawthorne mentions atropine-producing plants and the fact that Dimmesdale has suspicious symptoms. Still and all, literary critics contend that the medical interpretation disregards the book's real message—the moral and psychological ravages of sin.

E. Across the nation, reactions to the tragedy varied. Residents of the mining towns of central Utah gathered because they wanted to pray for the missing and the dead. Churches in San Francisco collected money and food so they could help families of trapped miners get through the Christmas season. Federal Mine Safety and Health Administration officials, speaking from Washington, criticized the company, which put coal production above safety.

DRESSED TO KILL

Using prepositional phrases and infinitives whenever appropriate, combine the following sentences into an explanatory essay that supports the old adage "clothes make the man." If you wish, add details of your own to further support the controlling idea.

1. It was easy.
2. You could tell the good guys from the bad.
3. This was in the old cowboy movies.

4. The good guys looked good.
5. The bad guys looked bad.

6. The good guys never lost their hats in fights.
7. And the good guys wore light-colored clothing.
8. The good guys were like Roy Rogers.
9. The good guys were like Gene Autry.

10. On the other hand, the bad guys lost their hats frequently.
11. And the bad guys always wore black.
12. The bad guys were like the crooked sheriff.
13. The bad guys were like the nasty rustler.

14. You might laugh at Hollywood stereotypes.
15. But some psychologists agree about this.
16. People do reveal their personalities with their clothing.

17. Police uniforms signal authority.
18. Clown costumes indicate silliness.

19. In the same way, the everyday clothes tell others who we are.
20. We wear the clothes.

21. People wear loud clothes.
22. The people have loud personalities.

23. Optimists tend toward bright clothing.
24. The bright clothing is happy.

25. And pessimists prefer grey clothing.
26. The grey clothing is neutral.

27. A generation of youth signaled this.
28. They were rebelling against their parents' values.
29. They signaled by adopting a new form of dress.
30. The new form of dress was highlighted by faded blue jeans.

31. Not all those who study clothing agree that this is so.
32. You can analyze people by their clothing.

33. Most do agree that this is so.
34. The clothes you wear identify your social status.
35. The clothes you wear identify your authority.
36. The clothes you wear identify your sophistication.

37. For instance, ties with big patterns identify lower-class males.
38. Neat paisley ties mark upper-class gentlemen.

39. One study of clothes reveals this.
40. Students apparently react to symbols of authority.
41. Students work harder for teachers who dress in suits.
42. Students don't work as hard for teachers in shirt-sleeves.

43. And do you want to move up the corporate ladder?
44. Then be prepared for this.
45. Dress properly in suits.
46. The suits are dark.
47. The suits are pinstriped.

48. Forget about bow ties.

49. Bow ties indicate this.
50. A man is a crook.

51. And never wear green.

52. For some reason, people who wear green are judged to be this.
53. They are less honest.
54. They are less likable.

55. It seems this is the case.
56. Gene Autry had the right idea.
57. Roy Rogers had the right idea.
58. You may think otherwise.
59. The good guys do look good.
60. The bad guys do look bad.

unit 9
NOUN SUBSTITUTES

Constructing Noun Substitutes

In everyday conversation and casual writing, we often state an observation in one sentence or clause and comment on it in the next:

1. Nuclear waste could be deposited in outer space. This could be one way of solving a difficult dilemma.
2. The university insists on controlling the private lives of its students, which is a laughable anachronism.
3. Laura was late for her trial, and it really made the judge furious.
4. Why don't more Americans listen to classical music? This is a mystery to Europeans.

But in more formal writing, you should generally replace vague words like "this," "which," and "it" by converting the previous sentence into a NOUN SUBSTITUTE.

In example 1, you can change the verb sequence "could be deposited" into the -ING NOUN "depositing."

Nuclear waste could be deposited in outer space. **This** could be one way of solving a difficult problem.

↓

Depositing nuclear waste in outer space could be one way of solving a difficult problem.

In example 2, you can convert the verb "insists" into the INFINITIVE "to insist" and add "for" before the subject:

The university insists on controlling the private lives of its students, **which** is a laughable anachronism.

↓

For the university to insist on controlling the private lives of its students is a laughable anachronism.

In example 3, you can make the first sentence into a THAT CLAUSE, a clause introduced by "that":

Laura was late for her trial, and **it** really made the judge furious.

↓

That Laura was late for her trial really made the judge furious.

In example 4, you can transform the question beginning with the question word "why" into a WH- CLAUSE by moving the verb "don't" to the other side of the subject, "Americans":

> Why don't more Americans listen to classical music? **This** is a
> mystery to Europeans.

↓

> **Why more Americans don't listen to classical music** is
> a mystery to Europeans.

These four kinds of structures—infinitives, **-ing** nouns, **that**
clauses, and **wh-** clauses—are called NOUN SUBSTITUTES. A noun
substitute has the meaning of a complete sentence, but it appears as
only a part of another sentence, in a spot normally occupied by a
noun or pronoun. In this way, noun substitutes allow you to integrate
into a single sentence the ideas expressed in two or more separate
sentences.

Not only do noun substitutes provide a means for converting
sentences into nouns, they also give you options for making that
conversion. It is often possible to make several different noun substitutes from the same sentence.

> You can slight the value of early detection programs for cancer.
> But this invites disaster and defeat.

↓

> **Slighting the value of early detection programs for
> cancer** is inviting disaster and defeat.

OR

> **To slight the value of early detection programs for can-
> cer** is to invite disaster and defeat.

OR

> **Whoever slights the value of early detection programs
> for cancer** invites disaster and defeat.

Wh- Clauses

Wh- clauses are closely related to questions. There are two kinds of
questions in English: those that must be answered with "yes" or "no"
and those that cannot be. "Did the Red Sox win yesterday?" is a

yes-no question, but "When is payday?" is not. Questions introduced by words such as **when** are called **wh-** questions.

To make a yes-no question into a noun substitute, first convert the question into a statement (with the verb following the subject) and then add **whether** or **whether or not** in front:

Will taxes be raised again this year?
This remains to be seen.

↓

Whether (or not) taxes will be raised again this year remains to be seen.

OR

It remains to be seen **whether (or not) taxes will be raised again this year.**

Does a government employee have the right to strike?
This is a constitutional question.

↓

Whether or not a government employee has the right to strike is a constitutional question.

All other **wh-** clauses come from questions that begin with one of the following words:

who, whoever   **where, wherever**
whom, whomever   **when, whenever**
whose   **why**
which, whichever   **how, however**

The next examples illustrate how a **wh-** question, converted into a noun substitute, can replace **it** or **this:**

What should Hollywood have learned from the failures of *Grease II* and *Airplane II*?
People won't always flock to see third-rate sequels.

↓

What Hollywood should have learned from the failures of *Grease II* and *Airplane II* is that people won't always flock to see third-rate sequels.

How much effect does TV have on the reading and writing abilities of young children?
Psychologists are trying to determine this.

↓

Psychologists are trying to determine **how much effect TV has on the reading and writing abilities of young children.**

Why were the hijackers allowed to go free?
This puzzled the public.

↓

Why the hijackers were allowed to go free puzzled the public.

What is it like to live and die with a baseball team through three decades of defeat?
Cleveland Indian fans know this.

↓

Cleveland Indian fans know **what it is like to live and die with a baseball team through three decades of defeat.**

Often you have the option of simplifying a **wh-** clause into a **wh-** infinitive phrase:

How can you create authentic French food with American ingredients and utensils?
Julia Child's book shows this.

↓

Julia Child's book shows **how you can create authentic French food with American ingredients and utensils.**

OR

Julia Child's book shows **how to create authentic French food with American ingredients and utensils.**

Infinitives and -ing Nouns

You make infinitives and **-ing** nouns from verbs. For instance, in the following, you can make "howled" and "whined" into **howling** and **whining:**

The dog howled and whined.
This kept the whole neighborhood awake.

↓

The dog's **howling** and **whining** kept the whole neighborhood awake.

In much the same way, the verb "move" becomes the infinitive **to move** below:

Aging ballplayers can move to Japan.
This is a sensible way to end a career.

↓

For aging ballplayers **to move** to Japan is a sensible way to end a career.

Because they are verbs converted to nouns, infinitives and **-ing** nouns have more verbal force than ordinary nouns: infinitives imply future action, and **-ing** nouns suggest that something is happening. This verbal force can help you get movement and vitality into your sentences. The phrase

a time **to live** and a time **to die**

loses much of its vitality when its infinitives are replaced by the abstract nouns "life" and "death":

a time for life and a time for death.

With the infinitives removed, we no longer sense the act or process, and perhaps no longer feel as keenly the contrast between living and dying.

In the same way, there are differences among the following:

Death with dignity and grace is an ancient idea.
Dying with dignity and grace is an ancient idea.
To die with dignity and grace is an ancient idea.

The word **death** suggests an abstract and impersonal event or state. But **dying** evokes the image of a living body's last moments as well as the course of its passing away, and **to die** almost gives you a sense of the purposefulness of death. Similarly, the noun in

Protest will get you nowhere.

lacks the sense of active personal involvement, the sense of your "doing it," that is conveyed by

Protesting will get you nowhere.

Using Noun Substitutes for Balance

Balanced infinitives of the type "To do this is to do that" are an effective means of implying a definition. The sentence "To vote Republican means to endorse big business" indirectly defines the Republican party as the party of big business. But this kind of definition often implies a comparison as well: the next sentence suggests the greatness of Julius Erving as a basketball player by comparing him to the greatest English poet:

To say that Julius Erving jumps is **to describe** Shakespeare as a guy who wrote poetry.

Infinitives—and indeed other noun substitutes—can also occur in a series. In the following example the last infinitive strengthens the link between the two sides of the sentence without destroying the balance:

> **To believe** that Christianity is concerned only with the afterlife is **to ignore** the ethical dimension of Christ's life, **to deprive** the gospel of its earthly and human significance.

A series of noun substitutes is a useful organizing principle for any type of information that suggests parallel points. In a first draft you might jot down such information in the form of sentences that obscure the parallelism:

> The new law would require the president to inform American citizens when he had grounds for believing that they were victims of eavesdropping by agents of another country. Then the agents involved must be requested to stop the eavesdropping, and they are to be ordered out of the country if they persist.

But in revising this passage, you might realize that the law would require the president not only **to inform** American citizens but also **to request** foreign agents to stop the eavesdropping and **to order** them to leave. Accordingly, you can construct an infinitive series to show the parallel points:

> The new law would require the president **to inform** American citizens when he had grounds for believing that they were victims of eavesdropping by agents of another country, **to request** the agents involved to stop the eavesdropping, and **to order** them out of the country if they persist.

For a slightly different effect, try **that** clauses:

> The new law would assure **that** American citizens are informed by the president when he had grounds for believing they were victims of eavesdropping by agents of another country, **that**

the agents involved are requested to stop the eavesdropping, and **that** the violators are ordered out of the country if they persist.

*   *   *

In brief, noun substitutes like **-ing** nouns, infinitives, **that** clauses, and **wh-** clauses can help make your writing more specific and more precise. Try using noun substitutes whenever you spot a vague "this," "which," or "it" in your own writing. Besides adding movement and vitality to your writing because of their verbal force, noun substitutes can be balanced to imply definition or placed in a series to suggest parallel points.

CONSTRUCTING NOUN SUBSTITUTES

Combine each set of sentences below into a single sentence using the kind of noun substitute specified in the example.

Example I: -ing Nouns

    1. Someone purchases original prints.
    2. This is the cheapest way to acquire fine art today.

↓

Purchasing original prints is the cheapest way to acquire fine art today.

OR

The cheapest way to acquire fine art today is by **purchasing original prints.**

A. 1. A tennis player wins at Wimbledon.
   2. This is the crowning achievement in tennis.

B. 1. She pretended to be one of us.
   2. She took part in all our pranks.
   3. This helped hide her identity as a policewoman.

C. 1. You can bury a dead cat at midnight.
   2. Or you can rub the spot with grasshopper spit.
   3. This might cure warts as effectively as medical treatment.

D. 1. You reduce your weight.
   2. It is not just a matter of this.
   3. You clip a diet out of a magazine.

E. 1. You try to bring about changes in education.
   2. This has been compared to a move.
   3. You move a cemetery.

Example II: Infinitives

1. You are born and raised in the West.
2. This means you are suspicious and fearful of claustrophobia.
3. Claustrophobia envelops the East.

↓

To be born and raised in the West means that you are suspicious and fearful of the claustrophobia that envelops the East.

OR

To be born and raised in the West is to be suspicious and fearful of the claustrophobia that envelops the East.

F. 1. You make your own pasta from scratch.
   2. It means you add a whole new dimension to Italian cooking.

G. 1. Someone says this.
   2. History is a record of dates and battles.
   3. This ignores most of history's significance.

H. 1. Honda's response to the "Buy American" campaign was this.
   2. Honda built its new assembly plant in Ohio.

I. 1. A restaurant becomes a five-star restaurant.
   2. This means the restaurant has consistently maintained superior standards.
   3. The standards are of quality in food and service.

J. 1. The faculty do not have their classes evaluated by students.
   2. This is to reject the best kind of advice.
   3. How can the faculty improve their teaching?

Example III: That Clauses

1. The earth's climate changes.
2. The earth's climate even now may be changing rapidly.

3. This is widely recognized.

↓

It is widely recognized **that the earth's climate changes and even now may be changing rapidly.**

OR

That the earth's climate changes, and even now may be changing rapidly, is widely recognized.

K. 1. Even in some elementary schools, children have easy access to drugs.
   2. This is no longer a secret.

L. 1. Al Capone tried to keep his criminal record clean.
   2. This helped him control his underworld empire without police interference.

M. 1. The editors of the *Washington Post* hoped this.
   2. The story would be accepted by the public.
   3. The editors of the *Washington Post* doubted this.
   4. The story would be embraced by the president.

N. 1. The percentage of left-handed Americans is increasing dramatically.
   2. This shows something.
   3. We're obviously becoming a left-handed nation.

O. 1. Television is still reluctant to entrust much responsibility to women.
   2. This is demonstrated by the fact that news anchor teams are always composed of either two men or one woman and one man but never two women.

Example IV: Wh- Clauses

1. Should a state university invest in stocks sold by companies?
2. The companies do business with racist governments like South Africa.

3. This has become a matter of controversy on several campuses.

↓

It has become a matter of controversy on several campuses **whether a state university should invest in stocks sold by companies that do business with racist governments like South Africa.**

OR

Whether a state university should invest in stocks sold by companies that do business with racist governments like South Africa has been a matter of controversy on several campuses.

P. 1. Where did Moriarty make his mistake?
   2. He underestimated the skill of his nemesis, Sherlock Holmes.

Q. 1. How did she manage to get straight A's without studying?
   2. This was a mystery to her roommate.

R. 1. Who claims the word of God as his personal domain?
   2. That person is more likely to be a fanatic than a saint.

S. 1. How soon is socialized medicine coming to America?
   2. This depends on the time.
   3. When will the majority of Americans get tired of paying astronomical doctor's bills?

T. 1. Should prisoners be used for medical experiments?
   2. This is not only a legal question.
   3. This is also a moral question.

MUZZLED

Using noun substitutes whenever appropriate, combine the following sentences into an essay that convincingly argues against the banning of sexist covers on record albums. Add examples or reasons of your own whenever you can.

1. We have all seen them.
2. They are on the covers of record albums.
3. They are photographs of women.
4. Or they are drawings of women.
5. The women are beaten by men.
6. Or the women are chained by men.
7. Or the women are otherwise manhandled by men.

8. And we can't help believing this.
9. Many of the artists do not care about morals.
10. Many of the artists do not care about art.
11. Many of the artists care only about money.
12. The artists are like pornographers.

13. Thus we understand the moral outrage of the feminist groups.
14. The feminist groups seek to outlaw the distribution of all such albums.
15. The feminist groups seek to outlaw the sale of all such albums.

16. Yet we must know this.
17. What these groups are advocating is censorship.

18. They would impose their own brand of morality on the record-buying public.
19. This would restrict the artist's freedom of expression.

20. Surely this is possible.
21. A great work of art can contain a scene.
22. In the scene a woman is tortured by a man.

23. In fact, an artist might even create such a scene.
24. The purpose would be to show the depravity of the scene.

25. To make it illegal for the artist to show such scenes is this.
26. It is taking away the freedom of expression.
27. Freedom of expression is the right of all American men and women.

28. Therefore, we must resist the attempt to censor record album covers.

29. In the same way, we must resist any effort that threatens freedom of speech.

CREATING NOUN SUBSTITUTES

In each of the following sentences, replace the pronoun in boldface with a noun substitute—an **-ing** noun, an infinitive, a **that** clause, or a **wh-** clause. In sentences where the pronoun is "it," you have the additional option of keeping "it" and inserting the noun substitute elsewhere in the sentence. Try experimenting with different types of noun substitutes.

Example

It was a courageous act.

↓

It was a courageous act **for the Egyptian president to visit Israel.**

OR

What Sadat did to end centuries of hatred and hostility was a courageous act.

OR

Defying the advice of many of his friends and doing what he believed he had to do was a courageous act.

A. You should have decided **that** before you mailed the letter.

B. **This** is what she would like to have done, had she not been afraid of seeming to be rude.

C. **It** threatened to endanger our relationship.

D. What none of us could understand—and still don't—was **this.**

E. **It** is not to state a general truth but rather to exhibit a personal prejudice.

F. **That** is one reason why Americans spend $8 billion a year on weddings, not counting gifts for the young couple.

G. In view of **this,** the Planned Parenthood clinic performs a useful service.

H. **It** is rarely mentioned in arguments about coed dormitories.

I. To speak another language means **this.**

J. **This** is a good example of the American preoccupation with sports.

MARGARET SANGER: FIGHTER FOR WOMEN'S RIGHTS

Select from the sentences below the most important ideas and information for an essay of no more than 250 words on the role of Margaret Sanger in the struggle for women's rights. Then, using noun substitutes whenever appropriate, create from those ideas and that information an effective explanatory essay.

1. Margaret Sanger was a maternity nurse.
2. She was working on New York's Lower East Side in 1912.
3. She realized this.
4. Women had no control over their own bodies.
5. Women had no control over their own lives.

6. The women she treated had too many children.
7. The women didn't know this.
8. How do they prevent unwanted pregnancies?

9. She saw one young woman.
10. The woman was near death from self-induced abortion.
11. The woman begged the doctor to tell her this.
12. How was she to stop having children?

13. "Tell Jake to sleep on the roof," the doctor said.

14. Three months later she died.
15. She died from an attempted abortion.

16. These women were so desperate.
17. These women were so ignorant about their bodies.
18. Margaret Sanger decided this.
19. She would do something about it.

20. Sanger began to wage a war of information.
21. Sanger began to wage a war against ignorance.
22. Sanger began to wage a war to liberate women.

23. She published a magazine.
24. The magazine was *The Woman Rebel.*
25. The magazine was designed to furnish information about birth control.

26. But the distribution of birth control information was a federal offense at the time.
27. It was considered the same as using the mail for this.
28. Obscene material was distributed through the mail.

29. Sanger was arrested.
30. It was one of eight times she was arrested.
31. And it was one of eight times she would stand trial.

32. The charges were eventually dropped.
33. The publicity helped Sanger fulfill her initial purpose.
34. The purpose was to let women know this.
35. The women could do something about birth control.

36. Sanger turned information into action.
37. Sanger opened the first birth control clinic in the nation.
38. The opening was in 1916.
39. The clinic was in Brooklyn, New York.

40. On the first day more than 150 women crowded in.
41. Most women were carrying babies.
42. Most women were holding their children by the hand.

43. Nine days later the police came.
44. Their purpose was to close the clinic.
45. Their purpose was to arrest Sanger.
46. They charged that Sanger "maintained a public nuisance."

47. But the people began to see.
48. The people heard about her work.
49. Hers was an idea whose time had come.
50. This didn't matter.
51. What did the law say?

52. Her case came up for appeal.
53. Public sympathy was with her.
54. The New York Court of Appeals judge decided this.
55. The judge granted doctors the right.
56. The right was to give advice about birth control.

57. Sanger formed conferences to further spread her cause.
58. She formed them through the 1920s and 1930s.
59. And in 1936 she won her most striking victory.
60. Doctors were granted the right.
61. The right was to prescribe contraceptive devices.

62. Sanger's ideas were worth this to her.
63. They were worth a lifetime of fighting.

64. She fought for birth control.

65. But she also fought for another kind of control.
66. The control was of a broader kind.
67. She wanted to show women this.
68. How could they take control of their bodies?
69. How could they take control of their lives?

REVISING WITH NOUN SUBSTITUTES

Revise each of the following sentences in order to make the most effective use of noun substitutes—of **-ing** nouns, infinitives, **that** clauses, and **wh-** clauses. Rearrange parts of your sentence whenever appropriate.

Example

House sparrows are able to build nests, lay eggs, and rear their young on constantly moving objects such as oil pumps, and this has helped make them the most widespread land birds.

↓

Being able to build nests, lay eggs, and rear their young on constantly moving objects such as oil pumps has helped make house sparrows the most widespread land birds.

OR

(The fact) **That house sparrows are able to build nests, lay eggs, and rear their young on constantly moving objects such as oil pumps** has helped make them the most widespread land birds.

A. When you think difficult problems through, it requires time, solitude, and relaxation.

B. Studies show when you use the lap-shoulder belt it reduces the chance that you will be killed in a car accident by 60 percent.

C. You can contribute to the Conscience Fund of the U.S. Treasury Department, which is one way that citizens who suffer second thoughts about cheating on their tax return can soothe their conscience.

D. Getting their children into college used to be the goal of millions of Americans; nowadays, with the spiraling costs of higher education, it has become the bigger challenge to pay for college.

E. They must establish safeguards for the privacy of personal records; furthermore, to inform individuals how their files are being used and to let them know what is in the files should be the constitutional obligations of every employer.

F. People doze at the wheel, and this is the major reason that motorists run off the road and hit parked vehicles, according to a recent study involving 2000 accidents.

G. The number of major league ballplayers over 37 has nearly doubled in the last ten years, but this should not surprise anyone aware of the multiyear, multimillion-dollar contracts awarded to aging stars like George Foster and Steve Garvey.

H. Perhaps America should have a new national anthem, but the reason for this has never been convincingly demonstrated.

I. It was concluded by the panel that if you search for the causes of the decline in SAT scores, it is an exercise in conjecture.

J. Will the Supreme Court's decision on several cases of "reverse discrimination" affect access by minorities to higher education? It is not yet clear.

SMILING BABIES

Using noun substitutes whenever appropriate, combine the following sentences into an essay of approximately 400 words which argues that babies delivered by Dr. Leboyer's method are happier and healthier. Reduce the length of your paper by eliminating needless repetition and by excluding any facts or ideas that do not support your central argument.

1. "That's simply beautiful."
2. This was all the new orderly could say.

3. The baby girl lies in her mother's arms.
4. She lies quietly and contentedly.
5. She was born only two hours before.
6. Her eyes are bright and alert.
7. Her hands are relaxed and already groping around.

8. Her parents will probably name her Claudia.
9. They are both ecstatic over their first child.

10. This smiling baby seems almost too happy.
11. She is so new to the world.
12. She doesn't at all resemble most newborns.
13. Most newborns' faces are knotted in a frightened grimace.
14. Their bodies are tense and struggling.
15. They seem to be on guard.
16. They are like boxers.
17. The boxers defend themselves.

18. Lately, more and more of these happy babies have been born.
19. They have been born in Europe.
20. They have also been born in America.

21. Dr. Frederick Leboyer is responsible for this new phenomenon.
22. Dr. Leboyer is a French obstetrician.

23. Dr. Leboyer has revolutionized delivery room procedure.
24. He is the author of *Birth Without Violence.*
25. It is a beautifully poetic book about childbirth.
26. He advocates a homey approach to childbirth.
27. His approach is simpler.
28. His approach is quieter.
29. His approach is better.

30. Many traditional physicians express doubts about the Leboyer system.
31. But all results indicate this.
32. We can bear happier babies.
33. The babies stand a better chance of staying happy throughout their lives.
34. This is done by reducing much unnecessary trauma.
35. The Leboyer method is all about delivering happy babies.

36. Leboyer's mother spent 30 hours in childbirth with him.
37. Leboyer witnessed thousands of deliveries during his career.

38. Leboyer began to feel serious doubts about needless pain and trauma.
39. Modern medicine inflicts the pain and trauma upon the infant.

40. Traditional practice has always emphasized this.
41. How can the mother's pain be reduced?
42. Traditional practice considers only the baby's immediate physical safety.

43. Lamaze is another French doctor.
44. He also has a new theory.
45. His theory reduces the mother's pain.

46. Leboyer claims that standard techniques hurt the baby.
47. The techniques hurt the baby with physical "birth marks."
48. The marks are left by the instruments.
49. They also hurt the baby with psychological scars.
50. These scars are not so obvious, at first.

51. Leboyer maintains this.
52. The delivery rooms foster aggression and violence in the baby.

53. The rooms have cold, glaring lights.
54. They have sounds.
55. The sounds may be shouts of instruction.
56. They may be shouts of encouragement.
57. The baby is still defenseless against such onslaughts.

58. Dr. Leboyer wants to deliver a smiling baby.
59. He doesn't want to deliver a crying baby.

60. Most people like smiles.
61. These babies start to please others as soon as they are born.

62. He turns traditional methods topsy-turvy.
63. He does that to deliver smiling babies.

64. His method is simple.
65. It is safe.

66. According to people, it is beautiful.
67. The people have witnessed a Leboyer birth.

68. The traditional delivery room is flooded with blazing lights.
69. The lights reflect off every possible surface.
70. The room is also flooded with grating noises.
71. The noises are from clinking instruments and squeaky carts.
72. They are also from noisy people.
73. Leboyer delivers in a darkened room.
74. There are soft moans.
75. There are soothing whispers.
76. There is gentle music.
77. These are the only sounds.

78. Standard deliveries subject the baby to spine-jerking dangling.
79. They subject the baby to upside-down dangling.
80. Immediate cutting of the umbilical cord follows the dangling.
81. A rush of oxygen follows the dangling.
82. A sharp slap triggers the rush of oxygen.

83. Leboyer gently lifts the baby.
84. He rests it on the mother's stomach.
85. On the mother's stomach the baby is gradually exposed to the new world.
86. It still feels warmth.
87. The warmth is from the mother's body.

88. After a few minutes the cord is cut.
89. The baby is lovingly massaged to induce breathing.
90. It is not spanked.

91. This is done unless some problem demands earlier care.
92. Leboyer always proceeds in a manner.
93. The manner is necessary for the baby's safety.

94. The baby is then treated to a bath.
95. The bath is in comforting lukewarm water.

96. Leboyer emphasizes the slow emergence of a new human being.

97. He emphasizes the delicate emergence of a new human being.
98. He emphasizes the loving emergence of a new human being.
99. The human being is usually smiling within minutes after birth.

100. It's all so simple.

101. Leboyer gears his method.
102. He reduces the jolt of being transferred from a womb to a world.
103. The womb is warm.
104. It is secure.
105. The world must frighten the newborn.
106. The world is intense.

107. In fact, Leboyer tries to re-create the womb environment.
108. He tries to minimize the shock of transition.
109. He does this with near darkness.
110. He does it with hushed sounds.
111. He does it with massages.
112. He does it with warm baths.
113. According to Leboyer, his approach results in a baby.
114. The baby is healthier physically.
115. The baby is healthier psychologically.

116. Traditional doctors have raised objections.
117. The objections are apparently more out of reaction to something new.
118. They are not from legitimate grounds.
119. The only real proof will come when Leboyer's babies grow up.

120. For right now, who can deny this?
121. A loving, careful entry into life is better than one filled with bright lights.
122. A loving, careful entry into life is better than one filled with harsh sounds.
123. A loving, careful entry into life is better than one filled with a spanking as well.

part **TWO**

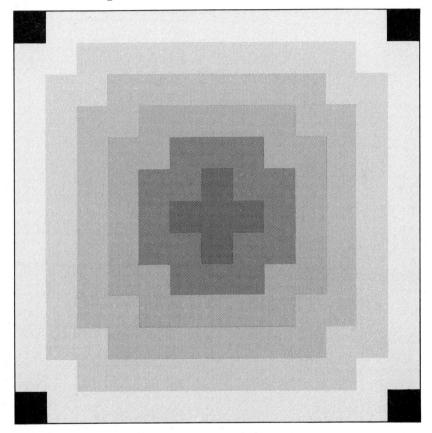

PARAGRAPH
STRATEGIES

unit *10*
COHERENCE

When we reread sentences that we've written, they may occasionally seem a bit disjointed and unconnected. That is, they may not make clear the relationships between our ideas. Take the sentences below, for example.

> Many people exercise every day and never lose weight. Exercising is important. The only sure way to lose weight is to stop eating.

While these sentences are tied together through the repeated phrase **lose weight** and through the similar words **exercise** and **exercising,** some connecting link seems to be missing. What the passage needs is a connective word or phrase to clarify the precise relationship between exercising, not eating, and losing weight. The versions below include such connectives:

Many people exercise every day and never lose weight. **No doubt** exercising is important, **but** the only sure way to lose weight is to stop eating.

OR

Many people exercise every day and never lose weight. Exercising is important. **Still,** the only sure way to lose weight is to stop eating.

Each of these revised versions is more coherent than the original one, because the connectives **no doubt, but,** and **still** clarify the contrast between the two approaches to losing weight. A paragraph is coherent when its ideas flow smoothly from sentence to sentence and when the reader is able to follow the train of thought without disruption. There are three major STRATEGIES OF COHERENCE for linking sentences to one another and for introducing new paragraphs: (1) the use of connective words and phrases; (2) reference to earlier words and phrases (by word repetition, through synonyms, and through pronouns); and (3) the arrangement of sentences into structural patterns, including the proper ordering of old and new information.

Using Connectives

Connective Words. Sometimes the logical connection between two sentences is so obvious that their relationship need not be signaled by a connective:

Most people can learn the basics of a craft quickly. In just weeks they can learn to carve, weave, or embroider.

Adding a connective like **for example** to such a passage is probably unnecessary:

Most people can learn the basics of a craft quickly. **For example,** they can learn to carve, weave, or embroider in weeks.

But whenever the connection between two sentences is not adequately established by the relationship in meaning alone, a formal transition can provide a link between them. The choice of a connective is determined by the specific relationship between the two sentences. Here are some common connectives for indicating specific types of relationships:

1. The second sentence gives an illustration or example: **first, thus, for example, for instance, for one thing, to illustrate.**
2. The second sentence adds another point: **and, also, too, then, second, equally, for another thing, furthermore, moreover, in addition, similarly, next, again, above all, finally.**
3. The second sentence restates, summarizes, or shows a result: **in fact, so, therefore, as a result, accordingly, of course, indeed, to sum up, consequently, in other words.**
4. The second sentence expresses a contrast: **but, still, yet, however, even so, by contrast, on the contrary, nevertheless, on the other hand.**

As you read the next paragraph, decide which connective from the list above best fits into the blank:

A prison should serve as a correctional institution where a criminal is taught to deal with the outside world. _____ _____, our prisons often harbor more crime within their walls than criminals find on the street.

To signal the difference between what a prison should be and what prisons often are, you probably chose a connective that expresses a contrast—either **yet, however,** or **nevertheless.** Which connectives would you select for the blanks in the following passage?

What explains the growing trend toward delayed childbearing? _____, the high divorce rate is making newlyweds think twice about starting a family right away. _____, many young couples want to be more financially secure before having children. _____, more married women prefer to devote time to their careers before having a baby.

For the first blank you might have chosen **first** or **for one thing;** for the second, **furthermore** or **for another thing;** and for the last, **above all** or **finally.**

Connective Phrases. In revising a paragraph, you may need more than a common connective to fill a gap between two sentences. You may need a longer phrase, a clause, or even a full sentence. In the next paragraph, for example, a transitional phrase inserted before the last sentence clarifies the link between restrictions imposed on marijuana and the federal order to reexamine its use:

Since the passage of the Controlled Substances Act in 1970, marijuana has been classified as a "dangerous drug," its possession subject to federal felony charges. This act has prevented the use of the drug even for medical purposes. A federal court in Washington has ordered a thorough reexamination of marijuana, including its potential for medical use.

Since the passage of the Controlled Substances Act in 1970, marijuana has been classified as a "dangerous drug," its possession subject to federal felony charges. This act has prevented the use of the drug even for medical purposes. **But now, in an attempt to separate fact from fantasy,** a federal court in Washington has ordered a thorough reexamination of marijuana, including its potential for medical use.

Using Reference

Aside from using connective words and phrases, you can create coherence by making reference to an earlier word or phrase—by word repetition, through synonyms, and through pronouns.

Word Repetition. The simplest way to use reference to achieve coherence is by repeating an important word (or several important words) within the paragraph. Repetition is especially effective when it occurs at points easily noticed by the reader. The point of the next paragraph, Agatha Christie's **mysterious disappearance,** is established in the first two sentences; but this point is further reinforced by the recurrence of these crucial words in the last sentence. The repetition contributes to the paragraph's coherence by forming a bridge between its beginning and end:

> Agatha Christie earned world renown as the author of numerous **mystery** tales. But none of these tales are more **mysterious** than that of her own **disappearance.** Waves of shock rumbled through the British public when, in December of 1926, the newspapers proclaimed that she had vanished. Not until several months later was she discovered, supposedly afflicted with amnesia and working as a nanny in a Yorkshire manor house. To this day, her fans are intrigued by the **mystery** of her **disappearance.**

Repeating a key word or phrase often helps to make an entire paper, as well as a single paragraph, more coherent. Try repeating in the last sentence of a paper a key word or phrase that you used in your opening paragraph, perhaps your opening sentence.

Synonyms. Like any potentially effective strategy, direct repetition can become tedious if overused. So consider a second kind of reference to create coherence—using a synonym. That is, try replacing one word with another that has the same or a similar meaning. In the next example the excessive repetition of the word **bicycle** becomes awkward and cumbersome. With synonyms substituted, the passage retains its coherence but is no longer repetitious:

> **Bicycling** in America has grown at an explosive rate. **Bicycles** used to be sold to parents for their children. Now those same parents are buying **bicycles** for themselves, as well as for their children. Young executives ride **bicycles** to work to stay out of traffic jams. Young parents are using **bicycles** to do their

shopping without competing for a parking place at the shopping center. College and high school students find **bicycles** an economical alternative to cars and buses. And even grandma and grandpa enjoy **bicycling** to picnics and barbecues.

↓

Bicycling in America has grown at an explosive rate. **Bicycles** used to be sold to parents for their children. Now those same parents are buying **them** for each other, as well as for their children. Young executives ride **bikes** to work to stay out of traffic jams. Young parents are finding **a way** to do their shopping without competing for a parking place at the shopping center. College and high school students find **biking** an economical alternative to cars and buses. And even grandma and grandpa enjoy **bicycling** to picnics and barbecues.

Synonyms can also cover a wider range of meanings. Throughout the next passage, for example, the various synonyms for **endanger** restate and reinforce the point of the paragraph, that the red wolf is an endangered species:

The red wolf is an **endangered** species. Its numbers have **perilously declined** both because of willful **slaughter** subsidized by government bounty and because of the wolf's **susceptibility** to the **deadly destructiveness** of intestinal parasites. And now the species may face total **extinction** because of its ability to interbreed with a closely related but far more numerous cousin, the coyote. Thus, having survived the worst that man and worms can do, the red wolf now faces what may be its final **extermination** in the **threat** of the **loss** of its own distinguishing genes.

Sometimes a synonym with a broader meaning summarizes one or more preceding statements. In the following passage, **such migrations** is used as a summarizing synonym:

Eels, whales, salmon, turtles, and birds—and even bees and butterflies—annually travel long distances, sometimes thousands of miles. While **such migrations** have been known since the beginnings of recorded history, there is still no clear explanation of how animals navigate.

Here **such migrations** establishes coherence by linking the second sentence to the first. Summarizing synonyms are commonly accompanied by words like **such, this, these,** and **of this sort.**

Pronouns. A third kind of reference is the use of pronouns, such as **she, he, it, they, this, that, some,** or **another.** A pronoun, too, is a kind of synonym, but it gets its meaning by referring to an earlier word or group of words. In the next example, the pronouns **they** and **their** refer to "Virgos":

> Virgos are simple and gentle people, with a need to serve humanity. Careful and precise by nature, **they** make excellent secretaries and nurses. The warm, shining eyes and the bright appearance of Virgos conceal **their** deeply burning desire for love.

In the next passage, not only does the pronoun **he** assure coherence, but its recurrence also links the successive sentences into a forceful and effective pattern. So you don't forget that **he** refers to **the Apostle Paul,** the last sentence repeats his name and neatly winds up the passage—perhaps with a touch of sarcasm:

> **The Apostle Paul** may have been an early example of a male chauvinist. **He** considers women the "weaker vessel," inferior to men. **He** advises wives to obey their husbands, because men are masters over their women just as Christ is master over the Church. **He** advises men not to marry, although **he** admits that marriage may be necessary for those who lust after women; for it is better to be married and sexually gratified than to be single and sex-crazed. But to be single and rid of women, says **the Apostle Paul,** is best of all.

Arranging Sentences

The third major strategy of coherence is the arrangement of sentences into structural patterns, including the proper ordering of old and new information.

Structural Patterns. Look for the possibility of patterning whenever you are discussing parallel points. Suppose, for instance, you have collected some notes on the thesis that in the early sixties pop music was shaped by radically different geographical and cultural influences, and you try a paragraph like this:

> The late sixties brought to pop music a fusion of radically different geographical and cultural influences. The influence of religion and mysticism, which came from the East, made popular such instruments as the tabla and the sitar. A Latin influence was southern in origin, branching into such forms as reggae and calypso, with its steel drums and marimbas. But folk music, perhaps the most important influence on pop music at the time, with its simple melodies and melodramatic lyrics, came from the West, particularly from Britain and the American Midwest.

Although this paragraph has a clear topic sentence and contains interesting details, the relationship of these details to the topic sentence could be more sharply focused. Since the topic sentence deals with "different influences," you can revise the paragraph by asking where those influences came from. Clearly, some came from the East, some came from the South, and some came from the West. Equipped with this new organizing principle, you might revise the passage as follows:

> The late sixties brought to pop music a fusion of radically different geographical and cultural influences. **From the East came** the influences of religion and mysticism, which made popular such instruments as the tabla and the sitar. **From the South came** a Latin influence, with its steel drums and marimbas, branching into such forms as reggae and calypso. And **from the West,** particularly from Britain and the American Midwest, **came** folk music with its simple melodies and melodramatic lyrics, to become perhaps the most important influence on pop music at the time.

Note that patterning does not mean mechanical repetition. The last item in this series is introduced by **and,** and it is separated from the verb **came** by the prepositional phrase **particularly from Britain and the American Midwest.** Here repetition of the pattern contributes to clear organization and a smooth flow of sentences; interruption of the pattern helps to add interest and variety.

By becoming pattern-conscious, you are in a better position to recognize the lack of coherence in your first drafts and to make the necessary revision. Consider the next paragraph:

> But what of the personal side of the story? What of retired mail clerks or janitors who have to contend with the continuous rise in the cost of living? They are no longer secure with a company's pension or with society's "gift" of social security. Government figures show that 5 million persons 63 years and older are living on an income under subsistence level.

The reader may sense that the last sentence has something to do with what comes before, but the connection is obscured because this sentence breaks the pattern established by the second and third sentences: **mail clerks or janitors** and **they.** A transition such as **in fact** or **to illustrate** would help little; but if we revise the last sentence so that it continues the structural pattern with **they** as subject, the paragraph becomes more coherent:

> But what of the personal side of the story? What of the retired **mail clerks or janitors** who have to contend with the continuous rise in the cost of living? **They** are no longer secure with a company's pension or with society's "gift" of social security. If **they** are among the 5 million persons 63 years and older who, according to government figures, live on an income under subsistence level, **they** can do no more than barely survive.

Old and New Information. A second way to create coherence through arrangement is by placing information in proper sequence. A sentence tends to contain both old information and new information. The repetition of old information—some reference to what has already been said—assures the continuity of thought. New information, on the other hand, carries the thought further. Ordinarily, you should try to place old information near the beginning of your sentence and new information toward the end, where the emphasis naturally falls. The next paragraph sounds odd partly because the second sentence, in which new information is placed before old information, violates this guideline:

> Perhaps *Naked Came the Stranger* was the greatest literary hoax of the century. *Newsday* staff members wrote its chapters, each writing independently and not knowing of the others' work. It was intended as an incoherent pornographic novel, to be published under the pseudonym Penelope Ashe.

The phrase ***Newsday* staff members** in the second sentence does not link up with anything in the first. By moving **its chapters** to the beginning of the second sentence, we not only order old and new information properly, but at the same time create a pattern of structurally parallel sentences: ***Naked Came the Stranger* was . . . . Its chapters were. . . . It was. . . .:**

> Perhaps ***Naked Came the Stranger* was** the greatest literary hoax of the century. **Its chapters were** written by *Newsday* staff members, each writing independently and not knowing of the others' work. **It was** intended as an incoherent pornographic novel, to be published under the pseudonym Penelope Ashe.

Connecting Paragraphs

Many of the same strategies of coherence that work within the paragraph to link sentences can also be used within larger units to link one paragraph to another. Often a simple connective like **however, of course, then,** or **for example** will provide sufficient transition between paragraphs. But sometimes a more extensive transition is called for.

For example, the second paragraph in the next passage lacks a transition. Since it appears to cite an additional argument against capital punishment, this paragraph could begin with a connective such as **furthermore:**

Capital punishment complicates the administration of justice; it leads to lengthy trials and unjustified verdicts, and it places a burden on appellate courts. It also forces taxpayers to support all those waiting their turn for execution on death row.

Furthermore, "cruel and unusual" punishment is explicitly barred by the Eighth Amendment to the Constitution.

But notice that the second paragraph introduces a much more fundamental argument against capital punishment than those cited in the first. When a person's life is at stake, lengthy trials and higher taxes seem trivial in comparison to constitutional questions. To focus on this difference between the trivial and the crucial, you might try a more elaborate transition:

Capital punishment complicates the administration of justice; it leads to lengthy trials and unjustified verdicts, and places a burden on appellate courts. It also forces taxpayers to support those waiting their turn for execution on death row.

But when a person's life is at stake, such inconveniences seem trivial. A far more fundamental objection to capital punishment is a constitutional one: the Eighth Amendment explicitly bars "cruel and unusual" punishment, **and execution is surely cruel and unusual.**

*   *   *

Your writing will be more coherent—and therefore easier to follow—the more closely you connect your sentences. Strategies that can help you achieve coherence include the use of connectives and connective phrases, reference to a previously stated word or piece of information by repetition, synonyms, or pronouns, and the arrangement of sentences into patterns, including the proper ordering of old and new information. These same strategies will also help connect your paragraphs to one another.

USING CONNECTIVES

Using Connective Words

Improve the coherence of each paragraph below by inserting one or more common connectives like **for example, furthermore, indeed,** or **by contrast.** You might want to review the list of common connectives found earlier in this unit.

Example

> Over half the states now accept simple incompatibility as legitimate grounds for divorce. Like some other well-meant reforms, no-fault divorce is proving to have unexpected disadvantages. It may be doing as much harm as good.

> Over half the states now accept simple incompatibility as legitimate grounds for divorce. **Yet,** like some other well-meant reforms, no-fault divorce is proving to have unexpected disadvantages. **In fact,** it may be doing as much harm as good.

A. Rape clinics teach women various methods of self-defense. Panic-stricken women cannot always use this training in a real situation.

B. Walking is a skill people learn as babies. There must be more to it than putting one foot ahead of the other. In any given year, some 15,000 American pedestrians are killed by motor vehicles.

C. The International Olympic Committee tries to enforce the amateur status of Olympic athletes. Many people charge that government-sponsored athletes from communist countries compete on the professional level.

D. The clang, clang, clang of the trolley could be heard in every major city of the nation before World War II. After the war, people moved to the suburbs and built superhighways; electrically powered vehicles were replaced by cars and buses. City planners are looking into the possibility of building new trolley systems, because they are cheaper and cleaner than other forms of mass transportation.

E. The porpoise is an especially appealing animal—intelligent, playful, and altogether winsome. No one but a brute would desire its extinction. Every time a large tuna boat makes its catch, hundreds of porpoises are killed. The U.S. government enforces strict regulations against the tuna fishermen. Many fishermen threaten to join the fishing fleets of other nations less concerned about the well-being of porpoises. Many have already gone. With every fisherman's departure, the plight of the porpoise becomes more desperate. If the American fleet is disbanded, the American regulations will have no protective force, and the porpoise is doomed.

Using Connective Phrases

Improve the coherence of each of the paragraphs below by constructing one or more connective phrases. Do not use only common connectives like **however** and **in other words** but create connective phrases of your own.

Example

Some arid regions of the world receive an average of only two- or three-hundredths of an inch of rain annually and may go on for years without getting a drop. Rain usually comes in torrential downpours.

↓

Some arid regions of the world receive an average of only two- or three-hundredths of an inch of rain annually and may go on for years without getting a drop. **But when the rain does come,** it usually comes in torrential downpours.

F. Travelers are surprised to find almost no eyeglasses on Chinese children. All children perform a series of eye exercises for 20 minutes each day in school to strengthen their vision.

G. In the 1970s the Supreme Court gave states and municipalities the power of discretion in establishing penalties for certain crimes. For example, it has given localities the right to establish their own obscenity laws, with the result that books and movies prohibited in one county may be available only a few miles away. The Court has allowed state and local powers to supersede federal powers.

H. Applying to graduate school is a time-consuming, expensive, and unpredictable venture. Undergraduates must take the required graduate examination and, after deciding where they would like to apply, write to the schools for application forms. They must ask three or four professors to write letters of recommendation and request the registrar to send off transcripts of their under-graduate records. The cost can be from as little as $2 to forward the transcripts to as much as $25 for application fees. There is no guarantee of acceptance.

MOTORCYCLE GANGS

Using connective words and phrases whenever appropriate, combine the following sentences into a paragraph that explains why it will be difficult for motorcycle gangs to change their public image.

1. Books have given motorcycle gangs a bad reputation.
2. Films have given motorcycle gangs a bad reputation.
3. Books and films show the gangs as this.
4. The gangs are constantly at war with each other.
5. Gang members brandish guns.
6. Gang members brandish clubs.
7. Gang members brandish switchblades.

8. True, motorcycle gangs are rebellious young men.
9. They are defiant.
10. They are reckless.
11. They are independent.

12. Motorcycle gangs often break the law.
13. They use hard drugs.
14. They abuse their women.
15. Sometimes they commit murder.

16. The gangs are not always tough and ruthless.

17. Money is often contributed to charity organizations.
18. Sometimes gangs volunteer their services to youth groups.

19. Motorcycle gangs have far to go.
20. Their image is to change.
21. The public is to accept them.

USING REFERENCE AND STRUCTURAL PATTERNS

Using Reference

Improve the coherence of each paragraph below by using pronouns or synonyms for reference.

Example

Dancing is a cultural universal. In many cultures dancing helps define group identity and enhance morale. Dancing has a central place in festive or religious events, and dancing may be an important factor in courtship.

↓

Dancing is a cultural universal. In many cultures **it** helps define group identity and enhance morale. **It** also has a central place in festive or religious events and may be an important factor in courtship.

A. Chicago, at the southern tip of Lake Michigan, has spent a half-century and billions of dollars developing a good water system.

Chicago draws a billion gallons a day from the lake, to serve over 5 million people. But now that Chicago's lake water has become almost too dirty for treatment, Chicago may be forced to get water elsewhere—and pay more for it.

B. Patchwork quilts today are among the antiques increasing steadily in worth. Once common in every household, the quilts were treasured, too, by the pioneers who made the quilts. The quilts provided color and gaiety for the crude, drab pioneer cabins. The quilts' combination of small, various-shaped pieces in geometric designs made use of otherwise useless scraps of fabric. And, since many patchwork pieces were cut from old clothing, the quilts even provided a sense of continuity with the past.

C. An American company under government contract is often faced with the choice of buying American-made goods, which are expensive, or foreign-made goods, which are cheaper. If the American company buys American goods, the company may anger taxpayers by failing to keep prices low. But if the company buys foreign goods, the jobs of American workers may be endangered. Confronting the issue, Congress has passed a law compelling American companies with government contracts to give preference to American goods and services.

Using Structural Patterns

Improve the coherence of each paragraph below by arranging sentences into structural patterns and/or by properly ordering old and new information.

Example

To become finalists in the competition for scholarships, the semifinalists must supply biographic information, maintain high academic standing, and perform well on a second examination. In addition, their high school principal must endorse them.

↓

To become finalists in the competition for scholarships, the semifinalists must supply biographic information, maintain high academic standing, perform well on a second examination, **and be endorsed by their high school principal.**

D. For the Northerners, Lincoln was a hero because he ended slavery and saved the Union. But because he threatened to destroy one of the staples of the economy, Lincoln was regarded as a villain by Southerners.

E. Because they are produced when conscious controls are lowered, doodles reveal personality in much the same way dreams do. Psychologists at Michigan State University found that students who draw houses on their lecture notes yearn for security, while aggressive personalities draw sharp objects. Spiders, bugs, and mice are drawn by deeply troubled people. And if you have a normal personality, you are likely to draw pictures of domestic animals—dogs, cats, and horses.

F. The weather forecaster on the evening news may have all the latest information from radar and satellites to give an accurate forecast. Old-timers claim you can be accurate just by watching natural signs. For an indication of fair skies ahead, look for gnats swarming in the setting sun. Noisy woodpeckers signal rain on the way. When bubbles collect in the middle of your morning coffee, fair weather is coming. But it's time to look for an umbrella when the bubbles ring around the edge.

TOMBSTONES

Using several different strategies of coherence—connectives, references, and structural patterns—combine the following sentences into a brief essay that explains how tombstones tell us as much about the living as the dead.

1. Tombstones would seem to record only remembrances.
2. The dead are remembered.

3. Tombstones are actually highly eloquent interpreters.
4. They interpret the culture of the living.

5. Tombstones change over the centuries.
6. These changes clearly reflect changes in values.
7. The values belong to the civilizations.
8. The civilizations created the tombstones.

9. The stones of colonial America are an instance.
10. The stones are frequently adorned with a head.
11. The head has wings.
12. The head depicts death.
13. Biographical facts are engraved on the stones.
14. These facts are often augmented by a warning.
15. They warn the passerby.
16. They warn of the inevitability of death.
17. These stones give mute witness.
18. The witness is to the solemn piety.
19. Our Puritan ancestors had solemn piety.

20. The willow and urn motif testifies.
21. The motif came a few generations later.
22. The motif showed a rendering of life out of death.
23. The rendering was symbolic.
24. The motif testified to the romanticism.
25. The romanticism was more hopeful.
26. The romanticism was of the early nineteenth century.

27. The Victorian preoccupation with status is demonstrated.
28. The early twentieth-century preoccupation is demonstrated.
29. The preoccupation was with material goods of the world.
30. It is demonstrated by tombstones and mausoleums of that period.
31. The tombstones and mausoleums are massive and ornate.

32. One wonders.
33. How will future generations interpret this?
34. They will interpret our own civilization.
35. They do this when they consider the anonymity of gravemarkers.
36. The anonymity is flat and uniform.

37. The gravemarkers are row upon row.
38. The gravemarkers are mechanically perfect.
39. The gravemarkers grace our modern "Memorial Parks."

CREATING COHERENCE

For any three sets from A–E below, make each of the three sentences into a coherent passage by creating an appropriate idea to follow the transitional word or words in parentheses.

Example

1. Most modern supermarkets are laid out in a carefully calculated manner. (For example, . . .)

↓

Most modern supermarkets are laid out in a carefully calculated manner. For example, meandering through the aisles the customer constantly bumps into attractive displays of those items the store most wants to sell.

2. Most modern supermarkets are laid out in a carefully calculated manner. (Even so, . . .)

↓

Most modern supermarkets are laid out in a carefully calculated manner. Even so, smart shoppers can guard against the lure of lavish displays and spend their money wisely.

3. Most modern supermarkets are laid out in a carefully calculated manner. (Indeed, . . .)

↓

Most modern supermarkets are laid out in a carefully calculated manner. Indeed, they are designed to trap unwary customers into buying many high-profit items they neither want nor can afford.

A. 1. Student government generates little interest among most students. (Furthermore, . . .)

2. Student government generates little interest among most students. (Yet, . . .)
3. Student government generates little interest among most students. (Its failure to attract support . . .)

B. 1. An educational computer center must be versatile enough to meet a wide variety of needs. (For one thing, . . .)
2. An educational computer center must be versatile enough to meet a wide variety of needs. (It must . . .)
3. An educational computer center must be versatile enough to meet a wide variety of needs. (But . . .)

C. 1. Americans spend more time at shopping malls than anywhere outside their homes and jobs. (Consequently, . . .)
2. Americans spend more time at shopping malls than anywhere outside their homes and jobs. (By contrast, . . .)
3. Americans spend more time at shopping malls than anywhere outside their homes and jobs. (In fact, . . .)

D. 1. Most doctors and lawyers do not advertise their services on radio or TV. (Even so, . . .)
2. Most doctors and lawyers do not advertise their services on radio or TV. (On the contrary, . . .)
3. Most doctors and lawyers do not advertise their services on radio or TV. (They . . .)

E. 1. Almost 35 million Americans have high blood pressure. (What's worse, . . .)
2. Almost 35 million Americans have high blood pressure. (As a result, . . .)
3. Almost 35 million Americans have high blood pressure. (In addition, . . .)

GENE BLUES

Read the following 21 sentences in order to get a sense of their meaning. Then, by (1) reordering sections A–D and (2) rearranging the sentences within each section, construct a coherent essay that explains why the creation of new forms of life through gene transplants is frightening.

A. 1. Because the transplanted genes are accepted readily by the bacteria and are able to reproduce themselves in succeeding generations, the result of the transplant is a permanent new life form.

2. No one knows how it would react to the environment outside the laboratory or to humans and animals.

3. These creations are a part of recombinant DNA research, which involves transplanting one or more foreign genes into loops of DNA in a bacteria.

4. All that is known about this new life are its observable physical characteristics.

B. 5. Perhaps scientists, who usually oppose public control of their research, have agreed so readily to these guidelines because they, too, fear the consequences of a mistake.

6. But since so little is known about the newly created organisms, how can scientists know that the safeguards are adequate?

7. And the safeguards do not apply to commercial companies, like Eli Lilly and General Electric, which are also conducting research in the field.

8. In response to these fears, the National Institute of Health offered a set of guidelines to ensure the safety of recombinant research.

9. They cannot.

10. One safeguard was a complete ban on the transplantation of cancer viruses.

11. No such mistakes have been made yet, though perhaps one is the limit.

12. Another safeguard required that only weakened *E. coli* bacteria be used, so that they could not survive for long away from the lab.

C. 13. Perhaps these creations could wreck the environment, eating up chemicals or destroying the soil.

14. Some people are afraid that cancer viruses transplanted into bacteria could spread cancer.

15. And, since most of the experiments use the bacteria *E. coli,* which live in humans, a new combination could turn out to be highly infectious to people.

16. They are afraid that a transplant between two completely different species, such as frogs and bacteria, could create new diseases to which humans would be susceptible.

17. Because of this uncertainty, fears have flared up.

D. 18. No one knows what would happen if some of these organisms were to escape from the laboratory, but doubtless there is a risk of disease or death in humans.

19. Scientists are creating new forms of life, and these new creatures do not have spikes through their necks, like Frankenstein monsters.

20. These forms of life involve gene transplants and are locked away in research laboratories, hopefully in safekeeping.

21. Yet they may be more dangerous than any Frankenstein monster could ever be.

unit*11*
REARRANGEMENT

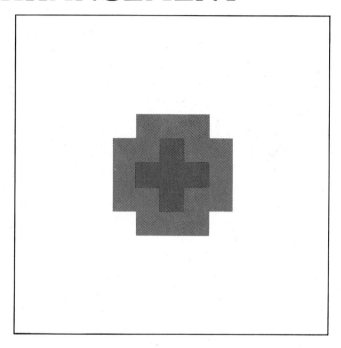

By changing the order of words within sentences, you can adapt
your writing to different situations. Just as the skilled orator sometimes speaks loudly and sometimes whispers, at one moment
pounds the podium and at another stands motionless, you can make
your writing more varied and more forceful by occasionally rearranging the normal word order of sentences. More importantly, with
skillful reordering you can better control the meaning of your prose.
Even slight changes in the expected word order can be powerful
ways of emphasizing important points, linking sentences to one
another, and expressing attitudes, as well as of achieving sentence
variety and producing interesting effects.

There are two basic facts about word order in English sentences
that are especially important for learning rearrangement patterns.
The first is that our word order is relatively fixed, with most sentences

following the pattern subject-verb-object (or complement). Any departure from this pattern tends to make a difference in a sentence —its meaning, emphasis, tone, or function in the paragraph. The second basic fact is that each major position in a sentence has a specific role of its own. The beginning and the end are the two most prominent positions and command the most attention. The beginning usually tells the reader what the sentence is about and in some way connects the sentence with what has been said before, to ensure continuity. The end or near the end of the sentence is the most emphatic position—this is where the most important word or words are usually placed.

What is true of the order of words within sentences is also true of the position of sentences within paragraphs. Although paragraphs have no "fixed sentence order," still some sentence positions within paragraphs have more strategic importance than others—positions such as the beginning or end of a paragraph, or the interruption of one sentence by another. Placed in these spots, sentences can sometimes do more work for you, especially by helping guide the reader's attention and attitude.

Rearrangement patterns practiced in this unit include shifted adverbs, patterns with introductory "what" and "it," passives, rhetorical questions, interruptive sentences, and "fronted" sentences. These patterns will help you to control the flow, emphasis, balance, and tone of your writing.

Shifted Adverbs

In earlier units you worked with modifiers like participles and absolutes that can often be moved from one sentence position to another. The sentence part that moves most freely is the ADVERB—a word, phrase, or clause that answers such questions as why, how, where, when, or how often. An adverb normally occurs next to the word it modifies; when shifted elsewhere in the sentence, the adverb usually becomes more prominent because—out of its normal position—it calls more attention to itself. Here is a sentence with the adverb **reluctantly** in its normal, unemphatic position, just before the verb:

The rescue team **reluctantly** suspended the operation.

If you choose to highlight the team's reluctance to stop the rescue effort, you can move the adverb **reluctantly** to the more prominent beginning or end position, depending on the context:

> The police had not given up hope, but for now the storm made any further search impossible. **Reluctantly,** the rescue team suspended the operation.

Connecting Sentences. But perhaps the most common reason for placing an adverb in an unusual position is to help connect one sentence to the next. In the following version **reluctantly** helps link "**suspended**" to "**hope**":

> The rescue team suspended the operation **reluctantly.** The police had not given up hope, but for now the storm made any further search impossible.

The next example further illustrates how the shifting of an adverb —in this case an entire phrase—can help the smooth flow of the sentences:

> Research on the atomic bomb proceeded quietly **in the laboratories of the University of Chicago**—unknown to all but the highest level military and government officials.

Note that moving the adverbial phrase **in the laboratories of the University of Chicago** to the beginning of the sentence places the word "**unknown**" next to the words to which it is most closely related—"**proceeded quietly**":

> **In the laboratories of the University of Chicago,** research on the atomic bomb proceeded quietly—unknown to all but the highest level military and government officials.

Controlling Tone. By shifting the position of an adverb, you can sometimes change the tone of a sentence as well, and thus express a different attitude toward what you're saying. Compare the following two positions of the adverb **usually**:

Harvey **usually** repays his debts on payday.

↓

Harvey repays his debts on payday—**usually.**

In the first version the writer seems to suggest that Harvey is—if not perfect—at least reasonably reliable about repaying his debts. But in the second version, the reader's suspicions are aroused by the emphasis on **usually,** an effect further enhanced by the pause (and the moment to have second thoughts) that the dash makes possible. The word **usually** can mean "more often than not," but here, given almost as an afterthought, it seems to suggest the meaning "not always." The tone of this version is one of doubt and mild distrust, a lack of confidence in Harvey.

Reversed Word Order for Emphasis. When you shift an adverb, it is often useful to rearrange other sentence parts as well. For example, in the sentence

The sound of shots came after midnight.

you can move the adverb **after midnight** to the front and then reverse the subject-verb order to create a dramatic effect:

After midnight came the sound of shots.

Here the effect is accomplished in two ways: first, the most striking word, **shots**, is placed in the final position for maximum emphasis; second, the sentence leads up to this key word through the unusual, reversed order of adverb-verb-subject.

When reversing the subject-verb order to achieve emphasis, be sure that your sentence begins with an introductory phrase and that its subject is important enough to deserve such emphasis:

Out of the lagoon and toward the village **crept the prehistoric creature** that for eons had slept undisturbed in ooze and slime.

Following the sheriff's arrival **came the announcement** we all dreaded—little Sarah had not been found.

Scholars disagree about the historical stature of Alexander the Great. Some consider him a drunken egotist, others a far-sighted humanitarian. **But beyond argument was** his military genius, proven by his 11 years of campaigning over 22,000 miles without a single battle lost.

You can shift an adverb clause as well as a word or phrase—an especially effective strategy when the adverb clause is intended to receive unusual emphasis:

Only if my safety is guaranteed in writing am I willing to join the experiment.

Not unless railroads resist pressures to modernize can the caboose be rescued from obsolescence.

Introductory "What"

The INTRODUCTORY "WHAT" pattern makes use of **what** and a form of the verb **be**, such as **is, was, are, were**. Imagine that you're writing an essay on predicting earthquakes and conclude that

Geologists can never predict exactly when an earthquake will strike.

In your second draft, so as not to suggest that geologists are totally inept, you might decide to give them credit for what they *are* able to predict, while maintaining your original point.

Geologists can often pinpoint where an earthquake will occur. But they can never predict exactly when it will strike.

If you decide that the connective "but" does not properly signal the contrast between what geologists can and cannot predict about earthquakes, you may add **what** and **is** to the second sentence. This will give "when" the strong emphasis it deserves:

> Geologists can often pinpoint where an earthquake will occur. **What** they can never predict **is** exactly when it will strike.

Similarly, the normal word order of the next example hides the most important word, "argument," in an unemphatic spot in the middle of the paragraph:

> After the last bunch of guys left the party, the house seemed unnaturally quiet. The argument when our parents came home was not so quiet.

But the pattern with **what . . . was** makes the "not so quiet" argument contrast sharply with the "unnaturally quiet" house:

> After the last bunch of guys left the party, the house seemed unnaturally quiet. **What** was not so quiet **was** the argument when our parents came home.

Introductory "It"

The INTRODUCTORY "IT" pattern involves the addition of **it** and a form of **be** along with **who** or **that.** Writing about a politician who had received more applause than even the president, you might say,

> The president was applauded enthusiastically, but the senator from Massachusetts received the largest ovation.

But by using **it was . . . who,** you can suggest an even stronger contrast between the two ovations:

The president was applauded enthusiastically, but **it was** the senator from Massachusetts **who** received the largest ovation.

In the same way, inserting **it is . . . that** into the next sentence turns a simple comment into a more emphatic assertion:

The room is tastefully decorated throughout, but the full-size grand piano gives the place its special charm.

↓

The room is tastefully decorated throughout, but **it is** the full-size grand piano **that** gives the place its special charm.

Passive

The passive is the most common, most useful, and probably most misused of all the rearrangement patterns.

To construct a passive from an active, move the subject noun to the end of the sentence and the object noun to the front; add a word like **is, are, was, were**, or **been** before the verb; and insert the word **by** after the verb:

Congress approved the new federal budget.

↓

The new federal budget **was** approved **by** Congress.

Commercialism and excessive violence are corrupting football.

↓

Football **is** being corrupted **by** commercialism and excessive violence.

Until recently, the American Telephone and Telegraph Company had dominated the telephone industry of the United States.

↓

Until recently, the telephone industry of the United States had **been** dominated **by** the American Telephone and Telegraph Company.

The passive helps you control *focus, flow,* and *balance.*

Controlling Focus. The passive is a tool for shifting nouns around in a sentence. Often what your paragraph is about—its focus or theme—is expressed by the nouns or pronouns near the beginning of sentences. The following paragraph is about Holiday Inns: note that references to this thematic focus—**Holiday Inns, It, Its 1800 motels**— all introduce sentences:

> Holiday Inns changed the concept of a motel from a sleazy road-side meeting place for lovers to a respectable lodging place for families. It is the "Innkeeper" not only of America but of much of the world. Its 1800 motels in nearly 60 countries offer tired travelers some 300,000 rooms—and convenience undreamed of 50 years ago.

But now let's suppose you want to include a further detail, perhaps after the first sentence:

> Kemmons Wilson, an enterprising real-estate developer from Memphis, started Holiday Inns in 1951.

Inserting this sentence would change the focus from "Holiday Inns" to "Kemmons Wilson" and then again back to "it" (Holiday Inns). But by shifting the sentence about Wilson into the passive, you can keep the focus and structural consistency of your paragraph intact:

> **Holiday Inns** changed the concept. . . . **It** was started by Kemmons Wilson. . . . **It** is the "innkeeper". . . . **Its** 1800 motels. . . .

Repetition of the pronoun "it" at the beginning of each sentence is of course not necessary for your paragraph's clear thematic direction; use of the passive has simply opened the door to further revision and improvement:

Holiday Inns changed the concept of a motel from a sleazy roadside meeting place for lovers to a respectable lodging place for families. Started in 1951 by Kemmons Wilson, an enterprising real-estate developer from Memphis, **the nation's "innkeeper"** has now become the innkeeper of much of the world. **Its 1800 motels** in nearly 60 countries offer weary travelers some 300,000 rooms—and convenience undreamed of 50 years ago.

Controlling Flow. Thematic focus is only one important fact about paragraph structure. Another one is the need for sentences to *follow from* what has been said before and to *lead to* what will be said next. Remember that the first part of a sentence usually contains information linked to earlier sentences, and any new information usually comes toward the end. Suppose what follows is your first draft of a report on an accident in your chemistry lab:

Yesterday a nasty explosion rocked Lab B in the Science Building. A small jar of old putric acid caused the blast. This chemical gets more volatile the longer it has been stored.

On rereading you may discover that the second sentence doesn't sound quite right: "blast," simply repeats "explosion" and would therefore be more appropriate at the beginning of the sentence, whereas the reference to "putric acid," the information of most interest to the reader, should appear at the end of the clause:

Yesterday a nasty explosion rocked Lab B in the Science Building. The blast **was** caused **by** a small jar of old putric acid, a chemical that gets more volatile the longer it has been stored.

Now if news of the explosion already happens to be known and you simply want to comment on its cause, the original three sentences can be further simplified into a single passive sentence that reads smoothly and directs the reader's attention to where it should be— on the word "acid":

Yesterday's nasty explosion at Lab B in the Science Building **was** caused **by** a small jar of old putric acid, a chemical that gets more volatile the longer it has been stored.

Controlling Balance. We normally put more words after the verb in a sentence than before it. So when you load a lot more words in the subject of a sentence than in the predicate, you will end up with a sentence that looks and sounds "front heavy." Making such a sentence passive will restore its proper balance. You can make the next sentence sound better by moving the short phrase "the unrest in the late sixties" to the front and the long, compound subject to the end, after the verb "caused":

Despair over the war in Vietnam, growing concern for civil rights, distrust of the Nixon administration, and general disillusionment with the government's ability to cope with problems caused the unrest in the late sixties.

↓

The unrest in the late sixties **was** caused **by** despair over the war in Vietnam, growing concern for civil rights, distrust of the Nixon administration, and general disillusionment with the government's ability to cope with problems.

The By Phrase. The **by** phrase of the passive construction can sometimes be shifted within the sentence to produce an effective stylistic variation:

Albert Einstein **is** called the greatest mind of the twentieth century **by those who know his work best.**

↓

By those who know his work best, Albert Einstein **is** called the greatest mind of the twentieth century.

More frequently—and more importantly—the **by** phrase can be omitted altogether, specifically when it merely repeats information contained elsewhere in the paragraph or when its information is trivial or inconsequential. If the sentence about Einstein were in a paragraph which made it clear that the comment was made by those who know his work best, the **by** phrase would be unnecessary:

Albert Einstein is called the greatest mind of the twentieth century.

In the next example, the phrase **by astronomers** can be dropped because it states an obvious fact:

Quasars, sources of energy in space, **were** first discovered **by astronomers** in 1960.

↓

Quasars, sources of energy in space, **were** first discovered in 1960.

But you should know that dropping the **by** phrase from a passive construction can sometimes be a way of hiding the truth. When Tommy reports to his Mom that a window "has been broken" or when a government official admits only that the FBI "was ordered" to conduct illegal wiretapping, both Tommy and the official are not telling the whole story. If you omit the **by** phrase from your own passive, make sure that what is omitted refers either to an obvious fact or to information that you deliberately want to withhold.

Rhetorical Questions

Sometimes writers ask questions that they do not really expect their readers to answer. More precisely, the answer may be so obvious that the reader mentally supplies it and thus helps the writer make a point. But even when the answer to a rhetorical question is not obvious, the question-answer format can help create drama, suspense, emotion—and agreement. No wonder that making statements in the form of questions has long been a favorite "rearrangement pattern" of preachers, advertisers, and politicians. Which option do you prefer? *"You* need America's railroads" or "America's railroads. **Who needs them?** *You* do." We think the second option, with the rhetorical question, is more effective.

A rhetorical question may be most persuasive when the writer puts the intended answer in the reader's "mouth." Here are some additional examples. Note that the rhetorical question often replaces statements beginning with "The question is/arises," "One wonders," or "One might ask."

> My roommate borrowed my new car three times last year and each time ended up in an accident. Now he asks for it again. I wonder whether he really expects me to say yes.
>
> ↓
>
> My roommate borrowed my new car three times last year and each time ended up in an accident. Now he asks for it again. **Does he really expect me to say yes?**

The following paragraph illustrates how rhetorical questions can be used both to consider alternatives and to drive home the obvious:

> An increasing number of women are taking hard-hat jobs. **Why do they do it? Is it for challenge? Pride? Adventure?** More likely, it's for the money. **Why settle for minimum wages working as a typist or receptionist when you can make five times as much as a construction worker or garage mechanic?**

The answer to a rhetorical question may be one of the few situations in your papers where your instructor will not only accept but welcome a "fragment"—a word or group of words less than a complete sentence, such as "Pride?" and "Adventure?" above, and the fragment in the next example:

> Why did President Lincoln's widow spend four months in an asylum in 1875? **Because she was temporarily insane, not because she was railroaded by her son.**

Interruptive Sentences

An interesting rearrangement pattern is the interruption of a sentence by another sentence. Because it is unexpected and unusual, a sentence that interrupts another is often more memorable than one placed in a normal position:

> Neighborhood crime watch programs are effective. Wherever they have been established, the crime rate has been reduced. But they can only be part of the solution to the fears many innocent citizens now suffer.

↓

> Neighborhood crime watch programs are effective—**wherever they have been established, the crime rate has been reduced**—but they can only be part of the solution to the fears many innocent citizens now suffer.

Like many appositives, interruptive sentences are normally set off by dashes. In fact, you can often reduce an interruptive sentence to an appositive. For this reason, a sentence with an appositive (the first example below) often resembles an interruptive sentence (the second example):

> A number of major corporations, such as Exxon, Bell, and Johnson & Johnson, encourage their employees to exercise at lunchtime in the belief that it will improve their afternoon productivity and their general health.

↓

> A number of major corporations—**Exxon, Bell, and Johnson & Johnson are a few**—encourage their employees . . .

But an interruptive sentence may be used for any commentary, even a rhetorical question. It enables you to make a pertinent remark exactly where you feel it is the most appropriate:

> I was interested—**wouldn't you be?**—in how Aunt Beulah's million-dollar estate was to be divided.

Fronting

Sometimes a word, phrase, or sentence is so crucial to a piece of writing that the writer wants it to be immediately noticed. You can "hit" your reader in a variety of ways—titles often serve this purpose, as do many visual devices. One uncommon but effective option is "fronting"—placing that critical word or sentence at the front of your paragraph or essay. Compare the effects:

> The very word "Cairo" evokes images of a vibrant, tumultous, exotic city.

> ↓

> **"Cairo"**—the very word evokes images of a vibrant, tumultous, exotic city.

The fronted word may be followed by a dash—as above—or by other punctuation marks such as dots **"Cairo"** . . . , colons **"Cairo":** or an exclamation mark **"Cairo"!**, depending on the intensity of response you hope to evoke. Your subject matter will often help you decide which punctuation is most appropriate:

> **The power of touch**. . . . If people only knew how it can help heal physical and emotional pain!

> **Reviving the draft!** Surely, Congress knows better.

Not only words and phrases but entire sentences may be moved to the front, if they deserve extraordinary emphasis. Fronted material is normally lifted out of the sentence, and it is followed by a pronoun such as "this" or "that":

> The best advice for handling an obscene or nuisance telephone call is to hang up immediately.

> ↓

> **Hang up immediately.** That's the best advice for handling an obscene or nuisance telephone call.

> The simple yet profound message millions are sending to world leaders is to prevent nuclear war.

>

Prevent nuclear war: this is the simple yet profound message millions are sending to world leaders.

*   *   *

Rearrangement patterns will work best if they are not overused. Since they alter the normal sentence order, your own use of these patterns should be justified by a need for smooth transition, rhythmic balance, or proper emphasis. But if you want more pizzaz in your writing—don't be afraid to experiment!

REARRANGING SENTENCES

Rearrange each sentence below as indicated by the example introducing each series.

Example I: Shifted Adverbs

International economics has become too complex for any single theory to explain or for any single government to control since World War II.

↓

Since World War II, international economics has become too complex for any single theory to explain or for any single government to control.

OR

International economics **since World War II** has become too complex for any single theory to explain or for any single government to control.

A. The public has grown understandably impatient with politicians and educators who make excuses for poor schools.

B. Class registration had not become computerized until quite recently.

C. Nobody is immune to unemployment when the economy is in trouble. Semiskilled or unskilled workers, who are first to lose their jobs and among the last to be rehired, are especially in danger.

Example II: Introductory "It"

Queen Elizabeth, the daughter of Henry VIII, finally brought England into the Renaissance and led it to greatness as a merchant power.

↓

It was Queen Elizabeth, the daughter of Henry VIII, **who** finally brought England into the Renaissance and led it to greatness as a merchant power.

D. The passion of Haley's narrative and its wealth of new material made *Roots* an event of social importance.

E. The oil crisis of 1973 prompted the 55-mile-per-hour speed limit, but the concern for highway safety made it permanent.

F. Pablo Picasso said, "Art is a lie which tells the truth."

Example III: Introductory "What"

Orwell's keen perception of how a totalitarian system works has made *1984* a significant novel.

What has made *1984* a significant novel **is** Orwell's keen perception of how a totalitarian system works.

G. The artist's intelligence, sensitivity, and range of vision make photography a form of art.

H. The electronics, not the music, is new in "synch-pop."

I. Alfred Nobel hoped to be remembered for his peace prize, not his invention of dynamite.

Example IV: Passive

Air travel, a more efficient means of transportation, doomed Europe's luxurious sleeping car express trains.

Europe's luxurious sleeping car express trains **were** doomed **by** air travel—a more efficient means of transportation.

J. Radio waves—a kind of electronic smog—endlessly bombard our cities, homes, and bodies.

K. Only crackpots who see what isn't there and publicity hounds who lie about what they see report UFO sightings.

L. In order to capture larger shares of the audience, many local TV stations have switched to the "Eyewitness News" format. On-the-scene reporting, informal atmosphere in the studio, expensive and elaborate sets, and attractive young newsreaders character-ize it.

Example V: Rhetorical Questions

The question is whether America's children are in deep crisis. You bet they are. That, at any rate, is the message from social agencies across the country.

↓

Are America's children in deep crisis? You bet they are. That, at any rate, is the message from social agencies across the country.

M. You may or may not have collected a good book lately. If not, join the crowd of antiques buffs hunting for good bargains at flea markets, garage sales, and estate auctions. It will brighten up your Saturday morning.

N. Gourmet lovers—and health nuts—are everywhere ignoring Shakespeare's admonition that we "Eat no onions nor garlic, for we are to utter sweet breath." There is no reason why they should not. Not only does garlic have the power to ward off vampires, but it also has medicinal value. If it can drive away maladies and vampires, no one cares if it drives away your friends.

O. Rags to riches stories, it seems, are relics of the past. Or maybe they are not. Maybe you can still get filthy rich in America. Some experts think so. They point out that the number of millionaires has more than tripled in just a decade, and the climate is just right for producing many more.

Example VI: Interruptive Sentences

No one knows why vampire bats drink blood, but their digestive systems are so specialized that they can't consume anything else. They have super-efficient kidneys, for example.

↓

No one knows why vampire bats drink blood, but their digestive systems are so specialized—**they have super-efficient kidneys, for example—** that they can't consume anything else.

P. Superstitions don't make sense, and there is no logical reason for their existence, and yet people believe them anyway, because their fathers and mothers did, or their friends do.

Q. As part of our "dress-for-success" trend, how you should dress for your court trial is now a hot fashion issue. Should you try to look rich? Or casual? Or conservative?

R. Resignation or retirement is now about the only way to weed out incompetent teachers. Firing a tenured teacher is virtually impossible. Most teachers fall into that category after just three to five years of experience.

Example VII: Fronting

Freckles don't die. They just fade away—sometimes.

↓

Freckles. They don't die. They just fade away—sometimes.

S. The worst day to schedule a job interview is Monday.

T. Whether you believe them or not, ghost stories carry a chill, an excitement, a fascination that has touched the human imagination since the beginning of time.

U. The philosophy that made Kodak a household word is to get lots of people to take pictures and make it as easy for them as possible.

WORDS AND THINGS

Using rearrangement patterns wherever appropriate, combine the sentences below into an essay that explains how words may originate.

1. A language is like a system.
2. The system is biological.
3. Its various parts are adapting to new situations.
4. They adapt constantly.

5. Words are the part of the system to study.
6. They are the most interesting part.

7. Words are the cells of language.
8. They are forming.
9. They are dying.
10. They are splitting up into parts.

11. Some words were originally the names of people.
12. An example is *sandwich*.

13. The Earl of Sandwich didn't like to interrupt his gambling with meals.
14. So he had his servants slap some meat between two slices of bread.
15. It was a snack at the gaming table.
16. The snack was handy.

17. Thus the earl became immortal.

18. *Hamburger* took its name from the city.
19. The city made it famous originally.
20. The city was Hamburg, Germany.
21. Hamburger is the world's most famous sandwich.

22. It is never called a sandwich anymore.
23. In fact, the *burger* part of the word means any kind of meat.

24. The meat is ground.
25. The meat is in a bun.

26. So we are inundated with *beefburgers.*
27. We are inundated with *vealburgers.*
28. We are inundated with *steakburgers.*
29. We are inundated with *doubleburgers.*
30. We are inundated with *cheeseburgers.*
31. We are inundated with *pizzaburgers.*
32. The latter is not a ground-up pizza.
33. But it is a meat patty.
34. The meat patty has cheese and pizza sauce on it.

35. Ground beef isn't a *burger* anymore.
36. The ground beef is in tomato sauce.
37. But it is a *Manwich.*
38. A *Manwich* isn't a sandwich.
39. But it is a meal.
40. Or so one manufacturer of tomato sauce would have us believe.

41. As long as the language is alive, its cells will continue to change.
42. The cells of the language are its words.
43. The cells will form.
44. The cells will die.
45. The cells will break up into parts.

REARRANGING IN CONTEXT

In each of the following paragraphs, rearrange one of the sentences according to the instructions in order to emphasize an important point, to sharpen paragraph focus, or to make a smooth transition.

Example

At the beginning of the twentieth century, America yearned to be a global power, which in those days meant having a large navy. But the American Navy was divided into two fleets, one on the East Coast, one on the West. The completion of the Panama

Canal in 1914 allowed the nation to fulfill its dream. By linking the two oceans, the canal made the separate fleets one great navy. (It was . . . that)

↓

At the beginning of the twentieth century, America yearned to be a global power, which in those days meant having a large navy. But the American Navy was divided into two fleets, one on the East Coast, one on the West. **It was** the completion of the Panama Canal in 1914 **that** allowed the nation to fulfill its dream. By linking the two oceans, the canal made the separate fleets one great navy.

A. Elias Howe is given credit for inventing the sewing machine. But Isaac Singer made it the most popular machine in history. With his partner, Edward Clark, Singer developed the marketing techniques of installment buying and trade-ins. He also overcame the nineteenth-century prejudice that allowing women to operate machines violated the laws of nature. (It was . . . who)

B. The term "yellow journalism"—journalism noted for its sensationalism rather than its truth—originated with a popular yellow-inked comic strip called "The Yellow Kid." Lurid murder stories and eye-catching colorful headlines characterize the practice. (Passive)

C. To some, the number of people on welfare is shocking. They complain that welfare recipients are lazy and don't want to work. They don't know that only 3 percent of those on welfare are able to hold a job. The rest are young children, mothers trying to care for them, and people with severe health problems. (What . . . is)

D. While many older films have faded or been completely destroyed, movie audiences can still see "Snow White and the Seven Dwarfs" in the same vivid color as its 1937 release. You might wonder how that is possible. The answer is that Walt Disney made sure the colors were separated and the original negatives kept in refrigerated vaults. (Rhetorical Question)

E. Several utopian communities thrived for short periods in nine-teenth-century America. One was New Harmony, Indiana. A group of religious zealots who formed a commune to await the Second Coming founded it. They were hardworking farmers and artisans doomed to a brief existence as a community because of their celibate lifestyle. (Passive)

F. Villagers from the little town of Catania frantically dug at a trench that would divert Etna's rivers of lava from their homes. They reluctantly gave up their efforts and allowed Catania to be over-run only when they saw that the new path endangered a neigh-boring town. (Shifted Adverb)

G. John James Audubon is revered by modern ornithologists who know his painstaking studies and detailed paintings of wild birds. They probably don't know that he shot his subjects before paint-ing them and that he once confessed he didn't feel right unless he killed a hundred birds a day. (What . . . is)

H. To some, competition is a great American virtue—as long as they are ahead; when the chips—and the profits—are down, they cry "unfair" and run to Uncle Sam for help. The unqualified success of imported cars prompted American automakers to press the government for import restrictions. The market share of imported cars increased from 15 to 30 percent in a single year. So much for fair competition. (Interruptive Sentence)

I. Even the word "hiccup" is funny. It imitates the silly sound you make when air bounces up and down inside you like it's on a trampoline. But hiccups are funniest when someone else has them—right? (Fronting)

TO TELL THE TRUTH

Using rearrangement patterns whenever appropriate, combine the sentences below into an essay that explains why tourists often fall from the Mayan pyramids.

1. The middle-aged American couple was enjoying a vacation.
2. The vacation was in an ancient Mayan city.

3. The couple grew tired of the sightseeing group.
4. They broke away to do some exploring.
5. They explored on their own.

6. They climbed a pyramid.
7. Its stepping stones were overgrown with weeds.
8. They wanted to reach one of the higher ledges.

9. The woman screamed suddenly.
10. Her husband had lost his balance.
11. He began to fall over.
12. He was grasping his chest.
13. She was reaching after her husband.

14. The two tumbled down to the horrified group below.
15. Their arms and legs were flailing.

16. What happened to the couple?
17. It is becoming more common.
18. At the same time the ruins are developing into tourist attractions.
19. About 50 tourists a year fall from the ledges.
20 Or they panic.
21. And they have to be carried down.

22. These accidents have led to fanciful conjecture.
23. The conjecture is about the origin of the ledges.
24. The conjecture is about this:
25. Why do people regularly fall from the pyramids?

26. Some Americans claim this.
27. And some Europeans claim this.
28. Ancient astronauts built the ledges.
29. The astronauts used the ledges for this purpose.
30. They anchored their spaceships.
31. The pyramids continue to rock and sway.

32. They do this as if they were still attached to interplanetary vessels.

33. The natives of the area blame the accidents on an ancient curse.
34. The Mayans placed the curse on the pyramids.
35. The curse protected hoards of gold.
36. The Mayans had hidden the hoards of gold in the pyramids.

37. Mexican scholars have recently revealed the truth about the origin of the ledges.
38. It seems to be this.
39. The Mayans practiced human sacrifice.
40. Human sacrifice was part of their religion.
41. The practice developed.
42. The Mayan population outgrew the protein supply.
43. The protein supply was available in the area.

44. The sacrifices became a means.
45. The means brought the population into harmony.
46. The harmony was with natural resources.
47. The means added to the food supply.

48. The priests stood on the ledges.
49. The priests removed the hearts of their victims.
50. Then the priests shoved the bodies down the steep sides of the pyramids.
51. The priests shoved the bodies to the hungry masses below.
52. The hungry masses below practiced cannibalism.

53. The Mexican government does not want to be left out.
54. The Mexican government offers its own reason for this.
55. Why do so many tourists fall off from the ledges?

56. The Mexican government blames the tourists themselves.
57. The tourists are not used to heights.
58. The tourists develop vertigo or acrophobia on the steep-sided pyramids.
59. Vertigo is a dizzy sensation.
60. Acrophobia is a fear of heights.

61. The truth may be stranger than fiction.
62. But the truth is less romantic.
63. At least in this case it is less romantic.
64. Curses are nice fictions.
65. Hoards of gold are nice fictions.
66. Ancient astronauts are nice fictions.

USING NOTES FOR REARRANGEMENT PATTERNS

Each of the following is a half-developed paragraph. The part not completed is given in the form of notes, such as you might jot down while preparing your own paper. Each note supplies some information that responds to a question such as Who? What? Where? When? Why? or How? (the "Five W's plus H" of journalism).

Use these notes to construct a sentence that will fit into the paragraph's context. In each case, one of the rearrangement patterns discussed in this unit is likely to be the most appropriate choice. When you are finished, polish the paragraph as needed.

Example

> Herbert Hoover, with his hands-off government policy, was unable to solve the problems of the Great Depression. (. . .)

> > Notes: Franklin D. Roosevelt did it
> > he finally put the nation back on its feet
> > did it with a series of government-sponsored projects

> Roosevelt took people out of the soup kitchens and put them to work clearing forests and building bridges, schools, and hospitals.

↓

> Herbert Hoover, with his hands-off government policy, was unable to solve the problems of the Great Depression. **It was** Franklin D. Roosevelt **who** finally put the nation back on its feet with a series of government-sponsored projects. **He** took people out of the soup kitchens and put them to work clearing forests and building bridges, schools, and hospitals.

A. The gondolas of hot-air racing balloons are equipped with controls that allow balloonists to change the altitude and direction of their craft—but not the speed, which is determined by air currents. (. . .)

> Notes: accuracy counts in balloon racing
> speed doesn't count

Victory belongs to the balloonist who lands closest to the target.

B. When it's time to celebrate the New Year, folks in Italy don't fool around—they go at it with a vengeance. Take New Year's Eve 1984. Sardinians tossed old belongings out of the house, with carpets, chairs, shoes, books, and vegetables flying from balconies and windows at the stroke of midnight. (. . .)

> Notes: the people of Rome were a bit roudier
> 49 of them ended up in the hospital
> they had injuries from fireworks
> but citizens of Naples had the best time
> 202 of them were wounded
> many of them were shot

Where, you ask, were the police? Well, they joined in—like the young Milan police officer who, drawing out his pistol to fire into the air, accidentally shot himself in the stomach.

C. The poison spewed along our city streets and expressways around the clock—lead in leaded gasoline—settles in the teeth and bones of children playing nearby, threatening to cause anemia and in some cases nerve and brain damage. (. . .)

> Notes: you may wonder if this is not an ironic coincidence
> lead poisoning may have contributed to collapse of Roman Empire
> the Empire had the mightiest civilization
> it enjoyed limitless wealth, pomp, and pleasure

Farfetched? Hardly. Historical records show that Roman food and wine were heavily contaminated with lead. And recent chemical analyses of Roman skeletons revealed abnormally high levels of lead—nearly 30 times that found in the bones of some prehistoric peoples.

GRAVE RESERVATIONS

Using rearrangement patterns whenever appropriate, combine the sentences below into a persuasive essay supporting Indian reservations. Supply additional details that will strengthen your argument.

1. Imagine this.
2. People live in a tar paper shack.
3. Or people live in a log cabin.
4. The shack or the cabin has only one small window.
5. A stovepipe is jutting out of the roof.
6. The roof is weighted down by old automobile tires.

7. Imagine this, too.
8. There is no electricity.
9. There is no running water.
10. Maybe there is not even an outhouse.
11. There are no less than six or seven people dwelling here.

12. This is a house on an Indian reservation in America today.
13. The house is typical.
14. The reservation is typical.
15. The reservation is impoverished.

16. Yet many Indians value their parcels of land.
17. Many Indians hold their parcels of land sacred.
18. The parcels are the last vestiges of a continent.
19. The Indians once freely roamed the continent.

20. It is for this reason.
21. One should preserve reservations.
22. One should protect reservations.
23. One should suppress any move.
24. The move would dissolve the reservations.
25. The move would force Indians into mainstream American culture.
26. Indians would be forced against their will.

27. The reservations' biggest problem is their poverty.
28. Many whites want to use poverty as an excuse.
29. The excuse is for abolishing the reservations.

30. This is true.
31. Indians are dependent on the federal government.
32. They depend on the government for housing.
33. They depend on the government for employment.
34. Sometimes they depend on the government for food.
35. Sometimes they depend on the government for clothing.

36. This is also true.
37. Infectious and communicable diseases are widespread among Indians.
38. In part, this is because of their flimsy shacks.
39. The flimsy shacks are often freezing in winter.
40. In summer, the flimsy shacks are often stifling.

41. This is equally true.
42. Large sums of money are spent on Indians by the Bureau of Indian Affairs.
43. In spite of this, the poverty never seems to go away.

44. Some people think the Indians should be driven off their reservations.
45. Some people think the Indians should be driven into white society.
46. Then the poverty would go away.
47. The people are mistaken.

48. The reservations themselves are not the major cause of Indian poverty.

49. This is a fact.
50. There are Indians who live in large cities.
51. The cities are far from the reservations.
52. Most of these Indians find themselves in urban slums.

53. But the reservations are a major source of Indian pride.

54. Reservations exist for a reason.
55. Reservations help preserve Indian heritage.
56. Reservations help preserve Indian culture.

57. Reservations exist for another reason.
58. Indian leaders do not want their people mixing with non-Indians.

59. Reservations exist for still another reason.
60. The federal government is under solemn treaty obligations.
61. The obligations are to keep the reservations intact.

62. One Indian leader said this.
63. An Indian is forced out of the tribe.
64. The Indian becomes "alienated, irritable, and lonely."
65. The Indian longs to return to the tribe.
66. The longing is desperate.
67. The return will restore the Indian's sanity.

68. The center of the Indians' universe is the tribe.
69. This is true today.
70. It was true in the past.
71. Without the tribe there is no culture.

72. But suppose there is no reservation.
73. Then there is no tribe.

74. So Indian poverty must be wiped out.
75. This is the way it should be done.
76. It should not endanger the existence of the reservation.
77. The reason is that the Indians have a primary goal.
78. Their primary goal is preserving their tribal lifestyle.

unit *12*
REPETITION

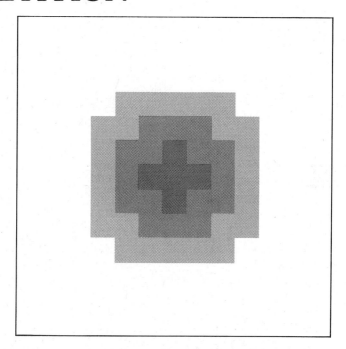

Repeating Words and Sounds

Advertisers know that repetition helps to sell products and services. So they often deliberately repeat words and sounds in order to drive home a message to potential buyers. Eastern Airlines claims that "you don't have to take **charter** flights to get **charter** prices," and Delta promises that "every **nonstop** to Florida is a **nonstop** party." TWA, paraphrasing football coach Vince Lombardi about winning, argues that "being the best isn't the only **thing.** It's every **thing.**" A manufacturer of bed linens urges you to "put a little **bloom** in your **room**" with its floral spread. Commodore claims that its popular computer "wr**ites,** r**ates,** cre**ates,** even telecommunic**ates.**" *Mademoiselle* advertises itself as "the magazine more **select** women **select,**" just as a peanut butter maker asserts that "**choosy** mothers **choose** Jif." Konica says that it's the "**oldest** and **boldest**" camera company. Not to be outdone, Kahns bills its hot dog as "the **w**iener the **w**orld a**w**aited."

Balanced Structures

Another form of repetition, equally popular with advertisers, involves not just single words or sounds but groups of words—phrases, clauses, even full sentences. What is repeated is both the structure and rhythmic pattern of the word group. For example, a New York hotel tries to attract tourists with this slogan: "Long after you've forgotten the time, you'll remember the place." If you read the slogan aloud, you'll hear that the clause **you've forgotten the time** corresponds in rhythm and structure to **you'll remember the place.** The correspondence is created by repeating some words (**you** and **the**) and by choosing others that are similar in cadence as well as in grammatical structure: **forgotten** and **remember** are both three-syllable verbs; **time** and **place** are both one syllable nouns. When a sentence or paragraph includes two or more elements similar in rhythmic pattern and in grammatical structure as well, the effect is called BALANCE. Here are some short sentences with balanced elements:

Don't let **a good ad** send you on **a bad trip.**

Gospel music is **good news** in **bad times.**

Othello is a board game that takes only **a minute to learn** but **a lifetime to master.**

Dodge and Plymouth dealers **take the shock out, put the value in.**

A good ad and **a bad trip, good news** and **bad times, a minute to learn** and **a lifetime to master, take the shock out** and **put the value in**—the contrasts in these phrases are reinforced by grammatical and rhythmic parallels.

Advertisers use balanced sentences because the repeated elements make the ads easy to remember. The travel agency that chose the balanced sentence "Don't let a good ad send you on a bad trip" would surely have rejected the unbalanced sentence "Don't let a good brochure send you on a vacation you won't enjoy." In the same way, "Gospel music is good news in bad times" loses its punch, along with its balance, when rephrased as "Gospel music is good news when you're feeling bad." Without balanced phrases, the Othello slogan falls flat: "Othello is a board game that takes only a minute to learn, but to master it requires a lifetime." And the car ad would hardly be interesting as "Dodge and Plymouth dealers take the shock out and let you have value, too." Now listen to the balanced phrases of a Rolls Royce advertisement: "The Silver Shadow II is a new air of comfort, a new sense of quiet, and a new feeling of command." The repeated pattern **a new . . . of . . .** gives the sentence the same luxury, ease, and controlled power that the Rolls itself claims to offer.

Some advertisers use repetition even more extensively by repeating words from one clause to the next and at the same time reversing word order to achieve an interesting effect. For example, a tobacco company claims that "You can take Salem out of the country, but you can't take the country out of Salem." The makers of a chocolate liqueur tell us that "Vandermint isn't good because it's imported; it's imported because it's good." And the distributors of Teachers Scotch whiskey use in their advertising slogan both balanced phrases and key words repeated in reverse order: "In life, experience is the best teacher. In Scotch, Teachers is the best experience."

The strategies of repetition that work in advertising copy can work just as well in your own writing to achieve emphasis, to gain coherence, and to create rhythms that are memorable, pleasing, and dynamic. You can use these strategies in both your sentences and your paragraphs.

Repetition for Sentence Emphasis

Repetition can help you to emphasize key terms in sentences:

The old man has **nothing** left, **nothing** except memories.

Of the many **gray, faceless** bureaucracies in Washington, the Veterans Administration is probably the **grayest** and the most **faceless** of all.

A director of the Central Intelligence Agency once said that his job in collecting information involved doing the in**decent** things as **decent**ly as possible.

As the sentence about the Central Intelligence Agency suggests, repetition also works effectively to reinforce contrasts. Repeating words and sounds is one way of directing the reader's attention to important differences. In the following sentence, the writer strengthens the contrast between her loafing **in the sun** and her friends' working **on the job** by repeating **spent long hot days:**

While all my friends **spent long hot days on the job,** I **spent long hot days in the sun,** soaking up a tan which made even the darkest-skinned girls envious.

In the next sentence, the writer is able to create a stark contrast between the two functions of Christmas by repeating the phrase **a time** and following each occurrence of it with a different prepositional phrase:

Christmas is not only **a time of good cheer** but also **a time for toy fads.**

When you revise, look for places where you can use repetition to achieve emphasis or to reinforce a contrast, as in the following:

The struggle to reduce the national debt will test the character of the American people. Whether the American nation is coherent will also be tested by this struggle.

↓

The struggle to reduce the national debt will test **the character of the American people** and **the coherence of the American nation.**

The balanced phrases **the character of the American people** and **the coherence of the American nation** make the second version more concise and more powerful than the first. You can often make one strong sentence out of two weak ones by using repetition. In the following two sentences, a student writer missed the opportunity to produce a compelling pair of infinitive phrases that would have reinforced her point:

Do you believe that children are immune to constantly repeated violence? Then you are ignoring the most basic principles of developmental psychology.

↓

To believe that children are immune to constantly repeated violence is **to ignore** the most basic principles of developmental psychology.

Repetition for Paragraph Emphasis and Coherence

Strategies of repetition are equally useful and even more varied on the paragraph level. One such strategy involves beginning consecutive sentences with the same word or group of words. In the following paragraph, for example, the opening two sentences begin in the same way to reinforce a contrast between the children of the rich and the children of the poor:

If you are born into an American family ranking in the top tenth of income, chances are 1 in 3 that you'll stay there. **If you are born into** a family in the bottom tenth, however, chances are less than 1 in 200 that you'll ever reach the top. So much for equality of opportunity.

In the next paragraph, the middle three sentences all start with the same construction:

If you don't vote, don't complain. **Never before** in history **have** American citizens held such power in their own hands. **Never before have** they had the opportunity to formulate such well-informed opinions. **Never before have** they been allowed such vigorous and unrestrained debate on the issues.

Not to vote is to throw away your simplest and most effective means of political influence.

The repetition of **never before have** lends both coherence and force to this brief paragraph. So does the repetition of **don't vote, don't complain** in the first sentence and of the infinitive phrases **not to vote** and **to throw away** in the last. Obviously, a writer must always choose how much repetition to use. For instance, the third and fourth sentences of the paragraph about voting could have repeated the longer phrase **never before have American citizens**:

If you don't vote, don't complain. **Never before** in history **have American citizens** held such power in their own hands. **Never before have American citizens** had the opportunity to formulate such well informed opinions. **Never before have American citizens** been allowed such vigorous and unrestrained debate on the issues. Not to vote is to throw away your simplest and most effective means of political influence.

Is this second version more effective than the first? Probably not, because the increased repetition makes it seem overdone. Like any writing strategy, repetition becomes ineffective when it is overused. Unfortunately, there are no exact rules to tell you when some repetition becomes too much repetition. The best advice is to trust your intuition and to remember that good writing involves both repetition and variation.

Just as you can repeat sentences that begin in the same way, you can repeat key words or phrases within a paragraph. Notice the different kinds of repetition in the paragraph below:

Spinning, spinning, the plastic plate twirls on the floor as the **beautiful** child sits mesmerized. **Eyes crystal blue, hair braided to the waist, features clear and shapely,** the little girl sits and watches—oblivious to the outside world. The plate continues to **spin** as a young woman enters the modern playroom and calls to her **beautiful** daughter. There is **no**

reply, **no** eye contact, **no** body movement—this **beautiful** child is autistic.

The repeated **spinning** of the first sentence suggests the child's fascination with the plate; **spin** picks up the idea again in the third sentence. A series of absolutes begin the second sentence. **No** is repeated in the last sentence to reinforce the child's complete isolation. And, most importantly, the word **beautiful** is repeated in order to contrast the child's physical appearance with her psychological condition.

Since the first or last sentence of a paragraph often announces its controlling idea, it is here that repetition will have its greatest impact. In the opening sentence of the next paragraph, the writer balances the phrase **financial security** with the phrase **personal security** in order to accentuate the controlling idea of the paragraph, that money can shelter you from life's harsh realities:

In today's world, **financial security** translates into **personal security.** A comfortable bank account and blue chip investments not only increase your future options but also protect your current lifestyle. Money makes it easier to live in a safe neighborhood, to buy nutritious food, and to afford a good education. While there is no absolute protection from all of life's hazards, wise financial planning can soften its harshest blows.

Aside from the balanced phrases of its opening sentence, this paragraph uses other strategies of repetition. The second sentence includes the paired coordinators **not only . . . but also,** which call attention to another set of balanced phrases—**increase your future options** and **protect your current lifestyle.** The third sentence includes a series of infinitive phrases, with the word **to** repeated before each series item: **to** live in a safe neighborhood, **to** buy nutritious food, and **to** afford a good education. The paired coordinators and repeated infinitives help to make the paragraph more coherent.

Here is one final example of a paragraph that is strengthened by repetition:

The great American sports hoax began when a stockbroker and football fanatic, Morris Newburger, decided it would be fun to create an imaginary college and a football legend. So every Saturday during the 1941 season, he called wire services with the results of games played by fictitious Plainfield College and its "stellar Chinese halfback," John Chung, who supposedly ate rice during halftime. A *Time* magazine reporter caught on to the hoax—but only after America thrilled to reports of an injured Chung, who had come off the bench to lead Plainfield to a 40–27 victory over Harmony College and an invitation to the Blackboard Bowl. Before the reporter could expose Newburger, the stockbroker issued one final story— that since a large number of players were declared ineligible because of failing grades, including Chung, Plainfield cancelled its remaining games. And so **ended the great American sports hoax.**

Because the last sentence reverses the phrasing of the first—substituting **ended** for **began**—it neatly concludes the paragraph, bringing it to a satisfactory close. The paragraph ends on the exact same phrase with which it began, **The great American sports hoax.**

Rhyming

One of the more interesting—and more risky—strategies of repetition involves rhyming words. Since rhyme is more appropriate to poetry than prose, you should use it sparingly. Despite the warning, you can sometimes make your writing particularly expressive with rhymed words, as in the next example:

After six years in Chicago, my sister Ann thought she had stumbled onto the ideal life when she was offered a job at a small university in Vermont. Vermont—the mere name evoked mystical and romantic thoughts. How wonderful to trade clogged city streets for winding valley roads, skyscrapers for mountains, neon **lights** for star-filled **nights!**

The rhyming of **lights** and **nights** suggests something falsely romantic about Ann's hopes and tries to prepare the reader for her later disappointment. But the rhymes in the next paragraph suggest, instead of false hope, a rebellious spirit trying hard within the conventions of standard prose rhythms and sound patterns to express the essence of rock and roll.

> Rock records are **made loud** to be **played loud.** The bass should **make** the floorboards **shake,** and the drums should **make** your marrow **quake.** The music seems both to taunt and seduce, to fetter and liberate. It is a howling spirit, ill at ease in these conventional times.

By rhyming **made loud** with **played loud** and **make . . . shake** with **make . . . quake,** the writer communicates a sense of the taunting and seductive, fettering and liberating spirit of rock music.

Ineffective Repetition

There are certain kinds of repetition that you should generally avoid. Unless you're trying to be humorous, it's a good idea not to repeat unimportant words like pronouns, not to place **-ing** words next to each other, or not to string together—except perhaps in a series—prepositional phrases beginning with the same preposition. Here are sentences that you can improve by eliminating their repeated elements:

> Karen was a close friend of a girl I was dating and, unknown to **me,** she had a crush on **me.**
>
> ↓
>
> Karen was a close friend of a girl I was dating and, though I didn't know it, she had a crush on me.

> I swerved back and forth, send**ing** chill**ing** droplets fly**ing,** sting**ing** my arms and legs.
>
> ↓

As I swerved back and forth, chilling droplets stung my arms and legs.

The speaker was the chair **of** the Department **of** Physics **of** Tulane University.

↓

The speaker was the chair of Tulane University's Physics Department.

I offered tickets **to** the concert **to** my friends **to** use on Saturday.

↓

I offered my friends tickets to Saturday's concert.

Ellipsis

With the final strategy of repetition, called ELLIPSIS, you omit certain words and phrases in repeated constructions. For example, you can delete the second occurrence of **was president** in "Theodore Roosevelt was president from 1901 to 1909, and Franklin Roosevelt **was president** from 1933 to 1945" in order to produce the more concise statement "Theodore Roosevelt was president from 1901 to 1909, Franklin Roosevelt from 1933 to 1945." In the same way, you can eliminate phrases within the following repeated structures and still retain the full meaning of the sentences:

Her hair is light brown, **and** her eyes **are** bluish-green.

↓

Her hair is light brown, her eyes bluish-green.

Some lawyers are arrogant, **and** some **lawyers are** simply reserved.

↓

Some lawyers are arrogant, some simply reserved.

One April morning, the president flew to Moscow, the vice president **flew** to London, and the secretary of state **flew** to Tokyo.

↓

One April morning, the president flew to Moscow, the vice president to London, and the secretary of state to Tokyo.

Like all strategies of repetition, ellipsis works particularly well in emphatic positions, such as the final sentence of the following paragraph:

One morning the valley's peace was interrupted by a grinding noise in the distance. Soon after, a yellow machine punctuated the horizon to the east, then another, and another. The invasion continued for six months, and then the army retreated, leaving behind a deep, blackened gorge of mud and slime. Thanks to strip mining, the vegetation is gone, the soil ruined, the entire valley turned into waste.

*   *   *

Balanced phrases, repeated key words, repeated structures, and ellipsis—these strategies can help make your sentences more varied and striking and your paragraphs more coherent and pointed. They can also enhance the sound and rhythm of your prose.

USING PATTERNS OF REPETITION

Combine each of the groups of sentences below into a single sentence by using one or more of the strategies of repetition—ellipsis, repetition of key words, repeated structures, or balanced phrases.

Example

1. For some students beer drinking has become a way of life.
2. And other students drink beer in order to escape.

Beer drinking has become a way of life for some students and a means of escape for others.

OR

For some students, beer drinking has become a way of life, for others a means of escape.

A. 1. Cincinnati is a city blessed with more than its share of good restaurants.
   2. Of smut, Cincinnati is blessed with less than its share.

B. 1. It is just as people live their lives in countless ways.
   2. So do people leave their lives in different ways also.

C. 1. For some Catholics the effect of celibacy is not just that priests cannot marry.
   2. But it is that married men cannot become clergymen.

D. 1. The going gets tough.
   2. That's when people who are tough start moving.

E. 1. Oklahoma became a state in 1907.
   2. New Mexico became a state in 1912.

F. 1. For days the Arctic explorers fought a running battle with drifting ice flows.
   2. They fought a running battle with light that dwindled, too.

G. 1. The photographer does not create the beauty of a landscape.
   2. Even so, he controls how it will be remembered.
   3. And, to some extent, how it will be interpreted later is controlled by him.

H. 1. To equalize economic opportunity, the Carnegie Council on Children recommends policies.
   2. The policies are fairly conventional in kind.
   3. But the policies are, in degree, fairly extreme.

I. 1. Most people make two mistakes in getting wine for a party.
   2. The first mistake is buying too little wine.
   3. Paying too much for the wine is the second mistake.

J. 1. Anorexia nervosa starts as an innocent diet.
   2. Anorexia nervosa then turns into a ritual of systematic starvation.
   3. The victims will not free themselves from the ritual.
   4. The victims later cannot free themselves from the ritual.

WHO NEEDS DODOS?

Using patterns of repetition, combine the following sentences into an explanatory essay about how scientists plan to use turkeys to help germinate the seeds of a nearly extinct tree.

1. Scientists have long known of this.
2. There are close interrelationships in nature.
3. Scientists have only recently learned this.
4. The extinction of an animal may cause the decline of a plant.

5. Thirteen calvaria trees grow on the island of Mauritius.
6. The trees are beautiful and rare.
7. Mauritius is best known as the last refuge of the dodo bird.
8. The dodo bird was bulky and flightless.
9. Each of the 13 trees is over 300 years old.
10. Each of the 13 trees is dying.

11. Not a single young calvaria has sprouted in the last three centuries.
12. The dodo became extinct three centuries ago.
13. The calvaria seeds have thick shells.
14. Apparently no calvaria has sprouted for this reason.
15. The calvaria seeds must be worn down.
16. This must happen in the digestive tract of the dodo.
17. Otherwise the calvaria seeds cannot germinate.

18. But help for the calvaria may be on its way.

19. Turkey gizzards contain stones for crushing food.
20. These stones are much like the stones of the dodo.
21. Therefore scientists are now experimenting.
22. Scientists want to see whether the tree can survive.
23. The tree declined with the loss of the dodo.
24. Can the tree survive with the help of the turkey?

USING REPETITION FOR PARAGRAPH REVISION

The following three paragraphs lack either coherence or proper emphasis. Rewrite the paragraphs using one or more of the strategies of repetition—repeated key words, balanced phrases, repeated structures, or ellipsis—in order to tighten their structure or to emphasize important ideas. Make any other changes you can justify. Be sure to write out the complete paragraphs.

Example

Chief Justice Warren E. Burger has become increasingly critical of the American lawyer. According to Burger, attorneys entangle the American populace in litigation and substitute legal manipulation for justice. Various federal agencies, commissions, and even Congress itself, where they hold more than 300 of the 535 seats, are dominated by barristers. Complex laws and obscure regulations are created by counselors-at-law who work in government and so business increases for attorneys whose work is outside government. Above all, barristers flock to the big money of corporate law while 30 million poor Americans suffer from a counselor-at-law shortage. "The harsh truth," Burger told the American Bar Association, "is that we may well be on our way to a society overrun by hordes of lawyers, hungry as locusts."

↓

Chief Justice Warren E. Burger has become increasingly critical of the American lawyer. According to Burger, **lawyers entangle** the American populace in litigation and substitute legal manipulation for justice. **Lawyers dominate** various federal agencies, commissions, and even Congress itself, where they hold more than 300 of the 535 seats. **Lawyers** who work in government **create** complex laws and obscure regulations that increase business for lawyers who work outside government. Above all, **lawyers flock** to the big money of corporate law while 30 million poor Americans suffer from a lawyer shortage. "The harsh truth," Burger told the American Bar Association, "is that we may well be on our way to a society overrun by hordes of lawyers, hungry as locusts."

A. According to comedian George Carlin, football is a ruthless, warlike game, but baseball is a warm and pastoral game. Football, for example, is played on the gridiron, while baseball is a game that takes place on a field. A defensive football player tackles the opponent but, in baseball, an opponent is only tagged by a defensive player. A violation in football draws a penalty, but a mistake is merely an error in baseball. A football team can score on a bomb, but on a sacrifice a baseball team can score. And, of course, the object of football is to reach the end zone, while in baseball to run safely home is the idea.

B. Back in April of 1775, some 300 beaten British soldiers retreated 26 miles from Lexington and Concord to the safety of their Boston barracks. As many as 3000 participants, every April now for over 75 years, run from the Boston suburb of Hopkinton to the city's fashionable Back Bay, a distance of 26 miles, to help commemorate the British defeat. The event is the Boston Marathon. The winner's prize is a laurel wreath and a bowl of beef stew and a lot of money.

C. He began planning it a year before he did it. First he started saving his salary to pay for bail and lawyers' fees. Whatever he could find about prison life he began reading next. His lucrative job with the United States Steel Corporation in Chicago he then quit, moving with all his belongings back to his family home in the San Francisco Bay Area. There, one by one, his three younger sisters were taken aside by him and told what he had done and what he was going to do. Then, after hiring a prominent criminal lawyer, Joseph Otto Egenberger surrendered himself to local police as the murderer, 14 years earlier, of a 20-year-old University of California sophomore.

CAPITAL PUNISHMENT: BARBARIC AND IRRATIONAL

Using several strategies of repetition, combine the following sentences into a letter to the editor which shows why government-sponsored executions are barbaric and not very effective in reducing homicide rates. Try to emphasize the quiet voice and reasoned tone. If you wish, add details of your own that will enhance the logic of the argument.

To the Editor:

1. The death penalty is a barbarous punishment.
2. The death penalty is an archaic punishment.
3. The death penalty is inconsistent with modern justice.
4. Modern justice has complexities.

5. The death penalty reduces our laws to the tribal level of revenge.
6. Not only that, it rules out any chance for rehabilitation.

7. The death penalty forces the state.
8. The state must share the murderer's crime.
9. And the death penalty creates a legal mechanism.

10. If the mechanism is abused, it could put any citizen's life in jeopardy.

11. The death penalty is not a solution to the problem of homicide, finally.
12. A convicted murderer is executed.
13. It does not bring the victim back to life.

14. Proponents of capital punishment often argue.
15. They say we need a final penalty.
16. The final penalty will deter would-be murderers from killing.

17. There are studies that show this, however.
18. Fear of execution is not an actual deterrent to homicide.

19. Several studies have compared murder rates in some states to murder rates in neighboring states.
20. Some states use the death penalty.
21. Neighboring states have outlawed the death penalty.
22. The studies found no statistical difference in the frequency of murders.

23. Other studies have examined the short-term effects of capital punishment.
24. The effects were on daily homicide rates.
25. The studies discovered this.
26. The number of homicides decreased on days immediately after an execution.
27. The number of homicides increased on the day of the execution.
28. The number of homicides increased on the day immediately before an execution.

29. Proponents of capital punishment lack evidence.
30. The evidence justifies executions.
31. The executions serve as a deterrent to serious crime.
32. Therefore proponents of capital punishment often resort to another argument.
33. Some crimes morally require the death penalty.

34. But this argument is hypocritical in view of the facts.

35. For example, 466 persons were executed for rape between 1930 and 1962.
36. 399 of the 466 persons were black.

37. One wonders.
38. Are our courts slapping the death penalty on *all* those who deserve to die?
39. Are our courts slapping the death penalty on *only* those who deserve to die?

40. We are given such findings.
41. Why, then, is there still so heated a debate over capital punishment?

42. The answer may be this.
43. There is an urge for revenge.
44. It is deep within the human psyche.

45. People feel more and more helpless.
46. They are helpless in the face of rising crime rates.
47. Then they want to strike out.
48. They want to get even.
49. They want to find a simple solution.
50. They want to find a final solution.

51. It is unfortunate.
52. There are no simple answers.
53. There are complex problems.
54. And it is our duty.
55. We are rational human beings.
56. We must resist such appeals.
57. The appeals are irrational.

Sincerely,

USING REPETITION IN CONTEXT

Each of the five paragraphs below contains sentences (enclosed in brackets) that you can strengthen with one or another of the strategies of repetition—balanced phrases, repeated key words, repeated structures, or ellipsis. Revise these bracketed sentences. Be sure to write out the complete paragraphs, and make any other appropriate changes.

Example

>The central theme of the Frankenstein movies is that those who attempt to create life will instead unleash the destructive forces of the universe. The films always open with the mad Dr. Frankenstein and his assistant in the unnatural act of robbing graves. [Then, in a hidden laboratory, they fit together pieces of different corpses and a monster is created which is not bound by the laws of nature. After terrorizing the populace, the monster is finally trapped and killed, and his master is captured and he is punished. The story implicitly warns that to assume the power of God is an invitation to nature's wrath.]

↓

>The central theme of the Frankenstein movies is that those who attempt to create life will instead unleash the destructive forces of the universe. The films always open with the mad Dr. Frankenstein and his assistant in the unnatural act of robbing graves. Then, in a hidden laboratory, they fit together pieces of different corpses and create a monster not bound by the laws of nature. After terrorizing the populace, the monster is finally **trapped and killed,** and his master **captured and punished.** The story implicitly warns that **to assume** the power of God is **to invite** the wrath of nature.

A. After political campaigns that last more than a year and that involve pie eating and baby kissing, speech making and fund raising, you might think that candidates could begin relaxing once the election results are in. [Actually, the period between election and inauguration is difficult for winners and losers don't fare much better. The winners have more official problems than they can handle, and the losers have so many regrets that they can barely bear them.]

B. We are so used to blaming modern industrial growth for the destruction of the natural environment that we sometimes overlook the damage done by less sophisticated means. Yet every year cattle and sheep farmers in nonindustrial societies turn nearly 17 million acres of land into desert by overgrazing. [This process of "desertification" has destroyed three-fourths of the forestland in Argentina in 50 years, and in western India in a single decade one-third of the arable land has been destroyed. Unchecked industrial growth may be polluting the air, but the land is being ravaged by herd management which is unscientific.]

C. If the best example of a criminal who became a folk hero is Robin Hood, perhaps the strangest example is D. B. Cooper, a hazy figure who perpetrated America's only unsolved airline hijacking. In 1971, Cooper collected $200,000 in $20 bills after threatening to blow up a Northwest Airline 727, then parachuted from the plane over Washington's Cascade Mountains. [Cooper disappeared without a trace and the money disappeared without a trace.] No one is sure if the hijacker's name was really D. B. Cooper or if he even survived the jump. But Cooper, like Robin Hood, beat the system, and that was enough to elevate him to folk-hero status. [The Cooper legend has spawned T-shirts; it has spawned a popular song; and it has even spawned an annual D. B. Cooper look-alike contest in Ariel, Washington, a contest which was recently won by a basset hound wearing sunglasses.]

D. In 1948, South Carolina Senator Strom Thurmond ran for president on the ultraconservative States' Rights ticket, but in 1978, Senator Thurmond publicly identified himself with Edward Kennedy, an outspoken liberal. [In 1968, Thurmond helped shape Richard Nixon's "southern strategy," which discounted black voters, but he helped get a South Carolina black appointed to the U.S. Court of Military Appeals ten years later. What apparently accounts for these changes is not that the senator has abandoned his old political philosophy but that there is a new political reality he has recognized: fully 25 percent of South Carolina's registered voters are black.]

E. "Dare to be Dull," the small ad challenged its readers from an obscure corner of a San Francisco newspaper, inviting applications to the "Dull Men's Club." [This is a country of streakers and pet rocks, we have tanning clinics, and you find biorhythm societies. Who knows what will catch on next? The response to the ad was staggering. Enthusiastic letters came from men who were sick and tired of scrambling to know and do whatever was "in" at the moment. "I'm out of it and proud of it," remarked one respondent. "Dull is beautiful," another one said. A third one asked: "Can women join?" The reply came,] "This is exclusively a gentlemen's club. What could be duller than that?"

CAPITAL PUNISHMENT AND THE LIBERAL BREAST BEATERS

Using strategies of repetition whenever appropriate, combine the following sentences into a letter to the editor which claims that our high homicide rates are caused by a court system gone awry because of liberal ideals of social justice. Try to emphasize the letter's slashing tone and immoderate voice. If you wish, add details of your own.

To the Editor:

1. There is a current debate over capital punishment.
2. It has brought out the usual number of liberal breast beaters.
3. It has brought out the usual number of teeth-gnashing liberals.
4. They are eager to whine about the poor little condemned criminal.

5. We are asked to shed tears for the cold-blooded criminal.
6. The criminal is supposedly a victim of society.
7. Or the criminal is supposedly a victim of childhood trauma.
8. Or the criminal is supposedly a victim of an incurable addiction to drugs.
9. Or the criminal is supposedly a victim of uncontrollable impulses for violence.
10. At the same time, our crime rates are soaring.

11. Are you one of those people easily impressed by a flurry of statistics?

12. The liberal camp offers the flurry of statistics.
13. If so, consider these figures.

14. In 1979 alone, nearly 17,000 people committed murder in the United States.
15. Yet in 1980, fewer than 500 were waiting in U.S. prisons.
16. Fewer than 500 had been sentenced to death for capital crimes.
17. The crimes had occurred in the previous decades.

18. And most of the criminals on death row are not in imminent danger of execution.
19. This is because the wheels of the law turn very slowly.
20. This is because appeals take years to run their course.

21. Liberals have persuaded the courts to do this.
22. The courts refused to allow the execution even when this was the case.
23. The condemned criminal asked to be executed.

24. I agree with the liberals in this.
25. The taking of human life is a serious matter.
26. At the same time I choose to reserve my tears for the innocent victim.
27. And for the victim's family my pity is reserved.

28. In fact, I feel that taking another person's life is serious.
29. Precisely because of this, I support the return of the death penalty.

30. The death penalty fits the crime.
31. The death penalty is the only punishment to do so.

32. And the death penalty is the only punishment strong enough to offer hope.
33. The hope is for the deterrence of future homicides.

34. It is sadly ironic.
35. There are those who had an aim.
36. The aim was to heighten the value of life.

37. The value of life would be heightened by abolishing the death penalty.
38. Instead, they have cheapened the very values.
39. They hold the very values so dear.

40. Americans are tired of living in fear for their lives.
41. They live in fear because of the leniency of the courts.

42. Any punk can murder now.
43. Punks who murder suffer only a minor inconvenience.
44. The minor inconvenience is a few years in prison.
45. At most it is a few years in prison.

46. There is a lack of risk.
47. This lies at the bottom of our soaring homicide rates.

Sincerely,

unit*13*
EMPHASIS

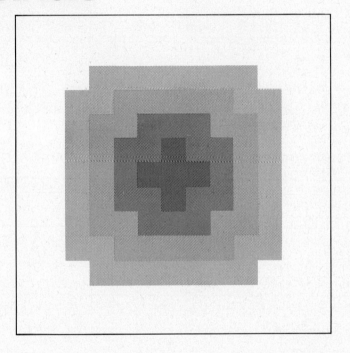

In any piece of writing, some words and some sentences are more important than others. To call the reader's attention to what is particularly important, you can choose from six major strategies of emphasis: (1) using visual devices; (2) making direct assertions; (3) breaking established patterns; (4) adding and rearranging words; (5) interrupting sentence progression; and (6) taking advantage of emphatic sentence and paragraph positions.

Visual Devices

The simplest device of emphasis involves visually marking the important element. You can mark a key word or sentence by printing it in italics or boldface type, by capitalizing its letters, or by underlining it. The underlined words in the following passage, for example, help emphasize the contrast between "says" and "does":

> Although the terms are often used interchangeably, there's a big difference between a comedian and a comic. A comedian, like Johnny Carson, <u>says</u> funny things. But a comic, like Carol Burnett, <u>does</u> funny things.

Punctuation marks are another kind of visual device for emphasizing a word or sentence. For instance, a command followed by a period, as in "Watch out." is not as forceful as the same command followed by an exclamation mark—"Watch out**!**" In the same way, a comma is usually less emphatic than a dash or colon:

The verdict was what he had expected**,** death.
The verdict was what he had expected**—**death.
The verdict was what he had expected**:** death.

The last two sentences place greater emphasis on the word "death" because a dash or colon creates a longer pause than a comma. The longer the pause, the more emphasis the following word "death" receives.

Direct Assertions

Another simple device of emphasis is the direct assertion. It works by openly telling the reader that something is important:

> Now we come to deterrence, the **central** issue in the debate over capital punishment, the single **most important** question in determining whether the state is entitled to take human life.

Direct assertions take the form of words or phrases like **especially, particularly, primarily, most of all,** and **above all:**

> America's finest dramatists are Edward Albee, Arthur Miller, Tennessee Williams, and**—above all—** Eugene O'Neill.

Most tourists who visit London want to see St. Paul's Cathedral, Westminster Abbey, and Buckingham Palace. But they **especially** look forward to climbing the infamous Tower of London.

Breaking Established Patterns

In addition to visual devices and direct assertions, emphasis can be achieved by disrupting an established pattern. Patterns are established both by the context of your writing and by the English language itself. In your own writing, the kinds of sentences you construct condition your reader to expect more of the same. When what comes next is not the same, when the pattern you establish is suddenly broken, the disruption is likely to be noticed by your reader and therefore to become a source of emphasis. For this reason, a short sentence that follows one or more longer sentences is often emphatic:

When two of the world's most famous scientists collaborate to produce a book aimed at expanding contemporary ideas about the nature of living things, the book should be well worth reading. **But this one isn't.**

A short question is sometimes even more emphatic than a short statement. In the passage below, the brief concluding question forces the reader to wonder if strenuous exercise is really healthy:

The increased number of joggers, the booming sale of physical training devices, the record number of entrants in marathon races—all clearly indicate the growing belief among Americans that strenuous, prolonged exercise is good for their health. **But is it?**

The short, abrupt element used for emphasis need not be a statement, question, or even a complete sentence. Exclamations and other deliberate sentence fragments are often just as effective in drawing the reader's attention:

Except for its most severe forms, wife beating used to be tolerated by society. Such abuse was commonly considered the right of a man who "owned" his wife. **What rubbish!** But what topped it all was that some wives accepted their husbands' violence as proof of love.

You can achieve emphasis not only by disrupting your own writing patterns but by departing from the basic sentence patterns of the language. The most basic sentence pattern of English begins with a subject followed by a verb and then an object or complement. In fact, the subject-verb-object sequence is psychologically so strong that readers tend to notice any departure from it. It follows, then, that you can create emphasis by moving the subject or verb or object out of its ordinary position. For example, questions and commands tend to be more emphatic than declarative statements because the verb has been moved to the front of the sentence. But you can create emphasis even within statements by changing the order of the words or by interrupting the movement of the sentence.

For example, the statement below adheres to the common subject-verb-object (or complement) word order:

My idea of a good life is interesting work, enough money, and plenty of exercise.

To give greater emphasis to the series **interesting work, enough money, and plenty of exercise,** shift it away from its ordinary end position to the front of the sentence; the series will gain added emphasis if it is followed by a dash and then a summarizing word like **this, that, these, none,** or **all:**

Interesting work, enough money, and plenty of exercise—that's my idea of a good life.

This pattern—an opening noun or noun series followed by a dash and then a summarizing word or two—can be used to emphasize any element in a sentence. The first example below draws attention to the series of paintings, while the second emphasizes the location of the paintings, "the Chicago Art Institute":

> **Toulouse-Lautrec's *At the Moulin Rouge,* Grant Wood's *American Gothic,* and Edward Hopper's *Nighthawks*—all these** great paintings are on display at the Chicago Art Institute.

> **The Chicago Art Institute—that's** where great paintings like Toulouse-Lautrec's *At the Moulin Rouge,* Grant Wood's *American Gothic,* and Edward Hopper's *Nighthawks* are on display.

Another way of creating emphasis is by beginning a sentence with an adverb that allows you to shift the verb in front of the subject. Such adverbs include words like **only** and **first,** negatives like **nowhere, not until**, and **never,** and certain prepositional phrases. In each sentence below, the initial adverb gains emphasis because it is immediately followed by the verb, not the subject.

> **Only recently have** scientists begun to investigate occult phenomena like ghosts and goblins.

> **First came** the governor and then her aides.

> **Nowhere else is** there a conference as enjoyable as the one held each July in Laramie, Wyoming.

> **Not until election night did** political pollsters realize the extent of the Reagan landslide.

> **Never again will** a single person be able to control a major city as Mayor Daley controlled Chicago.

> **Around the table sat** the four women who would make the decision.

Shifting the verb before the subject can be particularly emphatic at a climactic point like the end of a paragraph:

A good base stealer relies as much on intelligence as on speed. He must study pitchers and learn their motions, so that he will know when they intend to pitch to the plate. He must know how far to lead without being picked off, so that he can gauge his start to the next base. And he must know when the next batter will pass up a good pitch, so that he can take off and run. Only then **does** speed become important.

Adding and Rearranging Words

Even without changing the order of subject and verb, you can usually control sentence emphasis by adding and rearranging words. In the following sentence, for example, the word "merchants" is not strongly emphasized:

The merchants protested the new taxes.

But there are several ways to make "merchants" more emphatic:

The merchants **were the ones who** protested the new taxes.
It was the merchants **who** protested the new taxes.
The ones who protested the new taxes were the merchants.

Of course, you might want to call attention to a word other than "merchants." To emphasize "protest," you can say:

What the merchants **did was** to protest the new taxes.

And to emphasize "the new taxes," you have several choices:

What the merchants protested **were** the new taxes.
The new taxes **were what** the merchants protested.
It was the new taxes **that** the merchants protested.

Interruptives

You can create emphasis not only by adding and rearranging words but also by interrupting the movement of a sentence. Whenever a word, phrase, or clause interrupts sentence movement, the interrupting element—as well as what immediately follows it—gains in emphasis. The interruptive produces even more emphasis when separated from the rest of the sentence by a pair of dashes:

Amnesty International—**now more than 200,000 strong**—uses the force of public opinion to combat the violation of human rights.

Freud would have remained in Vienna, had not the Nazis—**much against his desires**— forced him to leave.

An interruption creates the most emphasis when it occurs at an unusual point in the sentence or just before the last and the most important piece of information:

A good-looking cop stopped her, lectured her on highway safety, gave her a speeding ticket, and than—**listen to this**—invited her out to dinner.

Even a full sentence, provided it's not too long, can work effectively as an interruptive to create emphasis:

There are now so many private security guards—**they have increased 75 percent since 1970**—that guards outnumber police.

The chaos of the American economy—**it suffered from stagnating productivity, double-digit inflation, and mil-**

lions of jobless—did much to elect Ronald Reagan president in 1980.

Emphatic Sentence and Paragraph Positions

When you create emphasis by breaking an established pattern or by using an interruptive, you can usually take advantage of naturally emphatic sentence and paragraph positions. Since the most emphatic place in a sentence is toward the end, try to position your most important element there. If the basic word order of the language places in the end position an element you don't want to emphasize, consider moving it elsewhere. In the sentence below, you can shift the phrase "on the opposite wall" out of its end position so as to place greater emphasis on more important words:

> What is probably the world's most famous painting—Leonard da Vinci's *Mona Lisa*—hangs on the opposite wall.

↓

> **On the opposite wall hangs** what is probably the world's most famous painting—Leonardo da Vinci's *Mona Lisa*.

To take another example, in the first version below the key phrase "the 'Who's Whoooooo' " is inappropriately placed in the unemphatic middle of the sentence:

> A guide to haunted houses, called the "Who's Whooooooo," is now offered by the U.S. Travel Service, the national tourism office which promotes travel by providing free advice on where to go and what to see.

But you can shift "the 'Who's Whoooooo' " to the end of the sentence to give it the emphasis it deserves:

> The U.S. Travel Service, the national tourism office which promotes travel by providing free advice on where to go and what to see, now offers a guide to haunted houses—**the "Who's Whoooooo."**

On the paragraph level, the change in emphasis brought about by the rearrangement of elements often changes meaning. The two paragraphs below each contain the same information—each says that skateboarding is both exhilarating and dangerous—but they differ in emphasis and ultimately in meaning. Read the paragraphs to determine how they differ:

1. Skateboarding may be the most exhilarating of all sports but it is also the most dangerous. Apparently the thrill comes from the speed—some champs do 65 miles per hour now—and from the challenge posed by the unlimited possibilities for new stunts. Although few have tried "pipe riding" or the "gorilla grip," in one recent year skateboarders still suffered over 130,000 injuries —20 of them fatal. Enthusiasts insist that what you can do with skateboards has no limit. At least 20 of them learned otherwise.

2. Although it may be the most dangerous sport, skateboarding is also the most exhilarating. Injuries do occur—over 130,000 in one recent year, 20 of them fatal. But consider the thrill that comes from the speed—some champs do 65 miles per hour now—and from the challenge posed by the unlimited possibilities for new stunts, like "pipe riding" and the "gorilla grip." While some practitioners will inevitably perish in trying new tricks, enthusiasts insist that what skateboards can do has no limit.

The first paragraph emphasizes that skateboarding is dangerous, the second that skateboarding is exhilarating. Danger is emphasized in the first primarily through the structure of the opening and closing sentences. In the opening sentence, the word **dangerous** appears in the emphatic end position as the climax of parallel phrases: "the most exhilarating . . . the most **dangerous.**" The danger is intensified by the short, crisp closing sentence. Its final word—**otherwise**—leaves the reader with the knowledge that death does indeed set limits upon skateboarding. By contrast, the second paragraph takes advantage of emphatic sentence and paragraph positions to indicate that the dangers of skateboarding are less important than its exhilaration. In the opening sentence, the phrase "the most dangerous sport" appears in an unemphatic subordinate clause, and emphasis falls instead on the word **exhilarating:** it appears in a main clause and it is the last word of the sentence. The second sentence acknowledges that injuries occur, but the connective **But** at the start of the third sentence indicates that the thrills of skateboarding outweigh its dangers. Finally, in the last sentence, the word **perish** is placed in the unemphatic middle of a subordinate clause, while the key words **no limit** occupy the paragraph's single most emphatic position—its end. Clearly, controlling paragraph emphasis is one way of controlling paragraph meaning.

*   *   *

In the following exercises and then in your own writing, try using strategies of emphasis to direct your reader's attention to what is most important.

CREATING EMPHASIS

For each of the five paragraphs below, create the emphasis called for in the instructions in parentheses at the end of the paragraph.

Example

> Archeologists might presume Ronald McDonald was a god if they were to dig out the ruins of America 1000 years from now and discover all those M-shaped golden arches spread across the continent. (Reorder the clauses to emphasize "a god.")

↓

> If archeologists were to dig out the ruins of America 1000 years from now and discover all those M-shaped golden arches spread across the continent, **they might presume Ronald McDonald was a god.**

A. Thirteen-year-old Cynthia Blake of Argo, Illinois, refused to take coeducational swim classes because her religion said it would be immodest to show her body in the presence of the opposite sex. The school principal said that Cynthia was not going to graduate without four years of physical education, because the state law requires it. (Rearrange the last sentence to emphasize that Cynthia was not going to graduate.)

B. Dozens of students at a New York university were once coerced into taking part in psychology department experiments that involved electric shock machines. The coercion consisted of giving students a choice between writing a term paper and participating in the experiments. This was some choice they were given. (Change the last sentence to an emphatic fragment.)

C. Gales of laughter followed when the Ouija board told Jane she would never marry. Asked to explain why, the board spelled out laboriously, letter by letter, "Because you will die." We all thought it was a lot of nonsense. It reminded us all of black magic. But imagine my shock when, three years later almost to the day, I read in the alumni journal that Jane had died of an incurable disease. (Change either the third or fourth sentence, or both, to an emphatic fragment.)

D. Carl Sandburg was a sensitive poet yet a brilliant scholar. He wrote of democracy yet lived like a king. He was a socialist yet hobnobbed with the rich and powerful. He wrote lively stories for children yet didn't like children. He wrote of love for humanity yet carried grudges all his life. Sandburg was a man of contradictions. (Introduce the last sentence with a direct assertion of its importance.)

E. Women are not new to terrorism. Charlotte Corday stabbed Marat to death in his bath during the French Revolution, and Maude Gonne took part in the Irish Rebellion of 1916. But now more and more women become members of terrorist groups. One psychologist studying the phenomenon of increasing female terrorism links it to the determination of women to prove they are as good as men even at crime. (Change "even at crime" into an interruptive.)

KILLER CAMILLE

Using appropriate strategies of emphasis, especially by shifting sentences from one position to another and by changing word choice when appropriate, construct from the facts below a paragraph or brief essay which emphasizes that, as a result of Hurricane Camille, 23 people died.

1. This occurred in September 1969.
2. Hurricane Camille came roaring into the Eastern Gulf of Mexico.
3. The winds of Hurricane Camille gusted up to 200 miles per hour.
4. There were urgent warnings to evacuate endangered areas.
5. The director of the National Hurricane Center simply told residents to "run for their lives."
6. Almost 75,000 residents responded to the warnings.
7. Almost 75,000 residents fled inland to higher ground.

8. Other residents chose not to flee.
9. Among those who chose not to flee were 25 guests of the Richelieu Hotel.
10. Of the 25, 23 did not survive Hurricane Camille.
11. The Richelieu Hotel was a solid-looking, brick-and-concrete structure.
12. The Richelieu Hotel was located 100 yards from the gulf.
13. 25 guests planned a festive hurricane party.
14. The hurricane struck before the party began.
15. The 25 guests had decorated the lounge with crepe paper, balloons, and streamers.
16. The 25 guests had set up tables for poker and refreshments.

CHANGING PARAGRAPH EMPHASIS

Rewrite each of the three paragraphs below in order to change its emphasis as specified by the instructions at the end of the paragraph.

Example

Fresh air—there doesn't seem to be enough of it around any more. At least that's what nonsmokers are claiming as they carry on their fight to breathe freely. Now they can cite you in a court of law if you violate the nonsmoking territories set aside for them in "places of public assembly." But there's one thing they can't make you do. They can't make you quit. (Emphasize nonsmokers' rights.)

↓

Fresh air—there doesn't seem to be enough of it around any more. So nonsmokers carry on their fight to breathe freely. To be sure, they can't make you quit. But now they can do something about it if you violate the nonsmoking areas set aside for them in "places of public assembly." **They can cite you in a court of law.**

A. As we toured the city, we stopped to watch a blind native sitting in a courtyard. He sat there in the sun in an attitude of reflection with his knees crossed and his head resting on his hand. He was covered with swarms of flies but seemed impervious to them, making no attempt to brush them off. We walked around to look at his face and realized his condition. (Emphasize that the man was blind.)

B. To get a nose job done, you need to stay in the hospital only a couple of days. You are understandably not comfortable, but there is no pain. Your face, particularly your nose, is bandaged up, requiring you to breathe through the mouth, which in turn results in swollen tonsils. In fact, your whole face may be swollen. Since your nose was broken, two black eyes will be inevitable, but they will disappear within two weeks. Some vomiting may result from the seepage of blood into the stomach, or the nose itself may bleed. All right. But look what you gain. When you look good, you feel good. With a nose that looks the way you want it to look, you gain more self-confidence and self-respect. Believe me, people will notice the difference, and they won't laugh at you any more. (Emphasize the discomfort.)

C. Legend has it that Robin Hood was a hero—a noble bandit who robbed from the rich and gave to the poor. The legendary Robin was chivalrous, manly, fair, and always ready for a good joke. And, according to legend, it was only because of Robin's loyalty to good King Richard that he was pursued throughout Sherwood Forest by the Sheriff of Nottingham, a villainous ally of Richard's evil brother John. But in reality Robin Hood was a small-time mugger, and his Merry Men a band of crooks and drunks. Once, sticky-fingered Little John ripped off $900 worth of household silver while his boss was out hunting. And Robin even conned the 18-year-old Maid Marion into living with him for seven years without marrying her. Some noble bandit! (Emphasize that Robin Hood was a hero.)

SHACKING UP

Create from the following sentences a humorous essay that explains why Americans are increasingly living together outside of marriage. To do so, first combine the sentences within each group and then rearrange the groups into a coherent order. Construct your sentences, paragraphs, and essay as a whole so that its humor falls in the most emphatic positions.

A. 1. The most recent census figures say this.
    2. More Americans are living together than ever before.
    3. They do not bother to get married.

B. 4. Sociologists are always eager to offer an opinion.
    5. Sociologists cite a number of reasons for the expanding popularity of living together.

C. 6. Janet Esposito and Dave Keefe are in the midst of this.
    7. Their parents call it an unholy alliance.
    8. Janet and Dave consider it a meaningful relationship.

D. 9. Even senior citizens have begun shacking up.
   10. The senior citizens are scandalizing their children in the process.
   11. The senior citizens are scandalizing their children's children in the process.
   12. The aim of the senior citizens is pooling their fixed incomes.
   13. The aim of the senior citizens is fending off loneliness.

E. 14. Sociologists point to the emancipation of women.
   15. Sociologists point to the rock music.
   16. Sociologists point to the ban on shotgun weddings.
   17. Sociologists point to soap operas.
   18. Sociologists point to the Pill.
   19. These are all partial explanations of the expanding popularity of living together.

F. 20. Janet and Dave have tried to explain this.
   21. The explanation is to their parents.
   22. Why are they living together?
   23. They have explained in terms of shared growth.
   24. They have explained in terms of mutual independence.
   25. They have explained in terms of freedom.
   26. The freedom is to be themselves without any of society's hang-ups.

G. 27. Of course, Janet's dad may be right.

H. 28. Janet's dad is convinced of this.
   29. It's all a conspiracy.
   30. The conspiracy is godless.
   31. The conspiracy is communist.
   32. Some people think that Janet's dad is not too bright.

I. 33. Small communal groups have sprung up across the nation.
   34. They dedicate themselves to plump Korean prophets.
   35. Or they dedicate themselves to transcendental meditation.
   36. Or they dedicate themselves to organic gardening.

J. 37. Janet isn't speaking to her dad.
   38. Dave isn't speaking to Janet's dad.
   39. This is since Janet's dad broke Dave's nose.
   40. He did it with a left hook.
   41. Dave's mom isn't speaking to Dave.
   42. Dave's mom isn't speaking to Janet.

K. 43. The course of true love never seems to run smooth.
   44. Alas!
   45. This is the case even when love is freed from marriage vows.

L. 46. Most unmarried households are composed of young lovers.
   47. Janet and Dave are young lovers.
   48. Many others are getting into this new way of life.

CHANGING EMPHASIS WITHIN PARAGRAPHS

Revise each of the three paragraphs below in order to make the material printed in boldface more emphatic.

Example

It wasn't supposed to happen. Yet, while everyone turned the other way, thousands of tiny places across the country **stopped dying,** and thus quietly reversed what was supposed to be an "irreversible" population trend. What's more, the "boondocks" are growing twice as fast as metropolitan areas and, for the first time since frontier days, beginning to wield political and economic influence.

↓

It wasn't supposed to happen. Yet, while everyone turned the other way, thousands of tiny places across the country quietly reversed what was supposed to be an "irreversible" pattern. **They stopped dying.** What's more, the "boondocks" are growing twice as fast as metropolitan areas and, for the first time since frontier days, beginning to wield political and economic influence.

A. For a long time, **but not any more,** Japanese corporations used Southeast Asia merely as a cheap source of raw materials and as a training ground for junior executives who needed minor league experience. Japan has learned that Western Countries which have closed their doors on merchandise labeled "Made in Japan" willingly accept goods from an underdeveloped country like Thailand or Malaysia.

B. While the rest of the world played soccer, Americans played football, basketball, and baseball. But now soccer is rapidly escalating into a major sport in the United States for reasons as simple as the game itself—school officials like it and kids like it. High school athletic departments, strapped for operating funds, can fully outfit a soccer player for less than the price of a football helmet. **And kids need only the desire to run** to play soccer. What they don't need is to be big.

C. Hoping to call the world's attention to the crisis of its water supply **(a crisis more threatening than the oil shortages of the 1970s),** the United Nations has declared the 1980s the "water decade." For the world uses and abuses its water supply faster than the hydrosphere can replenish it through evaporation and precipitation. Already the problem is so severe that desperate remedies are in order. In China, a half-million people dug a canal to water a parched province. In Arizona, people must get licenses before they can dig wells.

RENT CONTROL

Using several appropriate strategies of emphasis, construct from the material below a persuasive essay that argues for one of the following propositions (choose one): (1) rent control laws should be enacted by the U.S. government or (2) rent control laws should not be enacted by the U.S. government. Since a successful persuasive essay takes into account the arguments of the opposing side, use the content of *all* 21 sentences below. You will also want to add words, phrases, and perhaps even whole sentences in order to state and develop your proposition and to make your essay coherent.

A. General facts:
　　1. Rent control, as its name implies, is simply a form of price control.
　　2. Rent control fixes a ceiling on the amount of rent landlords may charge tenants.
　　3. In the past, the government has enacted rent control laws in cities with a housing vacancy rate under 5 percent.
　　4. Rent control also fixes the rates of future rent increases at what lawmakers consider "reasonable" so that landlords will get a fair return on their investment.
　　5. Rent control means that a family in Minneapolis or Memphis paying $250 a month cannot legally be made to start paying $475.
　　6. Rent control means that the family must be told in advance if its rent is to be increased at all.
　　7. Low-income housing is desperately needed in most American cities.
B. Facts favoring rent control:
　　8. Rent control effectively protects low- and fixed-income renters, especially during inflationary times.
　　9. Rent takes as much as two-thirds of the income of older people.
　　10. Many low-income families already set aside 34 percent of their salaries for rent.
　　11. Without rent control, rent rises faster than increases in wages or pensions.
　　12. *Business Week* reported that an 87-year-old pensioner and

his wife, residents of a Santa Monica high-rise for older people, watched their monthly rent double in just four years.

13. Rent control assures such people that their rent will be no higher than a rate fixed by the government and legally binding on the landlord.

14. A national system of rent control wouldn't cost the taxpayer a cent.

C. Facts against rent control:

15. Although rent control was designed to protect the rights of the renters, it serves instead to deny the rights of the landlords.

16. The idea of rent control may be noble, but there are problems in making it work; for example, "reasonable rates" and "fair returns on investments" are vague terms that are difficult to define.

17. Since these terms will be defined by government officials, it is likely that the rates will be set below what landlords consider reasonable.

18. Landlords say that, with rent control, rents do not rise fast enough to make the construction of new buildings worthwhile.

19. One California developer estimated that he needs to raise rents from 10 to 12 percent annually just to stay even.

20. Thus, rent control inhibits new construction.

21. With rent control, even the existing low-income housing deteriorates because there is less money available for landlords to pay for adequate maintenance.

unit *14*
TONE

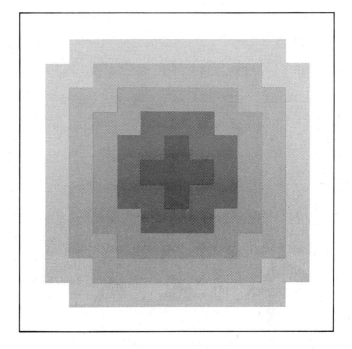

The tone of your writing indicates your feelings toward your material and your readers. Because tone reflects your frame of mind, it reveals whether you are being humorous or somber, playful or serious, whether you are angry or tranquil, bitter or confident. Through tone, your attitude toward what you are writing about and your relationship to your audience become clear.

Tone in Sentences

Controlling tone is largely a matter of selecting words, structuring sentences, and choosing details so as to make them consistent with each other and with the purpose of your writing. Suppose, for example, you are writing a paragraph or brief essay on the increased sales of vitamin E. In your opening sentence you intend to include these two facts:

> The sales of vitamin E have doubled in the past five years.
> The increase in sales has been helped by statements from health food enthusiasts and doctors.

You might put these facts together into a sentence like this:

> The sales of vitamin E, helped by statements from health food enthusiasts and doctors, have doubled in the past five years.

This sentence is impartial in tone because it doesn't reveal your attitude toward the increased sales of vitamin E. If you began with such a sentence, your reader would not know, at least at first, whether you thought the American public was wise or foolish in doubling its consumption of the vitamin. Of course, there's nothing wrong with being impartial. If you either have no opinion or want to seem factual and objective, rather than personal and subjective, impartial sentences are precisely what you want to write.

Words and Details

But let's suppose that you want a sentence reflecting your belief that vitamin E sales have surged because of a deceptive and misleading advertising campaign. One option is to state your position openly and explicitly:

> The sales of vitamin E, helped by the **deceptions and lies** of health food enthusiasts and doctors, have doubled in the past five years.

Strong in tone and clear in attitude, this hard-hitting sentence may be exactly the way you want to begin your paragraph. Its tone would be especially appropriate for readers who share your negative attitudes toward vitamin E. But for readers who don't begin on your side, the sentence may sound too strong, too opinionated, perhaps even biased. If so, you may try to *suggest* your feelings instead of stating them:

> The sales of vitamin E, helped by the statements of health food **freaks** and **quack** doctors, have doubled in the past five years.

In this version you have not called the statements deceptions and lies, but with the words **freaks** and **quacks** you have indicated your reservation about the worth of the vitamin and your contempt for those who promote it. Indeed, this sentence is almost as strong in tone as the explicit statement above, so strong that your reader may consider it exaggerated and may even begin to question its truth and your credibility. One way to guard against your reader's suspicions is to temper the sentence by making it more suggestive and less explicit:

> The sales of vitamin E, helped by the **claims** of health food **faddists** and doctors, have doubled in the past five years.

This sentence is more negative than your original version, but it is not as hostile as your second or third sentence. Its tone is negative because **faddists**, unlike **enthusiasts**, is a word with unfavorable associations and because **claims**, unlike **statements**, encourage the reader to doubt their truth. The sentence can be made still stronger in tone without making it seem biased by inserting the detail that only a few doctors make claims for the vitamin:

> The sales of vitamin E, helped by the claims of health food faddists and **a few** doctors, have doubled in the past five years.

But even if more than a few doctors support vitamin E, there are other ways to play down their support:

> The sales of vitamin E, helped by the claims of health food faddists and **some** doctors, have doubled in the past five years.

There is a big difference in tone between **some doctors** and just **doctors**. The phrase **some doctors** implies, as **doctors** alone does not, that there is another group of doctors who have made no claims for vitamin E and who may perhaps reject such claims. But the support of doctors for vitamin E can be played down still further without making your statement seem exaggerated or biased:

> The sales of vitamin E, helped by the claims of health food fad-dists and **even** some doctors, have doubled in the past five years.

The word **even** suggests your surprise that doctors, who should know better, have made such foolish claims.

Now let's suppose that you wanted to create a sentence favorable in tone toward the increased sales of vitamin E. You would do so by choosing words and details with more positive associations:

> The sales of vitamin E, helped by statements from health food **experts** and doctors, have doubled in the past five years.

OR

> The sales of vitamin E, helped by **reports** from health food experts and doctors, have doubled in the past five years.

OR

> The sales of vitamin E, helped by the **testimony** of health food experts and doctors, have doubled in the past five years.

Because **experts** seem more trustworthy than simple **en-thusiasts** and because both **reports** and **testimony** carry more weight than mere **statements**, the three sentences above are more favorable in tone than the original toneless version. But you can go even further in creating a positive tone by making the doctors who support vitamin E more prestigious:

> The sales of vitamin E, helped by the testimony of health food experts and **a number of** doctors, have doubled in the past five years.

OR

The sales of vitamin E, helped by the testimony of health food experts and a number of **leading** doctors, have doubled in the past five years.

OR

The sales of vitamin E, helped by the testimony of health food experts and a number of leading **medical authorities**, have doubled in the past five years.

The phrase **a number of doctors**, even if it actually refers to but three or four doctors, sounds more impressive than **a few doctors, some doctors**, or **doctors** alone. And **leading** doctors are supposed to be more reliable than doctors who are not leaders, although certainly not as reliable as leading **medical authorities**.

Sentence Structure

You may have noticed that so far in every example the basic sentence structure has been the same ("The sales of vitamin E . . . have doubled in the past five years"), and the tone has been changed only through the replacement of some important words. But you can also control tone by changing your sentence structure. For example, you can make your dislike of "health food freaks and quack doctors" even more obvious by moving this phrase from the relatively weak middle part of your sentence to its more emphatic end position:

In the past five years the sales of vitamin E have doubled, **thanks to the claims of health food freaks and quack doctors**.

But you can make your tone even angrier by moving this phrase to the beginning of the sentence and setting it off with a dash, almost as if it were an exclamation:

Claims by health food freaks and quack doctors— that's what has helped double the sales of vitamin E in the past five years.

Formal and Informal Tone

The previous sentences about vitamin E range from negative to positive in tone, but they are alike in that each is formal, serious, and relatively impersonal. If you want to make your sentence less formal and more personal, you have a number of options. The simplest way to personalize its tone is to introduce yourself into the sentence as **I**:

> **I** find it hard to believe, but the sales of vitamin E, spurred on by the claims of health food faddists and doctors, have doubled in the past five years.

> OR

> The other day **I** read that the claims of health food faddists and doctors have helped double the sales of vitamin E in the past five years.

> OR

> **I** never thought that any vitamin would become glamorous, but vitamin E certainly has. Thanks to the claims of health food faddists and doctors, its sales have actually doubled in the past five years.

The sentence can also be made more informal if you establish a relationship between yourself and the reader. One way of relating to your reader is by asking a question:

> **Why have the sales of vitamin E doubled in the past five years?** Largely because of the claims of health food faddists and a few doctors.

> OR

> **Who is responsible for the skyrocketing sales of vitamin E over the past five years?** Mainly health food faddists and a few doctors.

An even more direct way of relating to readers is by addressing them as **you**:

You may be surprised to learn that over the past five years the sales of vitamin E have doubled, in large part because of the claims of health food faddists and doctors.

OR

Did **you** know that, thanks to the claims of health food faddists and doctors, the sales of vitamin E have doubled in the past five years?

The informality of your writing will usually be increased by contractions, slang, and short, simple words instead of longer, more complex ones. Informal writing often includes exclamations, deliberate sentence fragments, and short as opposed to long sentences:

It's hard to believe but **it's** true. In just five short years the sales of vitamin E have doubled! **Why?** Because doctors and health food **buffs** have been telling people that **it's** good for their health.

OR

This may surprise you but twice as much vitamin E is sold today as five years ago. **Twice as much!** And **I'll** tell you why. It's because people have **swallowed** what some doctors and natural food **fans** have told them.

The more informal your writing becomes, the more it will sound like spoken rather than written language. Whether you want to give your writing the informal qualities of spoken language or the formal qualities of written language depends on what strategies you decide are most effective for achieving your overall purpose.

Tone in Paragraphs

The paragraph provides even more options for controlling tone than the sentence. Here is a paragraph on student loans that seems impartial in tone:

Many college graduates claim bankruptcy in order to avoid repaying money borrowed from the federal government to finance their education. In fact, over $500 million is now owed the government by more than 300,000 student borrowers. Statistics show that students are not good risks. Whereas the student default rate now stands at 12.2 percent, banks report that nonstudent loan delinquency seldom exceeds 3 percent. Apparently, the lack of money is not the only reason for nonpayment. Through its computers, the Department of Education discovered that 300 of its employees, some currently earning up to $33,000, had defaulted on student loans.

This is the kind of paragraph that might be written by a newspaper reporter striving to be objective. It does not indicate, through its word choice, sentence structure, or selection of details, either approval or disapproval of the students who default on their loans or of the government which apparently tolerates it. But the paragraph does indicate, especially through its formal wording and complete absence of humor, that the student loan situation is important enough to be taken seriously by the reader.

The same paragraph can be rewritten to make it less serious and more playful, to create a tone of mild amusement with the students who take advantage of the government:

One of the more popular pastimes of college graduates is claiming bankruptcy to avoid repaying money borrowed from the government to pay their college costs. Right now Uncle Sam is out some $500 million owed by more than 300,000 student borrowers. Unfortunately for the federal treasury, students are not the best loan risks. Whereas the student default rate has hit 12.2 percent, banks say that nonstudent loan defaults seldom go above 3 percent. Among the most interesting facts turned up by computers of the Department of Education is that 300 of its own employees, some making as much as $33,000, had managed to avoid repaying their student loans.

The paragraph is no longer wholly serious because the failure to repay student loans has become merely a **popular pastime**, presumably little more important than such other pastimes as golfing or watching TV. And that well-paid government employees have defaulted on student loans is nothing to take seriously, just an **interesting fact**. Much of the original wording of the paragraph has been made less formal in keeping with the paragraph's changed tone. The **government** has been reduced to **Uncle Sam**, always a slightly comic figure. The formal phrase **to finance their college education** has become **to pay their college costs**. In the same way, words like **exceeds, discovered**, and **earning** have been replaced by their informal equivalents—**go above, turned up**, and **making**. Through its tone the paragraph communicates the writer's attitude that there's nothing to get excited about. Just sit back and smile.

Of course, there may be good reason for concern. In that case the writer will eliminate whatever seems casual or informal in the paragraph and, most importantly, add details that make clear the serious consequences of allowing students to continue defaulting on their loans:

> At a time when funds are sorely needed for federal programs to protect the environment and to quicken the economy, college students are refusing to repay money borrowed from the government to finance their education. The situation is serious. Either by claiming bankruptcy or by simply ignoring requests for repayment, over 300,000 student borrowers have deprived the American treasury of half a billion dollars. Whereas banks report only a 3 percent delinquency rate on nonstudent loans, the student default rate has climbed to an astounding 12.2 percent. Withholding money owed the government has become so widespread that the Department of Education discovered defaults on student loans by 300 of its own employees, some earning up to $33,000. If defaults continue, the student loan program which has helped so many responsible men and women may be dismantled because of an irresponsible few.

There is nothing amusing in this paragraph. From the first sentence to the last, it is serious, even urgent in tone. Its urgency is created in part through the opening assertion that the money collected from student loans could be used for programs that most Americans believe to be vital—programs affecting the environment and the economy. The sense of urgency is maintained up to the paragraph's most striking point, deliberately placed in the emphatic concluding sentence: the entire student loan program is jeopardized by defaults. No longer is nonpayment a popular pastime bothersome only to Uncle Sam; it is now a grave threat to the education of millions of Americans. The paragraph's urgency of tone is controlled not only through the choice of words and the selection of details but through sentence structure as well. The first and last sentences both make use of strategies of repetition, which are especially appropriate in formal and serious prose. The first sentence uses the balanced phrases **to protect the environment** and **to quicken the economy**, and the last sentence contrasts **responsible** with **irresponsible**. The pattern of paired coordinators, another mark of a serious and deliberate prose style, is found in the construction of the third sentence. The short second sentence, "The situation is serious," is constructed to gain emphasis and impact from its position between two longer, more complex sentences. Through its tone the whole paragraph communicates the writer's feeling that there is cause for deep concern.

The next paragraph also expresses concern but without the positive suggestion that we can act to improve the situation. Instead, the tone of the paragraph is bitter and cynical:

Whatever else they got out of their four years at State University, college graduates have surely learned how to rip off Uncle Sam. In fact, claiming bankruptcy to escape repaying their student loans must now rank with pot smoking and wife swapping as the favorite pastimes of college grads. Some 300,000 of them have already bilked the federal treasury of $500 million, and you can bet that's not the end of it—not with one out of every eight student borrowers refusing to pay. The Department of Education took the time to find out that 300 of its own employees, some making salaries well over the national average, had squirmed out of debts they promised to repay. The only question is who deserves more of our scorn—the swindlers from college or the fools from Washington?

The tone of the opening sentence indicates what the rest of the paragraph makes clear—the writer hates colleges and college students. The first sentence suggests that students are likely to learn little from college except how to scheme and cheat, and the second sentence extends student immorality into the areas of drugs and sex. But the writer's contempt for college students is matched by a loathing of government officials, the ones who finally "take the time" to discover what any ordinary American would have recognized long before. Assuming the role of that ordinary American, the writer chooses not to use fancy, intellectual terms like **default, delinquency**, and **dismantled**; instead, the words are coarser, tougher —**rip off, bilked, stupid, twice as fat, squirmed, swindlers**, and **fools**. Despite the tough, earthy language and the writer's attempt to relate to the readers—"**you** can bet that's not the end of it" and "who deserves more of **our** scorn"—the paragraph communicates a sense of futility and bitterness. Its tone suggests the writer's attitude that there's nothing to do about the entire rotten mess but to get angry.

*　　*　　*

The four paragraphs on student loans illustrate some of the options for defining and controlling the tone of your writing. Try experimenting with word choice, detail selection, and sentence structure until you have created the tone best suited for communicating your attitudes and feelings.

CONTROLLING TONE

Each of the following three paragraphs has a particular tone. Let's assume you've decided that this tone is inappropriate for the purpose of your essay. By using different words, reconstructing sentences, adding and omitting details, or making any other changes, rewrite each paragraph to give it the tone suggested by the directions.

Example

"Lennonizing," the ruthless and tasteless exploitation of John Lennon's death for the sale of records, books, and mementos, became a lucrative overnight industry. It inspired such quickie song tributes as "We won't say Goodbye, John" and "Elegy for the Walrus." Book publishers cashed in on the bonanza with instant masterpieces like *John Lennon: Death of a Dream,* published within days of—but written weeks or months before?—Lennon's assassination. And even the *National Enquirer* got into the morbid act by publishing—with its usual execrable taste—a four-color photograph of John Lennon at the morgue. (Rewrite the paragraph to make its tone friendlier.)

"Lennonizing," the **commemoration** of John Lennon's death in records, books, and mementos, became a **popular** overnight industry. It inspired such **spontaneous** song tributes as "We won't say Goodbye, John" and "Elegy for the Walrus." It **prompted** book publishers to **respond immediately** with biographies such as *John Lennon: Death of a Dream,* published within days of—**though evidently researched weeks or months before**—Lennon's assassination. And even the *National Enquirer* **paid its tribute—in its usual dramatic fashion—**by publishing a four-color photograph of John Lennon's body **as mourners said their last farewell** at the morgue.

A. After four days of college life, I've had enough and I'm ready to leave. My clothes have been disappearing one by one into my laundry bag, but they are not clean, folded, and ready to wear the next morning as they were at home. After almost a week without my favorite television programs, I still haven't adjusted to the loss. The supply of snacks ran out yesterday, leaving me totally dependent on the trash that the dining hall calls food. Worst of all, I haven't been able to figure a way to bring my old jalopy to campus, so I have nothing to do with my spare time. Oh, how I wish I were home. (Rewrite the paragraph to make it more playful, less serious.)

B. Not only did Stephen Foster's heart not yearn for the "Swanee" River before he made it famous in his song "The Old Folks at Home," the overrated songwriter never even saw the muddy stream. His first version of the song used the Pee Dee River, but Foster decided a softer sounding name would make him more money, so he found the Suwannee River on a map and then falsified its name. He never even bothered to find out that the Suwannee runs through the swamps of northern Florida and Georgia without so much as touching a plantation. (Rewrite the paragraph to make its tone less nasty.)

C. Of course, it's possible that some of the sightings of flying saucers are actually close encounters of the third kind—encounters with extraterrestrial life. Scientists do believe that 80 of the 300,000 planets in our galaxy have intelligent life. It is even likely that 40 of them have civilizations more advanced than our own. But each of those 40 planets is at least 11,500 light-years from earth. So, besides the time—a lot—it would take the energy equivalent of 139,000,000,000,000,000,000 kilowatt-hours of electricity to move a spaceship to this planet in order to fly around a swamp and excite earthlings. And that's just for a one-way trip. In other words, it's more probable that flying saucer sightings are close encounters of the fourth kind. Close encounters with swamp gas. (Rewrite the paragraph to make its tone more serious and less skeptical.)

THE DASTARDLY DUCKS

Combine the sentences below into a humorous paragraph or short essay by choosing the funniest of the words given in parentheses.

You may add or delete details as well as change any words, phrases, or sentence constructions.

1. There are (people, dedicated souls, busybodies).
2. They (are opposed to, fight, wage holy war on) pornography and vice in the media.
3. They should (take a closer look at, scrutinize, feast their eyes on) the Donald Duck comic books.

4. These (disgusting, seemingly innocent, unwholesome) books present a picture of the family and of American capitalism.
5. The picture is (dirty, sordid, foul).

6. The Duck family itself is (fragmented, incomplete, motherless).
7. Donald Duck raises three ("nephews," kids he tries to pass off as his nephews, young boys who are obviously illegitimate).

8. (Moreover, Not only that, If that weren't bad enough), the kids' upbringing is (hurt, tainted, poisoned) by Donald's relationship with Daisy.
9. Daisy is a (loose, sexually active, promiscuous) duck.

10. In fact, you can't turn a page in the comic book without (observing, seeing, spotting) a duck.
11. The duck is (unclothed, naked, nude).
12. Even the ducks that (dress, are attired, have the decency to wear clothes) cover only their tops.
13. They never cover their more (essential, private, significant) (bodily areas, parts, places).

14. The only example of a successful (businessman, businessduck, capitalist) is Scrooge McDuck.
15. Scrooge McDuck is (frugal, miserly, money-grubbing).
16. Scrooge McDuck is a (millionaire, tycoon, plutocrat).

17. (All in all, If everything is taken into account, Thus), Donald Duck comics (have, offer, market) vice and corruption.
18. It is as much vice and corruption as a (copy, issue, volume) of *(Hustler, Playgirl, Reader's Digest)*.
19. The (copy, issue, volume) is (average, representative, typical).

CREATING TONE

Each of the following three paragraphs is relatively impartial in tone. By using different words, reconstructing sentences, adding and omitting details, or making any other appropriate changes, rewrite the paragraph to give it a more definite tone. You may create the tone called for in the directions, or you may create any other tone you want.

Example

> A football widow is not a woman whose husband perished on the stadium parking lot. No, it's just that her husband watches football on television every Saturday and Sunday and every Monday night during the football season. She has her weekends all to herself because, when she tries to talk to her husband, she is usually told to start crocheting a sweater for the neighbor's poodle. Instead, she'll probably join a bridge club, go bowling with her friends, or bake batches of chocolate chip cookies. (Rewrite the paragraph to make it more serious and more angry.)

↓

> A football widow is not a woman whose husband died on the stadium parking lot, although she often wishes he had. She is a woman whose husband is addicted to watching football on television every Saturday, every Sunday, and every Monday night from late August to early January. She is a woman afraid to talk to her husband—except to offer him a brew—for fear she will be ignored, shut up, or told where to go. And sometimes she does go—to the bridge club, to the bowling alleys, or to have an affair with her daughter's math teacher.

A. Each year, fraternities and sororities replenish their ranks through a process known as "rush." Ostensibly a group of open houses and parties for the purpose of making friends and learning about the Greek system, rush is also a screening process for choosing acceptable pledges. It is a procedure whose structure is bound by tradition, allowing the participants to be closely scrutinized in a variety of social situations. The brothers and sisters compare the newcomers, from the first beer bash through the final dinner party, seeking people with a strong affinity for their group. These people are tendered an invitation to join the fraternal organization at the close of rush activities. (Rewrite the paragraph to make it either more hostile or more favorable in tone to fraternities and sororities.)

B. Each spring, during the period that has become known as "college weeks," some 250,000 college students crowd into Daytona Beach, another 100,000 invade Fort Lauderdale, and still another 10,000 fly on to Bermuda. Resort owners welcome the business the college students bring. In Bermuda, for example, owners not only try to attract the students to the island but keep them happy and occupied when they have arrived. They offer the students everything from free harbor cruises to limbo contests and get-acquainted dances. But the same owners breathe a sigh of relief when the invasion is over. (Rewrite the paragraph with a tone that suggests more clearly why the owners are relieved to see the students leave.)

C. We've all used mnemonic devices, memory aids, to help us recall information. Probably the most famous is the tune by which everyone learns the ABC's. A recently published book entitled *A Dictionary of Mnemonics* lists hundreds of memory devices used by schoolchildren and scholars from the Middle Ages to the present. It includes a rhyming poem for those who wish to list the rulers of England from the eleventh century, another that gives the value of pi to the twentieth decimal point, and a sentence whose initial letters indicate the order of the planets: "**M**en **v**ery **e**asily **m**ade **j**ugs **s**erve **u**seful **n**octurnal **p**urposes." (Rewrite the paragraph with a tone of doubt and skepticism about the value of mnemonic devices.)

THE CRIMSON TIDE

As you combine the following sentences into an explanatory essay, change the angry, sarcastic tone into one that gives at least some credit for the entertainment value of bloody movies. Add details of your own from current movies.

1. Blood has become a hot commodity.
2. No, the hot commodity is not a pint of A positive or B negative.
3. You may donate the pint of A positive or B negative to your local blood bank.
4. The pint of A positive or B negative could save a life.

5. The hot commodity now is cheap crimson liquid.
6. The liquid splashes from human bodies.
7. The bodies are severed and hacked.
8. The bodies are gouged and mangled.
9. The liquid splashes all over neighborhood movie screens.
10. At the same time, audiences look on.
11. Their eyes are wide.
12. Their mouths are gaping in horror.

13. Fourth-rate movie producers are turning filth into gold.
14. They appeal to the basest of human instincts.
15. In some cases a $300,000 investment yields a $50 million profit.

16. Only limits to the imagination set limits to the gore.
17. Some sick minds have the imagination.
18. We are now privileged to witness the gore.
19. Kids boil their parents to death in *The Children*.
20. This is "kid's stuff" in comparison.
21. A woman is impaled on a meathook in *The Texas Chainsaw Massacre*.

22. Take your pick.

23. Merely an arm or two is chopped off.
24. This is shown in a close-up.
25. This has lost its novelty.
26. Therefore producers of a recent hit have the sole survivor of a massacre behead the alleged murderer.
27. The recent hit is *Friday the 13th*.
28. The murderer is then seen walking around.

29. He is headless.
30. Its arms are still jerking in the air.

31. Is all this too ordinary for you?
32. Then you can watch cannibalistic ghouls.
33. Their rotting skins drip like candle wax.
34. They munch on their victims.

35. Or you can watch walking monsters.
36. Prehistoric fish have turned into walking monsters.
37. The monsters are forcing their attentions on reluctant women.

38. The greed of producers may never run its course.
39. Yet one wonders about this.
40. When will producers run out of human body parts?
41. The body parts are to be chopped or ripped apart in a novel way.
42. Then the current horror epidemic can become only a frightening memory.

REVISING FOR CONSISTENCY OF TONE

Each of the paragraphs below is confusing because of inconsistency of tone. Following the specific directions, revise each paragraph to create a consistent tone that makes your feelings and attitudes clear.

Example

Many states are instituting proficiency examinations for graduating high school seniors. They test, for example, the students' ability to read newspapers and magazines, to write checks, and to find names in phone books. Educators hope that proficiency testing is a first step in assuring that, when you've finally gotten the old diploma, you can really do some of the things you're supposed to be able to do in the twelfth grade. (Rewrite the last sentence to make it consistent in tone with the rest of the paragraph.)

↓

Educators hope that proficiency testing is a first step toward assuring that **graduation from high school means a student has achieved twelfth-grade skills**.

A. The government obviously resorts to secrecy whenever its agencies conduct research which the public has good reason to suspect is either cruel or unethical. The army has secretly subjected dogs to torture endurance tests and, in the 1950s, hid from the public its testing of LSD and other dangerous drugs on unsuspecting American soldiers. Of course, the army is not the only governmental agency guilty of concealing its inhumane and immoral experiments from the public. Even the Department of Transportation admitted that for years it has used human bodies in auto crash tests to study the effectiveness of air bags. I tend to believe, and so do many of the people I've talked with, that the interest of the public would best be served if the government occasionally made available the nature and purposes of any experiment that might conceivably prove to be questionable. (Rewrite the last sentence to make it consistent in tone with the rest of the paragraph.)

B. Although successful people and failures both agree that luck and connections are the main ingredients of success, they view these factors differently. The guys 'n' gals who've never made it to the top say that forces they can't control prevented them from doing more. They view luck as a turn of the roulette wheel or a throw of the dice, as an almost magical force. They believe that connections are an accident of birth. But that's not the case for those who've made it. Oh, no! Those who have succeeded attribute their accomplishments to their own talent and effort. They see luck in terms of timing, of taking advantage of opportunities as they arise. And according to these Joes and Janes, connections are not really a birthright. No way! They're the result of keeping your nose to the grindstone. One essential difference, then, between those who succeed and those who fail seems to be the extent to which they accept responsibility for controlling their own lives. (Rewrite the middle of the paragraph to make it consistent in tone with the first and last sentences.)

C. The national parks, which were set aside by an act of Congress to keep the American wilderness going, have become tame and polluted, little more than drive-in Holiday Inns complete with newfangled, computerized reservation setups. Trails that were once loads of fun to explore have been paved over for the convenience of tenderfeet. Park rangers now spend more time picking up litter and putting out fires than caring for Yogi Bear, Boo Boo, and all their friends and relatives. Walking among the candy wrappers, beer cans, and spray-painted boulders—some of them decorated with really interesting designs!—campers smell gas fumes more often than the scent of pine. Even the whispering wind is likely to be drowned out by the roar of trail bikes or by the chatter of portable radios. When will Americans shape up? (Rewrite the paragraph to make it consistent in tone. Decide whether to make its tone serious or playful and formal or informal.)

CHOOSE ME

Selecting from the facts below (you may change those facts in any way you choose), construct two pieces of writing, each no longer than 300 words:

A. A required autobiographical statement to accompany your application for a college scholarship.
B. A letter to the cousin of one of your close friends. Although you've never met the cousin, this person is supposed to be both lots of fun and really good-looking. The cousin is coming to town for a week, maybe more, and the purpose of your letter is to convince your friend's cousin to go out with you on the first night of the visit.
    1. I am 18 years old, finishing my senior year in high school.
    2. I have applied to four colleges: Beloit College, University of Minnesota, Purdue University, and West Virginia University.
    3. In college, I plan to major in history.
    4. I have maintained a B+ average in high school, but my average in history courses is a straight A.

5. I play the clarinet in my high school orchestra. I received the music award in my sophomore year.
6. In my junior year, I starred in my school's production of the play *Tea and Sympathy*.
7. I am average in weight and height. I jog daily and I occasionally play tennis and volleyball.
8. My favorite sports are swimming and waterskiing.
9. I broke both my ankles last fall.
10. To relax outdoors, I like to read books of travel or history under a tree and to go fishing at the creek; to relax indoors, I play table tennis and watch TV. My favorite programs are "60 Minutes," "Dallas," and "Hill Street Blues."
11. My eyes are blue, my hair brown, my complexion clear.
12. Sponsored by Buzz Auffenneuter's Central Electronics, I participated in a dance marathon last year which raised $235 for the volunteer fire fighter's fund.
13. I am allergic to cats.
14. I founded the Young Historians Club, and I edited the only issue of the club magazine *Historiana*.
15. I was recently named president of the local chapter of the Young Conservatives Club. Last fall, I campaigned in my neighborhood for Senator Burch.
16. For the past three summers, I've supervised the delivery and distribution of magazines, newspapers, and paperback books for Edna's News and Novelties.
17. My analysis of Lincoln's Gettysburg Address, entitled "A Mirror for Gettysburg: Lincoln and His Archetypes," won the annual Richard F. Davis award for the best essay by a senior.
18. I often feel shy and uncomfortable in the company of members of the opposite sex, but I always consent when my friends want to "fix me up" with dates.
19. I have no neuroses or unnatural phobias, except for a fear of forgetting my name when introducing myself to a date.
20. One of my goals is to teach high school history; another is to enter local politics and eventually run for the state senate.
21. Like my parents, I have deeply held religious convictions. I attend weekly services at the Green Street Church of Christ.
22. I do not intend to marry and settle down until after I have earned my college degree.

23. I listen to fifties jazz, mainly early Brubeck and Kenton. I can barely tolerate country music, and I absolutely hate rock 'n' roll, disco, punk, and bluegrass.
24. I love historical movies, particularly *Anne of a Thousand Days, A Man for All Seasons,* and *Dr. Zhivago.*
25. I have an older brother, Vince, who lives in Detroit, and two younger sisters—Alice and Constance—who live at home and attend junior high school.
26. Based on my past performances, my teachers and coaches predict success for me in the future. They often compliment me on my diligence, my perseverance, and my good sense.

unit*15*
PARAGRAPH PATTERNS

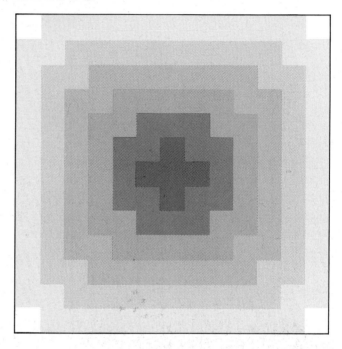

Writers use paragraphs primarily to help the reader. Since each paragraph begins with white space that the writer creates by indenting or by skipping a line, a new paragraph provides a brief rest for the reader's eye and brain. Even more important, the start of a new paragraph helps the reader recognize that a change is taking place —perhaps in place or time, perhaps from one idea to another or from a generalization to an example, perhaps from the body of an essay to its conclusion. Because paragraph divisions indicate that one thing is ending and another is beginning, they help the reader understand the organization and meaning of any piece of writing.

Paragraphs have various functions in an essay. Some paragraphs introduce an essay, others conclude it, and still others connect one part of an essay to another. But the most common kind of paragraph serves primarily to help support or develop the essay's controlling idea. Such supporting paragraphs may be descriptive or narrative, but in most cases they are explanatory: they help develop the controlling idea of the essay by either informing or persuading the reader. Whether your aim is to inform or to persuade, the explanatory paragraph can be organized in many different ways. There are, however, four especially useful patterns of organization: the direct pattern, the turnabout pattern, the climactic pattern, and the interrogative pattern.

The Direct Paragraph

The DIRECT PARAGRAPH, as its name implies, begins with a statement of its controlling idea (that is, with what is sometimes called the topic sentence). The controlling idea in a direct paragraph will usually be stated in the first sentence, rarely later than the second. What follows in the paragraph will develop the controlling idea—by defining it, qualifying it, analyzing it, and, most frequently, illustrating it. To create a direct paragraph, then, you should begin by clearly stating your controlling idea and then continue by developing it. For example, if your controlling idea is that "an omelette can contain many different ingredients," then start your paragraph with a sentence which includes that assertion and proceed by giving examples of the different ingredients:

> **The wonder of omelettes is that so many things can be put into them.** Take cheese, for example. All sorts of cheese, like Swiss or provolone, American or mozzarella, slide deliciously into the omelette's fold, enhancing the texture of the eggs. And vegetables, from the predictable onions and mushrooms to the less common spinach and kohlrabi, add vital flavor. Still more lavish, for those who are not vegetarians, is the addition of a meat, possibly pepperoni or bacon or ham. But the omelette's most exotic components might be the fruits that give it tang: raisins, tomatoes, avocados. Maybe someday an enterprising chef will discover that candy and liquor can be mixed with eggs to produce a vodka-and-fudge omelette.

The paragraph about omelettes ends with a culminating illustration of its controlling idea: it may be possible to make an omelette even out of vodka and fudge. But you may choose to construct your direct paragraph so that it ends not with a final example but with a restatement of the paragraph's controlling idea. The more complex your controlling idea, the more appropriate it becomes for you to restate it at the conclusion of your paragraph. In the paragraph below, the controlling idea that the free road map is becoming extinct is stated in the first sentence and then restated in the last:

> **The free road map is becoming a cultural dinosaur—a thing of the past, a victim of changing priorities.** Until recent years, service station attendants dispensed road maps as freely as they washed windshields. In fact, one oil company official boasted that "free road maps are an institution peculiar to Americans." Well, the institution peaked in 1972 with the production of 250 million maps and then began its decline. Far fewer maps are distributed today, and almost none of them are free. Citing high production costs and the energy crisis, oil companies claim that the demise of road maps is actually patriotic. After all, they explain, maps promote travel and travel wastes energy. With this kind of logic, **is it any wonder that the free road map is nearly extinct**?

Whether or not its controlling idea is restated in the final sentence, the direct paragraph has an obvious advantage over all other paragraph patterns: the direct paragraph is clear, straightforward, and easy to follow. It is a pattern well suited to inform and clarify because, from the start, your readers know exactly where you're taking them. For this reason, the direct paragraph minimizes the chances for misunderstanding or confusion.

But while the direct paragraph is often the best pattern for informing and for clarifying, it is usually not as effective for persuading as the other common paragraph patterns—the turnabout paragraph, the climactic paragraph, and the interrogative paragraph.

The Turnabout Paragraph

The turnabout paragraph differs from the direct paragraph in that it does not begin with a statement of its controlling idea. Instead, the turnabout paragraph begins with an observation or suggestion that is often the direct opposite of its controlling idea. That is, if the controlling idea of a turnabout paragraph is that "ballet dancing demands as much strength, stamina, and athletic skill as football," the paragraph is likely to begin by suggesting the opposite: "At first glance, there seems to be no similarity between the pro football players who abuse each other on Sunday afternoons and the professional ballet dancers who perform in *Firebird* and *Swan Lake.*" In the same way, a turnabout paragraph whose controlling idea is that "most modern American writers live relatively happy lives" might open with an observation that points in an opposite direction: "It's the suicides that have made the headlines: Ernest Hemingway putting a double-barreled shotgun to his forehead, John Berryman leaping into the Mississippi River, Sylvia Plath sticking her head in an oven." The turnabout paragraph below, which develops the idea that "alcohol may help the memory," appropriately begins with a suggestion to the contrary:

> Everyone knows that college students drink Budweiser or Johnny Walker Red in part to escape the pressure of studying. Drinking is a good way to forget about chemistry or composition for a while, right? Well, this generalization may not be true. Drs. Elizabeth Parker and Ronald Alkana ran experiments showing that ethanol—pure booze—might aid memory if it's taken in moderate amounts immediately after learning something. At least that's what seems to have happened with drinking mice: they remembered an electric shock for an average of 110 seconds longer than their sober friends. So if alcohol affects human beings as it does mice, **we may one day be drinking to remember rather than to forget**.

Unlike the direct paragraph, which moves in one direction only, the turnabout paragraph moves first in one direction and then in another. Because it changes direction, the turnabout paragraph may confuse your readers unless you help them follow its movement. The first way to help is by indicating that they should not unhesitatingly accept your opening observation as true. You can encourage readers to question the truth of your opening observation by introducing it with a phrase like **Many people believe that . . .** or **It is**

commonly assumed that . . . or **According to most observers . . .** You can create further doubt by using equivocal words like **appears, seems, may, might**, and **evidently**. The second way of helping readers follow a turnabout paragraph is by signalling when the turn comes. Readers must know when your paragraph turns from a statement that only appears to be true to one that is actually true. The clearest signal is the simple word **but**. Other signals of a change in direction include connectives like **yet, however**, and **nevertheless**, subordinators like **although, even though**, and **while**, and prepositions like **despite, contrary to** and **by contrast to**. Occasionally, you may choose to signal a turn with a full sentence like **But this plausible explanation is simply not supported by the evidence** or—as in the previous paragraph on drinking—**Well, this generalization may not be true.** However you signal your turn, it should usually come in the first half of your paragraph. The third and most important way to help readers follow a turnabout paragraph is by clearly stating the controlling idea of the paragraph in the final sentence. Even if your controlling idea has been stated earlier in the paragraph, it's almost always best to conclude a turnabout paragraph with a statement or restatement of its central point.

The turnabout paragraph below employs all three ways to help readers follow its movement. The word **seem** in the first sentence encourages readers to doubt the observation by "those of us tied to routine jobs" that truck drivers are "independent rogues." The word **but** in the second sentence clearly signals the turnabout. And the controlling idea—that truckers too are bound by routines and regulations—is plainly stated in the final sentence.

> To those of us tied to routine jobs in offices or factories, truckers **seem** to be tough, independent rogues of the open road, driving their own rigs and setting their own rules, like the cowboys of old who rode the open range on horseback, beholden to no one. **But** truck drivers themselves will tell you that —the public's perception be damned—trucking is a business and not too good a one at that for the small, independent trucker. Since the seventies, it seems, most independent drivers have been forced out of business by skyrocketing costs and increased federal regulation of the industry. **So the truckers**

you see on the road now generally work for large firms and are as tied to routines and regulations as those of us in office or factory jobs.

Carefully constructed turnabout paragraphs have one major advantage over direct paragraphs: they tend to be more persuasive. If your aim is primarily to inform or to clarify, then the direct paragraph that opens with a statement of its controlling idea is your best bet. But if your aim is to persuade, to move your readers from one position to another, then the direct paragraph with its blunt opening may not be psychologically appropriate. Instead, you might try the turnabout paragraph. Because it presents one point of view before advancing another, the turnabout paragraph suggests your willingness to see both sides of a question. Once you have convinced your readers of your sense of fairness, you will find them more likely to accept your viewpoint. In your next persuasion paper, try using the turnabout pattern in a paragraph intended to refute a commonly held position.

The Climactic Paragraph

Like the turnabout paragraph, the climactic paragraph is especially appropriate for persuasion. Because it begins with examples and supporting details that build gradually toward the statement of a controlling idea in the last sentence, the climactic paragraph psychologically prepares your readers for the idea you want them to accept. But because such a paragraph withholds a statement of its controlling idea until the very end, the climactic pattern has a built-in element of surprise and drama that makes it equally appropriate for the opening or closing paragraph of your essay.

To construct a climactic paragraph, begin with examples, illustrations, or supporting details. Only after you have supplied enough examples—usually between three and five—should you state the controlling idea in the climactic final sentence of the paragraph. In the paragraph below, for example, there are three instances of the influence of situation comedy before the idea itself is stated clearly in the paragraph's concluding sentence:

At every dropped dish or bungled plan in "Mork and Mindy," Mork would curse in his native Orkan tongue; for more than a year, "Shazbaht" was the favorite expletive of the preadolescent set. In one episode of "Happy Days," Fonzie took out a library card; across the country, libraries showed an eye-popping 500 percent increase in applications for loan privileges. For the seven years of "The Mary Tyler Moore Show," Mary Richards struggled as an assistant producer and then producer of the news at fictional station WJM-TV in Minneapolis; journalism schools received a growing number of women applicants choosing broadcast-news production. **It seems that situation comedies grip their audiences in at least two ways: they both keep us entertained and change the way we live.**

If the climactic paragraph tends to be more persuasive than the direct, it may be because the pattern of the climactic paragraph corresponds more closely to the pattern of much of our own thinking: we often begin by collecting data—an example or two here, an instance or two there—until we have enough evidence to make a generalization or reach a conclusion. By contrast, the direct paragraph presents the conclusion first and the evidence which supports that conclusion later: this pattern makes the direct paragraph clearer but probably less convincing. The climactic paragraph, when it is most convincing, leads the reader, step by step, to a conclusion which seems to follow naturally from the earlier examples and illustrations:

There is no such thing as the "1975 Public Affairs Act." Yet researchers have found that, when asked about it, one out of every three Americans will offer opinions about the act as if it really did exist. When asked about other, real issues, like the government's foreign policy, these same people are more likely than others to offer their opinion. The usefulness of public opinion becomes even more suspect when we learn from surveys conducted in the mid-1960s that two-thirds of all Americans thought that the Soviet Union was a member of NATO and that only one-quarter knew that mainland China was gov-

erned by Communists. **Given such ignorance, government policymakers must be careful not to rely too
heavily on public opinion polls.**

The Interrogative Paragraph

The interrogative paragraph differs from the other types of explanatory paragraphs because it opens with a question. The opening
question is used either as an introduction to the controlling idea of
the paragraph or as a transition from one idea to the next, rather
like a turnabout statement. For instance, if you were writing a
paper in order to convince your audience that the isolation of
neighborhood from neighborhood is too great a price to pay for
lower crime rates, you might begin by showing how several small
communities had, in fact, decreased street crime by fencing themselves off from surrounding communities and placing armed
guards at entrance points. Then, to move to your major point, you
could ask, "Is the price of safety really worth turning America into
a nation of armed camps?"

Instead of functioning as a transition, the opening question of the
following paragraph introduces the controlling idea, that De Camp's
book "explores what many consider to be the 'secrets' of the an-
cients, which turn out not to be so secret after all":

> Have you ever wondered how ancient peoples created such mar-
> velous feats of engineering as the pyramids, the Great Wall, and
> the fabled Tower of Babylon? If you have, then you should read
> *The Ancient Engineers,* by L. Sprague de Camp. The book
> explores what many consider the "secrets" of the ancients,
> which turn out not to be so secret after all. While the Ancient
> Egyptians, Chinese, and Babylonians did not have engineering
> know-how equivalent to ours, they were able to make optimal
> use of what they did know, largely because they had unlimited
> manpower and—what may be more important—infinite pa-
> tience. De Camp discloses that the Egyptians used 100,000
> laborers over a 20-year period to build the Great Pyramid. He
> also shows that the Chinese labored for centuries on the Great
> Wall, as did the Babylonians on the Tower.

Questions have a strong psychological hold on us. They provoke our interest and demand to be answered. That's why riddles are so popular. And that's why editors put questions like the following on their magazine covers: "Can A Change in Diet Help Prevent Cancer?" "Who Are the Wealthiest Stars in Hollywood?" "The IRS: Has It Gotten Too Powerful?" Editors hope you will buy their magazine to find out the answer.

Because of the psychological demand of questions, paragraphs that begin with them, like riddles, tend to involve readers more directly in your writing than do other paragraph patterns. Notice how the opening sentence of the next paragraph almost gets you responding silently, with your own question, "O.K., Why *do* track coaches watch so carefully as students walk by in the corridors?" The opening question not only introduces you to the controlling idea, it almost demands your response.

> Why do high school track coaches watch so carefully as students walk by in the corridors? To look for youngsters who are pigeon-toed, bowlegged, or flatfooted, of course. It seems such youngsters make the best sprinters. Coaches know that a normal gait, with toes pointed outward, slows you down. A normal gait forces your heels to slip forward as you raise up on your toes, detracting from the force of your push off. Those odd gaits, though, give you a firmer landing and kickoff, helping you to run faster.

Because its opening question can suggest the opposite of its controlling idea, an interrogative paragraph often resembles a turnabout paragraph, changing direction after the first sentence. But the change is generally less overt than in a turnabout paragraph.

Whether or not it resembles the turnabout paragraph, the interrogative paragraph can help you to persuade your readers to accept your viewpoint. If, for instance, you want to convince your readers to take up jogging, you might try an opening question like this: "Would you like to firm up flabby muscles, lose weight, handle stress better, and have more energy, too?" Before they can read the next sentence in your paragraph, "Then you should take up jogging," many of your readers will be responding affirmatively to the question and be ready to accept your point of view.

*   *   *

In your explanatory writing, you will probably construct more direct paragraphs than any other kind. But for variety and for drama, especially in your persuasive writing, now and then try the turnabout paragraph, the climactic paragraph, and the interrogative paragraph. Of course, there are many effective paragraphs that follow none of these common patterns. With the paragraph, as with the sentence, the final test is whether it does what you want it to.

CONSTRUCTING PARAGRAPH PATTERNS

The sentences are out of order in the groups below. Read through them in order to get the sense of their meaning. Then organize each group of sentences into an effective paragraph of the type indicated. Be sure to write out each paragraph.

Example

Alpine Slide

Organize these sentences into an effective *direct* paragraph.

1. Covering anywhere from 2000 to 4000 feet of mountainside, the ride lasts four minutes and costs only three dollars.
2. Riders cruise down curving chutes of asbestos cement in a fiberglass sled whose speeds, reaching 25 miles per hour, are regulated by a control stick, which can be pushed forward to accelerate or pulled backward to brake.
3. Once deserted during the snowless summer months, ski resorts now attract visitors with a new sport—the Alpine Slide.

Once deserted during the snowless summer months, ski resorts now attract visitors with a new sport—the Alpine Slide. Riders cruise down curving chutes of asbestos cement in a fiberglass sled whose speeds, reaching 25 miles per hour, are regulated by a control stick, which can be pushed forward to accelerate or pulled backward to brake. Covering anywhere from 2000 to 4000 feet of mountainside, the ride lasts four minutes and costs only three dollars.

On Ice

Organize these sentences into an effective *turnabout* paragraph.

1. Players feel pressured by their organization to put on spectacular shows, a practice which translates into more violence.

2. We assume that players almost instinctively react to a push or a shove with fists flying.
3. In fact, one team's publicity agent admitted that his organization stresses violence as a major attraction to spectators.
4. Yet, according to a Canadian criminologist who has studied fighting in hockey games, violence reflects not the killer instincts of players but the greedy policies of owners.
5. Violence is so common to hockey that we can't help believing that players crave nothing more than a good fight.

Name Calling

Organize these sentences into an effective *direct* paragraph.

1. There was a time when parents honored their newborn children by naming them after figures in the Old Testament, like Esther and Ezekiel.
2. During the years following World War II most parents thought twice before naming a son Adolph or a daughter Rose.
3. Like clothing and hairstyles, the naming of children has always reflected the fads and fancies of culture.
4. And, when President Nixon resigned from office rather than risk impeachment for Watergate-related crimes, it's a safe bet that the name of Richard declined in popularity.
5. Back in seventeenth-century Ireland, after the Protestant army of William III outmatched the Catholic army of the deposed James II, loyal Catholic parents never even considered naming a son William.
6. That fashion passed, but parents have continued to be in-fluenced—often negatively—by the reputations of famous men and women.

Bigfoot

Organize these sentences into an effective *climactic* paragraph.

1. Despite its variety of names, in every case it is an 8-to-10-foot-tall man-ape, a strange and hairy being that flees at the sight of humans.
2. In the Pacific Northwest, where it roams the great forests, it is commonly called Bigfoot.

3. The American Indians refer to it as Sasquatch, "the wild man of the woods."
4. Whether the creature exists or not, the proliferation of stories about it surely points to the human need to believe in the strange, the mysterious, the unknown.
5. To the Russians, it is the final descendant of the Neanderthal man and is known as Alma.
6. In Nepal, it is Yeti, the Abominable Snowman, a feared yet revered creature who wanders in the snows of the Himalayas.

Poets

Organize these sentences into an effective *interrogative* paragraph.

1. In the nineteenth century, poetry was just about the most popular literature, and some poets—like Byron, Shelley, Keats, and Tennyson—even became celebrities.
2. Can you associate the names Richard Wilbur, Adrienne Rich, Ted Hughes, or Leonard Cohen with an occupation?
3. In their own time, they were as well known as movie stars like Paul Newman, Debra Winger, Al Pacino, or Meryl Streep are today.
4. But such was not always the case.
5. You probably don't know that Wilbur, Rich, Hughes, and Cohen are among the most respected contemporary poets, because few people today read poetry or pay much attention to living poets.

MOO-CLEAR ENERGY

Combine the sentences below into a humorous essay that examines one alternative energy source—animal waste. Be sure to create at least one paragraph like those discussed in this unit—direct, turn-about, climactic, or interrogative. You might, for instance, consider opening the essay with a question.

1. Most energy research is directed at deriving power from the sun.
2. Most energy research is directed at harnessing the wind and waves.
3. At the same time some researchers think the following.

4. They've found a short-term answer to energy production.
5. The answer is in animal waste.

6. In fact, CRAP already converts cattle manure into methane.
7. And CRAP sells 1.6 million cubic feet of gas to utility companies.
8. CRAP is the Calorific Recovery Anaerobic Process, Inc.
9. CRAP is an Oklahoma-based company.

10. The gas is the output of its "harvest."
11. The "harvest" is of the waste of 100,000 cattle.

12. CRAP could supply nearly 5 percent of the nation's gas demands.
13. It could do this by recycling the estimated 380 tons of U.S. manure.

14. Valley View Energy Company is moving in a different direction.
15. Valley View is in Hereford, Texas.
16. Hereford, Texas claims to be the home of the world's biggest pile of cow dung.

17. Valley View plans to convert manure more directly into electricity.

18. The manure will be burned in beds of "fluidized" ash.
19. And the heat will power a turbine generator.

20. The Valley View plant will turn 1900 tons of manure into electricity.
21. It will do this daily.
22. The electricity will be for 100,000 homes in Austin, Texas.

23. CRAP and Valley View should prove profitable.

24. After all, there's plenty of cow-fuel available.

25. Ten pounds of manure come out of a cow.
26. This happens for every 25 pounds of grain that go into the cow.
27. This happens every day.

28. Now only one thing would be worse than an Arab oil embargo.
29. That would be an epidemic of bovine constipation.

CHOOSING PARAGRAPH PATTERNS

The sentences are out of order in the groups below. Read through them in order to get a sense of their meaning. Then organize each group of sentences into an effective paragraph. Decide whether you want to use the direct, turnabout, climactic, or interrogative pattern, or whether you want to organize the paragraph in some other way. Be sure to write out each paragraph.

Example

Street Talk

1. In street talk, *Mother's Day* comes once a month—not once a year as a holiday to honor maternity but "when welfare checks arrive."
2. In street talk, a *crib* isn't merely a cozy place to bunk a baby but a "nice apartment."
3. They do the same for the street language of the black ghetto.
4. And someone who's *shooting the pill* isn't destroying medicine but "playing basketball."
5. Metaphors, words that say other than what is literally true, make poetry lively and interesting.
6. Even dull, throbbing "hangovers" become *headbusters* in the vivid, metaphoric language of the street.

↓

Metaphors, words that say other than what is literally true, make poetry lively and interesting. They do the same for the street language of the black ghetto. In street talk, a *crib* isn't merely a cozy place to bunk a baby but a "nice apartment." And someone who's *shooting the pill* isn't destroying medicine but "playing basketball." In street talk, *Mother's Day* comes once a month—not once a year as a holiday to honor maternity but "when welfare checks arrive." Even dull, throbbing "hangovers" become *headbusters* in the vivid, metaphoric language of the streets.

The Beauty of the Beast

1. And, in *The Lost World,* Claude Rains and Jill St. John stumble upon a land full of genuine dinosaurs.
2. So was Godzilla.
3. Although they have been extinct now for more than 50 million years, dinosaurs or creatures like them continue to live in our books and movies.
4. The Creature from the Black Lagoon, its evolutionary growth stunted, was a throwback to the age of reptiles.

Everything You Almost Wanted To Know

1. Somehow it has become important to know Franklin Delano Roosevelt's favorite blues singer or Reggie Jackson's slugging percentage in 1975 or the kind of cookie Robert Redford likes best.
2. Maybe a couple of trivia enthusiasts even know that, during the last half of the 1970s, eleventh graders' scores on a standard math exam dropped a full four points.
3. Publishers have also gotten into the act with books of TV and movie trivia, sports trivia, music trivia, and any other trivia that is insignificant enough.
4. To aid these trivia buffs, call-in radio programs from Panacea, Florida, to Limerick, Maine, broadcast trivia questions and their trivial answers.
5. Considering that test scores are declining and that schools are failing to educate their students, it is ironic that so many people are getting excited about trivia.

Panda-Monium

1. You have undoubtedly heard it called a panda *bear*; even in China, its native country, its name is *beishung,* meaning "white bear."
2. It can stand on its hind legs, and its sharp claws allow it to climb up trees with agility.

3. In fact, its harlequin outfit—the basically creamy white body with black bursts on the ears, over the eyes, around the chest and back, down the forelegs, and along the hind legs—is the only trademark that recalls the panda's true family, the raccoon.
4. As it lumbers along, it walks on the soles of its feet just as bears do.
5. It is shaped like one—massive body, large head, short, stubby legs—and built like one—sometimes as long as 6 feet and as heavy as 300 pounds.
6. If you've ever seen the giant panda, you know how closely it resembles a bear.

Beastly Work

1. When Wolfgang and Sharon Obst were assigned by *Animal World* to film the Panamanian army ant, the days were always sticky, the grounds usually muddy, and the cockroaches sometimes 4 inches long.
2. At midnight, in the middle of the wilds, bitten by ants and mosquitoes, the Obsts had no power to film and no way to leave.
3. After the adventure of photographing zebras and impalas, rhinos and orangutans, you could surely expect to bathe in a cool mountain pool and then to sip martinis with the crew, *right?*
4. Adventure? Maybe. Glamour? Hardly.
5. During the entire week they spent simply searching for the ants, they had to lug all their paraphernalia with them—lights, camera, generator.
6. But at the crucial moment the generator blew.
7. You might think that filming exotic animals for shows like "Wild Kingdom" would offer adventure and glamour.
8. Then, having found the ants, the Obsts couldn't film them during the day (the little creatures are nocturnal), so they set up their equipment for night operation.
9. Not so.

Behind the Scenes

1. For the writer, there is the enviable opportunity of spending a few days with a Jack Nicholson or a Nancy Lopez.
2. For the reader, there is the comfort of identifying with the most

human characteristics—the flaws, the petty likes and dislikes—
of a favorite actor or athlete.

3. There must also be a heady pleasure in knowing that millions
of people want desperately to discover what a star is "really" like.
4. For the celebrity, there is all that free publicity.
5. What is the attraction of the "celebrity profiles" that fill so many
pages of our popular magazines?
6. And the writer is not obligated to be totally objective, like a
journalist, but is free to create impressions and narrate intensely,
like a novelist.
7. Yet at the same time the article reinforces the celebrity's fame,
so that the reader, sharing the celebrity's nervous tic or hatred
of turnips, feels better about his or her chances of becoming
famous.

THE BEAR FACTS

Combine the sentences below into an explanatory essay about how
and why teddy bears became popular. Since this is a subject most
of us can relate to personally, you may add details from your own
experience that make the essay more engaging. Be sure to construct
at least one paragraph like those discussed in this unit—direct,
turnabout, climactic, or interrogative.

1. Winston Churchill, Radar O'Reilly, and Christopher Robin have
something in common.

2. The former prime minister was an arctophile.
3. The company clerk in *M*A*S*H* was an arctophile.
4. And the protagonist of Winnie the Pooh books was an arctophile.
5. An arctophile is a lover of teddy bears.

6. And they're not the only ones.
7. This is so if recent statistics are a true indication of bear popularity.

8. The "bear" facts are these.
9. Toy-bear sales rose to over $125 million in 1984.
10. Over 40 percent of those sales were to adults.

11. The first American teddy-bear convention attracted nearly 25,000.
12. It was held at the Philadelphia Zoo in 1982.

13. Collecting bears is the fourth largest collecting hobby.
14. It comes after coins, stamps, and dolls.

15. And fan clubs abound.
16. "Bearaphernalia" abounds.

17. You'll find teddy logos on everything.
18. They're on masculine ties.
19. They're on feminine lingerie.

20. The teddy-bear mania began with this.
21. It was a hunting trip.
22. President Theodore Roosevelt took it in 1902.

23. It seems that this happened.
24. The president refused to shoot a bear.
25. This was under unsportsmanlike conditions.

26. A political cartoon popularized the event.

27. A Russian immigrant received permission from T.R. to call the stuffed bears Teddy Bears.
28. He sold the stuffed bears in his Brooklyn candy store.
29. He was named Morris Michton.

30. Michton eventually founded this.
31. It was the Ideal Toy Corporation.

32. Now we can buy Bride and Groom Bears.
33. We can buy Paddington Bears.
34. We can buy nurse bears.

35. And we can buy doctor bears.
36. We can buy these besides the simple teddies.

37. And don't forget Very Important Bears.
38. These include the movie star Humphrey Beargart.
39. These include the athlete Kareem Abdul Jabear.
40. These include the Jewish Bearmitzvah.
41. Bearmitzvah comes complete with tallis and yarmulke.

42. Bears may have become popular because of this.
43. They were associated with a popular president.

44. But they have remained popular because of this.
45. They fill a real need in people's lives.

46. Bears are comforting to hug.
47. And bears are comforting to talk to.
48. So people of all ages learn to rely on them.

49. Olympian Greg Louganis talked to his bear.
50. This was during gold-medal dives at the Los Angeles Olympics.

51. Actress Samantha Eggar took her Mr. Bear.
52. This happened on her honeymoon.

53. Bears have accompanied fighter pilots.
54. Bears have traveled with Arctic explorers.
55. Bears have driven with daredevil racers.

56. And we all remember hugging our own teddies.
57. This was when things got tough at nursery.

58. It is not unusual to rely on stuffed bears.

59. Marc Stutsky summed it up nicely.
60. Marc Stutsky is a noted psychiatrist.
61. He said the following.
62. Teddies "make scary things manageable."

63. Life might be "unbearable" without stuffed animals.

REVISING PARAGRAPHS

The paragraphs below are written as either *direct, turnabout, climactic,* or *interrogative.* Whatever the paragraph, rewrite it as a different type, changing sentences when appropriate. Make sure you write out the complete paragraph.

Example

Is romance a thing of the past? It is according to one Michigan State psychologist, who claims that romance is going out of our lives. According to him, the conditions for romantic love no longer exist, replaced in men and women today by a pragmatic cynicism in which they view each other with a cool and objective eye. He says that freer attitudes toward sex and contraception have also helped kill off romance. Would-be Dantes can now have affairs with would-be Beatrices rather than mope and pine away in poetry. (Interrogative Paragraph)

A Michigan State psychologist confirms what most of us already know—that romance is going out of our lives and that the conditions for romantic love no longer exist. According to him those conditions are replaced in men and women today by a pragmatic cynicism in which they view each other with a cool and objective eye. He claims that freer attitudes toward sex and contraception have also helped to kill off romance. It seems that would-be Dantes can now have affairs with would-be Beatrices rather than mope and pine away in poetry. (Direct Paragraph)

A. In the period following Vietnam, students are supposedly dull and conforming. But they may in fact be imaginative and rebellious, if the behavior of Caltech students is indicative. Recently, a group of Caltech students disassembled a senior's sports car and left it for him in his room, completely reassembled and the engine running. Not long ago, when McDonald's ran a promotional contest in California, Caltech students found a loophole in the rules and programmed a computer to spit out 1.2 million entries, winning thousands of dollars in prizes. One Caltech student, thought to be tapping professors' phones, admitted to the FBI that he was actually tapping the Strategic Air Command's hot line. Another, a senior, created a quantum mechanics problem for some undergraduates as a prank and ended up with a puzzle that stumped even a Nobel-Prize-winning physicist. Some dullards! Some conformists!

B. Children in Northern Ireland, the scene of a long, bitter, and bloody civil war, have been studied by a group of psychologists. They tell us that 75 percent of the ten-year-olds believe that any unknown object found in the street—like a cigarette pack, a letter, or a package—is likely to be a bomb. Moreover, 80 percent of the children believe that shooting and killing are acceptable ways of achieving political goals. In effect, terrorism seems to affect children psychologically more than it does adults.

C. Have people really progressed since primitive times, or does civilization simply cover our innate savagery? A recent British Broadcasting Company documentary indicates that we may not be as civilized as we think. In order to film a documentary on life in the Iron Age, the BBC hired a group of ten men and women to live in an ancient village just outside Stonehenge. There, the men and women had to live as their distant ancestors did: they wove cloth, made tools, farmed in ancient ways, and practiced the Celtic religion. After a year, their behavior changed. They walked more slowly and they talked more slowly. They slept longer and were less inhibited about nudity. They were more self-sufficient but also more primitive. At the planting ceremony, for instance, they forced one member of the group to be lashed as a sacrifice to ensure a good harvest.

D. Toy fads have their own peculiar logic, which manufacturers are seldom able to predict or even to explain. So Coleco Industries —the makers of Cabbage Patch Kids, those ugly, irresistible urchins who come complete with adoption papers, names, and birth certificates—wasn't surprised when its cuddly creations took the trade by storm one recent Christmas. It was simply another one of those hysterias that sweep the volatile toy market from time to time. Coleco just hopes that the Kids have the staying power of such perennial favorites as Barbie dolls, Raggedy Ann, and teddy bears and don't prove to be short lived like hula hoops, Pet Rocks, and Davy Crockett hats—toys that exploded on the scene then disappeared within a season or two.

THE HOME FRONT

Combine the following sentences into an explanatory essay about how civilians lived during World War II and how they produced the weapons of war. Be sure to create at least one paragraph like those discussed in this unit—direct, turnabout, climactic, or interrogative. If you can, add details from movies you've seen, from books you've read, or from what your parents or grandparents have told you about those times.

1. Large numbers of the civilian population took to the streets.
2. This happened in protest against our most unpopular war.
3. This happened during Vietnam.

4. Civilians stood firmly behind the government.
5. This was in order to help defeat Germany and Japan.
6. This happened a generation before.
7. This happened during World War II.

8. Most of the young men were in the military.
9. So women had to replace men in industrial jobs.

10. The women were symbolized by "Rosie the Riveter."
11. The women left their homes to work in factories.
12. "Rosie the Riveter" was a cartoon figure.
13. She wore coveralls and carried a pipewrench.
14. And she urged workers to greater production.

15. Women like Rosie learned how to solder.
16. They learned how to run lathes.
17. And they learned how to rivet metal parts together.

18. They did without new cars.
19. They did without new refrigerators.
20. They put up with shortages of certain foods.
21. And they put up with shortages of luxury items.
22. They bought gas and tires only when they had enough ration coupons.

23. They were like the rest of the civilians.
24. They often rode to work in a '38 Studebaker.
25. The Studebaker had bald tires.
26. It was short on gas.
27. But it was filled with people.

28. They put up blackout curtains at night.
29. They did this before they turned on the lights.
30. And they tuned the radio to hear Gabriel Heatter or H. V. Kaltenborn.
31. They had the latest news.
32. The news was from the European and Pacific Theaters of Operation.

33. They listened to "Amos 'n Andy."
34. They listened to "The Hit Parade."
35. They listened to "Gangbusters."
36. They listened to "Lux Radio Theater."
37. They listened after supper.

38. This was the way.
39. Millions of Americans spent the war years this way.
40. They waited for loved ones in uniform.
41. They listened to the radio.
42. And they took part in the greatest production effort.
43. It was the greatest production effort a people have ever made.

44. Women weren't the only ones who worked, of course.

45. Men shouldered much of the burden.
46. The men were exempt from the military.

47. High school kids spent evenings in tank factories and steel mills.

48. Old people in retirement took up trades.
49. The trades were half-forgotten.

50. They produced the weapons that fought the Axis.
51. They produced 296,029 airplanes.
52. They produced 86,333 tanks.
53. And they produced 319,000 artillery pieces.

54. They raised steel production by 70 percent.
55. They raised aluminum production by 429 percent.
56. And they raised magnesium production by 3358 percent.
57. They raised production over prewar years.

58. They saved tin cans.
59. They brushed their teeth with half brushfuls of toothpaste.
60. And they volunteered their time at the local USO.

61. They walked the darkened streets as air raid wardens.
62. They walked in the evenings.

63. Or they strained their eyes.
64. They peered through the night skies as aircraft warning watchers.

65. They waited.
66. They worked.
67. They lined up for hard-to-get items.
68. They had ration coupons in hand.
69. Sugar was a hard-to-get item.
70. Nylon stockings were hard-to-get items.
71. Tires were hard-to-get items.
72. And coffee was a hard-to-get item.

73. They were unlike the civilians during Vietnam.
74. They were a people united against a common enemy.
75. They were united in their desire to win a war.
76. They believed in the war.

*part***THREE**

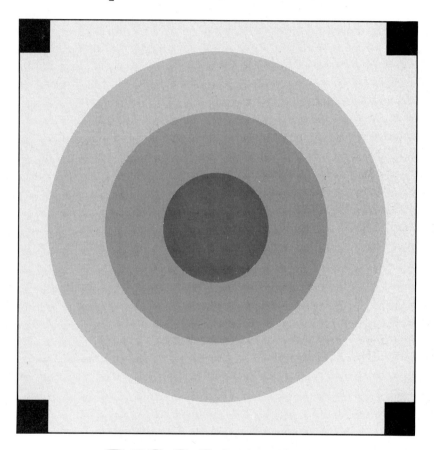

DISCOURSE
STRATEGIES

unit *16*
DISCOVERING AND GENERATING IDEAS

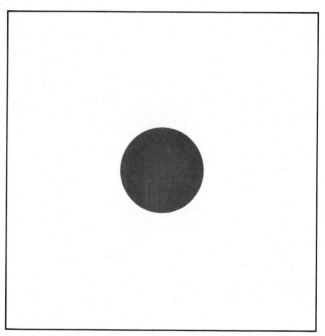

Sometimes we know exactly what we want to say. When taking notes in history class, writing a letter to a friend, or leaving a message for a roommate, we often know precisely what we want to write down. In instances like these we don't need strategies to help us discover and generate ideas.

But at other times we need help. In fact, most of the time—especially with college assignments—we have to work hard to come up with the material and content of our writing. This unit outlines five useful ways of finding and creating such material: listing, free writing, the reporter's formula, cubing, and collaborative learning. For any assignment, use whichever option works best for you.

Listing

Listing is the simplest strategy for discovering and generating ideas: all you do is make a list. The trick is to go quickly and, at this early writing stage, to reject nothing that suggests itself to you. On a piece of paper try to list, as rapidly as you can, any subject or topic that you might conceivably like to write about. Remember to write down every possibility, even those that begin to seem ridiculous on second thought. Take no more than five or ten minutes for this exercise, but be sure to list at least ten items. Then from your list choose a tentative topic for your paper. One or more of the general strategies suggested below—*brainstorming, focused free writing, cubing,* and *the reporter's formula*—might be useful as you begin to develop that topic. If you cannot choose a tentative topic or work up enthusiasm for the topic you chose, try making a second list—again in no more than ten minutes. If your second list also fails to yield a workable topic, try another strategy discussed below—free writing.

Brainstorming. Listing is a strategy that works not only when you are searching for a topic but at other stages of the writing process as well. You can list potential titles, openings, organizational patterns, supporting examples, and the like. One special kind of listing is known as brainstorming. Although brainstorming works best as a group activity and is especially appropriate within the composition classroom, it can be used outside as well as inside class. Brainstorming begins at the point when you have chosen a subject or topic, and the members of the group simply toss out ideas related to it. As one person volunteers a thought, it will encourage others to think of a related or opposing idea. The important point is to accept all ideas without qualification and for each group member to write them down. Later, at the end of the brainstorming session, you can decide which ideas are worth further thought and which should be discarded. To brainstorm by yourself, just write down all the topic-related ideas that come into your own mind, quickly and without evaluation. If ideas are slow in coming, try role-playing: imagine your reaction if you were someone other than yourself, perhaps of a different age or sex or educational level or nationality or occupation. Pretend that you are your mother or kid brother or minister or chemistry teacher or governor or coach and write down their reactions as you imagine them to be. Then, after the brainstorming session is over, review the ideas to decide which are worth carrying forward to the next stage of the writing process.

Free Writing

Free writing is a quick, efficient way of generating and discovering ideas and of getting them down on paper.

Free writing is nonstop writing. You begin by deciding how long you want to write nonstop—5 minutes? 10 minutes? 15 minutes? Then start writing or typing, and don't stop for any reason until the time is up. Don't stop to think; don't stop to correct your spelling, punctuation, or grammar; don't stop to consider questions about organization or meaning. Just let your mind and hand go in whatever directions they choose. If you get stuck after a sentence or two, don't worry—but don't stop writing. Just write "I'm stuck" or "My mind's a blank" or "Why am I doing this?" or "I can't think of anything to say." After several sentences like these, you'll almost surely begin writing something different and more interesting.

Free writing is called "free" for two good reasons. It's free in that it doesn't cost you anything. You don't have to turn it in to your instructor or even show it to your classmates, so there's no worry about a low grade or about being embarrassed. In fact, you do free writing for yourself, not for others. It's a way of discovering for yourself what you think and what you feel. Free writing is free also in that it often works best if you allow your thoughts to wander freely. So unless you have a tight paper deadline, let your mind and heart go in whatever directions they choose.

Here's the result of five minutes of free writing done by one of the authors of this book:

It's a nice day—spring must really be on its way. There's a green car outside my window along with a blue and yellow one. None of the trees have leaves yet. Stop looking out the window, stupid; you won't find any topics to write about there. What's on your mind? Anything? Anything?? Anything? Anything I can write about? I don't think so. I don't think so. Scared. Scared. Scared that I'll never complete this chapter on generating ideas. Why do I procrastinate? Why think of any excuse not to do it? Go across the street to get some food. Look through the college directory at names and addresses. Who's not living with whom this year? Go to the Coke machine. Why do I procrastinate? After all it's not that hard. And why do I care anyway who's divorced and who's not? Have I turned into some sort of voyeur in my old age? Where do I go from here? I wonder who's playing in the NCAA basketball tournament this afternoon. What a lousy year Indiana has had—but maybe they'll do OK in the NIT. How about Bobby Knight throwing a chair across the floor of Assembly Hall? I'd probably be a coach much like him. I remember the time I coached Stephen's baseball team for just one game and . . .

Whenever your allotted time is up, stop writing and read what you've written. Can you find anything promising? In particular, can you find an especially interesting or surprising statement? Is there a word or image or sentence provocative enough to make you willing to use it as the starting point of your paper? If not, you might try another round of free writing. But if you do find an unusual or puzzling or disturbing idea or attitude, then you may want to try focused free writing.

Focused Free Writing. In focused free writing, you follow essentially the same guidelines as for unfocused free writing:

1. Set yourself a time limit—usually 5, 10, or 15 minutes.
2. Once you begin writing, do not stop until the time is up. If you have nothing to say, just write "I have nothing to say" until you do.
3. Do not worry about errors or mistakes of any kind; don't take time to correct or even cross out anything you've written. Keep writing.

But when you do focused free writing, try—as its name suggests— to write on a single subject only and not let your thoughts wander off in other directions. Here is the result of five minutes of focused free writing in which the author tried to stay with the subject of spring:

> March 16, 1985. Will spring ever come? spring spring Why aren't I going to Florida this spring? To Fort Lauderdale or Daytona Beach? Why instead am I heading for Minneapolis? Isn't it crazy to be going to Minneapolis in March? But why have I never gone to Florida during spring break? Lots of my students go, why not me? Even when I was a student I never went. Were things so different then in the fifites? I remember a couple of my fraternity brothers going to Florida, but it seemed quite unusual, out of the ordinary. But now it's common—so common that even lots of high school students go. Heck, two of my children have gone. So next year why not a trip to Vero Beach Florida to watch the Dodgers? Or how about Key West to visit the Hemingway house? Or some place warm to forget about this god-awful Ohio winter. After all, don't I deserve a break? Shouldn't I get some sunshine and warmth before I'm too old to appreciate it? Appreciate it. Appreciate it. I don't know where to go from here. Well, the five minutes is just about up anyway.

Some people think that free writing, focused or unfocused, is the single most effective way of generating and discovering material to write about. There are even people who believe that 10 or 15 minutes of free writing once a day is the best way to become a better writer.

The Reporter's Formula

Once you've settled upon a topic, there are several strategies—in addition to focused free writing—for generating ideas. One popular strategy is called the reporter's formula because it is used by newspaper reporters in gathering material for stories. The reporter's formula consists of six one-word questions commonly known as the five W's and an H:

Who?
What?

Where?
When?
Why?
How?

To use the reporter's formula, apply each of the six questions in turn to your topic. Go slow: spend at least several minutes considering each question and writing down your response to it. Don't worry if the questions occasionally seem to overlap. After all, the purpose of the reporter's formula is to generate material; organizing it comes later. Finally, keep in mind that—depending on your topic—some questions are likely to generate more answers and more interesting answers than others.

If the six questions of the reporter's formula are applied to the author's topic "My Travels in England," they will generate information like this:

Who?   Who travels to England? Lots of people but I want to focus on my own three trips. Each time I went with my wife. Who didn't go? Our kids—they stayed home. Who planned the trips? Both of us.

What?   A trip that was both a vacation and an education. What made it so exciting? What is it that makes traveling about England so fundamentally different from traveling about the United States? In what sense does it differ from domestic travel? In what ways was it educational?

Where? We traveled primarily in the English countryside. We avoided big, crowded cities like Liverpool, Manchester, and Birmingham, and we didn't spend all that much time in London itself. Of course, we spent time in the Tower of London, Westminster Abbey, the Houses of Parliament, and St. Paul's Cathedral. But most of our time was outside London. What were the most enjoyable sites? The city of York with its magnificent cathedral. But all the cathedral cities were grand—Winchester, Salisbury, Canterbury, Ely, Lincoln, and Wells. The magnificence of Fountains Abbey. The disappointment of Tintern Abbey. The mystery of Glastonbury. Imposing Warwick Castle. The ruins of Kenilworth. The Lake District. Cornwall and Devon.

When?　During the summers of 1979, 1981, and 1984. For a week to ten days at a time. During June or July so the weather is warm (but never as hot as an Ohio summer).

Why?　At first because we had inherited a (for us) rather large sum of money, and we had no better way to spend it. (We never thought of saving it.) Why? Because my wife had the will and determination to insist that we go. Then, for the second and third trips, because it was exciting, exhilarating, romantic, charming, new. Why England rather than other countries like France, Germany, or Italy? Because we know more of English history. We know of the Civil War and the Restoration and the defeat of the Spanish Armada and Henry VIII and Queen Elizabeth and lecherous Charles II. And we know about English literature, so we enjoy visiting the home of John Keats in London, the Brontë cottage in Haworth, and the places in the Lake District associated with Wordsworth and Coleridge.

How?　By plane, of course; a ship takes too long. And then with a rental car. Never a tour—dullsville. There's more excitement and independence with a car—remember hitting the parked motorcycle in Newcastle and flipping over the Escort on a lonely road in Cornwall. And rarely staying in motels or hotels but rather in what the English call "B & B's"—beds and breakfasts. A B & B is a privately owned home with one or more bedrooms for rent on a nightly basis. The cost, which includes a full English breakfast, is usually much cheaper than a hotel. Besides, it's a great way of getting to know the English people.

You can see that the six questions of the reporter's formula can generate a wealth of material. Then it's up to you to go through the material you've generated in order to look for an idea that will serve as the focus or center of interest for the paper you will write. If an idea or impression emerges, consider using it as the basis for focused free writing or brainstorming. If no idea or impression emerges from the mass of material, then either try the reporter's formula again, perhaps on a different topic, return to unfocused free writing, or use yet another strategy for generating and discovering ideas—cubing.

Cubing

The strategy of cubing is a lot like the reporter's formula. Both strategies work best after you've selected a subject but before you've written a first draft. And both cubing and the reporter's formula help you generate and discover ideas by applying six questions or operations to your subject. In fact, the name *cubing* comes from the word *cube*—a six-sided figure. Try to visualize a cube—think of a square block—with one of the following operations written on each of its six sides:

1. Describe your subject.
2. Compare your subject.
3. Associate your subject.
4. Analyze your subject.
5. Apply your subject.
6. Argue for or against your subject.

To use the strategy of cubing, make sure you apply in order all six operations to your subject, spending no more than five minutes on any one operation. Here's an example of cubing applied to *The Sun Also Rises,* a novel by Ernest Hemingway:

1. Describe *The Sun Also Rises* (What does it look like? feel like? taste like? What about its shape, size, color, smell?):
   Well, it's a novel—and a short one at that. It's only 247 pages in my edition and large size print, too. There's a good deal of white space on lots of pages, a sign that Hemingway uses much dialogue. There's a picture on the front cover of a village (is it in Spain?) with the sun shining above it. On the back cover is a photograph and biographical sketch of

Hemingway, together with a list of other Hemingway books.

2. Compare *The Sun Also Rises* (What is it like? What is it unlike?):
    It's like other Hemingway stories in that it deals with war (Jake Barnes has been injured in World War I) and in that sports seems to be important. There is bullfighting, fishing, and boxing here, the same sports Hemingway uses elsewhere. It's like the fiction of F. Scott Fitzgerald in that it deals with Americans in the 1920s who are living abroad. It's unlike *The Scarlet Letter* or *Moby Dick* not only because of all the drinking, partying, and sex but because Hemingway doesn't seem primarily interested in religion or morality. (Is this right? Doesn't Jake define morality some place in the novel? I'll have to think about this later.)

3. Associate *The Sun Also Rises* (What does it remind you of? What does it make you think about?):
    It makes me think of Hemingway himself and wonder how close his own life comes to the events of the novel. After all, wasn't Hemingway getting divorced at about the time *The Sun Also Rises* was written? And didn't he dedicate the novel to his first wife out of guilt? It makes me think about living in Paris in the 1920s. It makes me wonder whether all of us have a handicap or limitation like Jake. Few of us were injured in a war, of course, but don't all of us have a limitation that we must try to live with? Either we're not as good-looking as we'd like, or not as intelligent or sociable or athletic.

4. Analyze *The Sun Also Rises* (What parts does it divide into? How can you take it apart? How is it made?):
    Hemingway himself divides the novel into three parts—Book I, Book II, and Book III. Each of the books has a series of chapters, except Book III. The novel also is broken into different geographical locations: it begins in Paris, moves to Burguete, Pamplona, and San Sebastian, and then concludes in Madrid. But all these locations fall into two categories: the cities like Paris, Pamplona, and Madrid where Jake confronts Brett; and the vacation spots like

Burguete and San Sebastian where Jake can temporarily escape from Brett. The characters in the novel also divide into two groups: those who fail to get their money's worth of pleasure out of life—like Robert Cohn, Mike Campbell, and Brett herself—and those who have learned to get their money's worth of pleasure out of life—like Count Mippipopolous, Pedro Romero, and—finally—Jake Barnes.

5. Apply *The Sun Also Rises* (How can you use it? What can be done with it?):

I think what you do with *The Sun Also Rises* is to experience it and enjoy it. But maybe you can use it to awaken your interest in fishing and bullfighting, if not in drinking. But since the novel is concerned above all with learning how to live, it may have more practical value. From it, you may learn that it is possible to get your money's worth of enjoyment from life—once you understand that you have to pay in some way for anything that's good. You may also learn the value of Jake's definition of immorality—"things that made you disgusted afterwards"—and decide to adopt it as your own definition.

6. Argue for or against *The Sun Also Rises* (Define an issue and take a position):

Yes, I think *The Sun Also Rises* is a great novel, one of the four or five best American novels ever written. No, I don't think it encourages immorality or dissipation: perhaps the most important word in the novel is "control." Not until Jake learns to control Brett, in much the same way as Romero controls the bull, does he begin to get his money's worth of pleasure out of life. Is the novel anti-Semitic? I think it might be, although the anti-Semitism is Bill's more than Jake's or Hemingway's. Is the novel finally affirmative or pessimistic? Absolutely and positively affirmative.

With the information and ideas you've generated through cubing, you should be ready to begin selecting and defining the central idea of your paper on *The Sun Also Rises*.

Collaborative Learning

Sometimes the best way of discovering and generating ideas takes the help of another person or two. Talking about your subject with a friend or classmate, either inside or outside class, often helps you to come up with information that would be unavailable otherwise. Reading what you've written to another person occasionally helps you to hear what you never heard when reading to yourself. But two forms of collaborative learning are especially effective when you are searching for material to write about—paired interviews and peer criticism.

Paired Interviews. In a paired interview, two people exchange ideas about a piece of writing in process. The interview can take place within the composition classroom or outside it; all you really need is a pair of writers willing to talk about their work.

Once you have a partner and the two of you have decided who will go first, the next decision is whether your work in progress is more a story or more an explanatory or persuasive piece. If you decide it's a story, your interview might consist of the following steps:

1. Summarize the plot of the story for your partner and then state the point or theme of the story, if it has one.
2. Ask your partner if he or she has ever had a similar experience and, if so, to tell you about it briefly.
3. Ask your partner which part of the story he or she would most like to read about and why.

But if you are writing an explanatory or persuasive essay rather than a story, try these three steps:

1. Explain to your partner what you are going to write about and what you are going to say about it (your topic together with your central idea or proposition).
2. Ask your partner what he or she knows about your topic that you may be able to use in your essay.
3. Ask your partner what he or she would especially like to know about your topic.

After the interview, which should take between five and ten minutes, reverse roles with your partner so that he or she goes through steps 1–3. When both interviews are completed, try to incorporate into your writing plans whatever new approach and new information you gained from collaborating with a fellow writer.

Peer Criticism. Like the paired interview, peer criticism can take place outside the writing classroom but it works best within it. The essence of peer criticism is that writers try to help each other by honestly but tactfully responding—*in writing*— to a series of questions about writing in progress. Peer criticism works best with a group of three or four writers who have a rough draft to share with each other. One by one, each member of the group gives a copy of the draft to the others to read; the draft may be read aloud while the others follow along. After the reading, the group members write out their response to several questions—usually three or four—that either the instructor or the writer has chosen. If the draft is a narrative, the following kinds of questions are appropriate:

1. How did you feel when you finished the story?
2. What did you like best about the story?
3. What part of the story do you wish had been developed more fully?
4. What did you think after you had read the first couple of sentences?
5. What do you think the story is really saying?
6. What do you most clearly remember about the story?
7. How might you change the story if you had written it?
8. When did you realize the nature of the story's central conflict?
9. How did you react to the story's title?
10. What do you think of the story's main character?

For an explanatory or persuasive paper, the questions below will be more useful:

1. What did you learn from reading this paper?
2. What kind of audience is this paper written for?

3. How might this paper be made more informative or more convincing?
4. What do you think is the central purpose of the paper?
5. What do you most clearly remember about the paper?
6. What did you like best about the paper?
7. Which is your favorite sentence or paragraph?
8. Where do you need more information or more evidence?
9. What were you thinking as you finished reading the paper?
10. Where do you wish the paper had provided more specific examples?
11. What did you think when you had read the opening sentences?

Whether your draft is narration, explanation, or persuasion, try to ask some of your classmates the questions that will be most useful to you in writing your next draft. Of course, it will be entirely up to you whether to accept their recommendations: the final responsibility for the paper is yours. But the honest responses of our peers can often help us discover ideas and approaches that we had either overlooked or never even considered.

*   *   *

No one of the five major strategies for discovering and generating ideas is intrinsically superior to the others. Try them out to see which works best for you in any given writing situation. All of them will be useful at one time or another.

LISTING

1. In no more than ten minutes, write down a list of at least 20 topics that you might possibly like to write about someday. Go fast, write down any topic that comes to mind, and don't reject any possibility. Here is one person's list:

   traveling in Canada, especially the Maritime Provinces
   my favorite movies
   memories of the Jefferson School playground
   an undefeated season
   Venice, my favorite city
   white water rafting
   blind dates
   the Indy 500
   why I like *Citizen Kane*
   why was I so insecure in high school?
   the junior prom
   Michael Jackson
   "General Hospital" and "All My Children"
   graduation day
   the trip to Chicago
   the time I had the fight with Phil
   the last time I saw Barbara
   too much drinking
   The Catcher in the Rye
   hitchhiking to San Francisco
   my high school reunion
   working at Wendy's

   Now make a list of your own and, from that list, select the two or three topics that strike you as most promising. For each of those topics, write down a list of three or more possible paper titles.

2. In no more than ten minutes, write down a list of five or more topics that you probably know more about than most of your friends. Go fast, don't be modest, and write down any topic that comes to mind. Here is one student's list:

myself
my family
Perry, New York—my hometown
waterskiing
baby-sitting
making pecan pies
being a waitress at a pizza restaurant
"Hill Street Blues"
Harlequin romances

Now make a similar list of your own.

3. In no more than ten minutes, write down a list of five or more subjects you would like to know more about. Go fast, be honest, and write down whatever comes to mind. Here's one person's list:

What's the best way to get to know the girl who sits just in front of me in zoology class?
Are guys really more interested in sex than girls?
What's the major difference between front-wheel-drive and rear-wheel-drive cars?
Why does this school make me take a course in composition?
Do coaches really tell college athletes which profs to take and which to avoid?
What am I going to do for a job this summer?

Now make a similar list of your own. If you have the chance, exchange your list with other students in your class or dormitory.

4. *Brainstorming.* Choose any topic you generated by a listing activity, and brainstorm about it for 10–15 minutes. List any idea or question or thought that comes to mind without evaluating it. Here are the results of one person's brainstorming on the topic of the Indy 500:

400,000 people or more
"the greatest spectacle in auto racing"
gasoline alley—what really happens there?

"Gentlemen, start your engines"
Will a woman driver qualify this year?
new speed records—how high will they go?
"Back Home Again in Indiana"
Do people really go to see drivers killed and hurt?
How important are the pit crews? And how are they chosen?
just 800 left-hand turns
the deafening noise—frightening the first time you hear it
all the bright colors—but none of the cars are green because
   green is supposed to be an unlucky color. Why?
How do you get to be an Indy driver?
Is it tough being a rookie?
How much does it cost to build a car good enough to qualify?
How does qualifying work anyway?
How do Indy cars differ from grand prix cars?
Why is auto racing more popular now than ever?
Why don't European drivers compete at Indy?
Why do people keep coming back?
What do people do in the infield—watch the race or drink and
   fool around?
What happens to the racetrack the other 365 days of the year?
Are there many father-son teams like the Unsers?

Now brainstorm for 10–15 minutes on a topic of your choice.

FREE WRITING

1. *Free Writing.* Give yourself exactly ten minutes, and during that
   time write down—without stopping for any reason—whatever
   thought comes into your head. Start anywhere, but stop when the
   time is up. Then reread what you've written in order to find in
   your free writing a word, an image, a sentence, an idea, or an
   attitude that you might like to explore further. Decide whether to
   try a second round of unfocused free writing or whether you are
   ready to move to focused free writing.

   2. *Focused Free Writing.* Give yourself exactly ten minutes, and
      during that time write down—without stopping for any reason

—whatever thought comes into your head on *one* of the following topics:

The word, image, sentence, idea, or attitude that you would most like to explore from your earlier free writing.
Whatever's on your mind right now.
The topic you discovered through the listing activities described above.
What you most vividly remember from junior high school.
The person you care for most in the world.
What you think you'll be doing a year or two from now.
A topic of your choice.

When your ten minutes are up, reread your focused free writing sample in order to decide on your next step. Should you do more free writing? Should your focus this time be broader or narrower? Or should you move to another strategy for discovering and generating ideas—listing, cubing, the journalist's method, or another?

THE REPORTER'S FORMULA

Use the reporter's formula—the questions "Who?" "What?" "Where?" "When?" "Why?" and "How?"—to generate material about one of the following topics:

a topic of your choice
the last time you cried
how to lose a high school election
breaking up is hard to do
buying a used car
the difference between right and wrong
what I enjoy more than anything else in the world

When you have answered each of the six questions, go through your material carefully in order to decide upon a focus or central idea for your paper.

CUBING

Use the six operations of cubing—describe the subject, compare the subject, associate the subject, analyze the subject, apply the subject, and argue for or against the subject—to generate material about one of the following topics:

a topic of your choice
the last time you hit someone or someone hit you
differences among high school coaches
the double standard for males and females in sexual behavior
your favorite movie or record album or TV show
Huckleberry Finn, The Great Gatsby, or any other book
loneliness

When you have applied the six operations of cubing to your subject, go through your material carefully in order to decide upon a focus or central idea for your paper.

COLLABORATIVE LEARNING

When you have written a first draft of a paper assignment, select from the questions on pp. 344–345 the four that you would most like several of your peers to answer. Either bring your questions to class during the workshop on peer criticism or exchange them with peers outside the classroom.

unit *17*
SELECTING AND
ORGANIZING
IDEAS

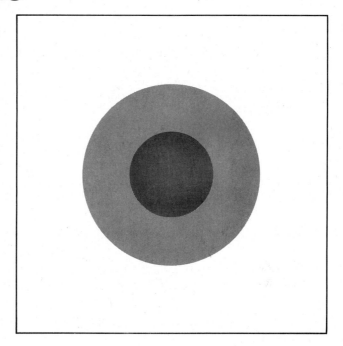

You usually start writing a first draft only after you've collected some information. You do enough reading, remembering, and thinking until you've accumulated a set of related ideas and supporting details, often in the form of notes. Then the process of selection and organization begins. Suppose that, beginning only with the vague purpose of writing about Charles Lindbergh's historic transatlantic flight in 1927, you collect the following notes:

Lindbergh was 25 years old when he flew from New York to Paris. The solo flight was from Long Island to Orly Airport.

It took 33 hours.

Onlookers thought he was doomed to failure.

He had flown and navigated mail planes for years.

He had been a stunt pilot on the barnstorming circuit.

He had set out to win the $25,000 prize offered for the first nonstop flight across the Atlantic.

He had studied all the planes available and chose the Ryan monoplane.

He had it modified and supervised all the modifications.

The wingspan was extended 10 feet for more lift.

He added stronger landing gear.

The fuel capacity was increased from 50 to 450 gallons.

He had enough fuel for a 300-mile navigational error.

He replaced the original seat by a cane chair to save weight.

He installed a 200-horsepower radial air-cooled Wright Whirlwind engine.

The plane had a 130-mile-per-hour top speed.

He had no radio.

He navigated with a magnetic compass and mariner's sextant.

He flew 10 feet above the waves to keep track of wind direction and wind speed.

He had a bottle of water and five sandwiches—two ham, two beef, and one egg with mayonnaise.

His first landsight was Ireland, just as he had planned.

After the flight, he was made a hero, and songs were written about him.

One song was "Lucky Lindy."

Which of these ideas and details you select and how you arrange them depends on your purpose. If you had been a newspaper reporter in 1927, your story would probably begin with a paragraph whose purpose is to communicate the basic facts of Lindbergh's flight. The basic facts will emerge from your notes if you use the reporter's formula—a set of six questions known as the "Five W's plus H": Who? What? Where? When? Why? and How?

Who?   Charles Lindbergh, a 25-year-old former mail pilot.
What?   Flew nonstop across the Atlantic.
Where? From Long Island to Paris.

When?   Landed this morning after a 33-hour flight.
Why?   A $25,000 prize.
How?   In a Ryan monoplane, solo, navigating with a compass and
           sextant.

With the answers to these six questions, you can construct an appropriate opening paragraph for a longer article on Lindbergh's flight:

> Charles Lindbergh, a 25-year-old former mail pilot, landed in Paris this morning after a 33-hour solo flight from Long Island. Lindbergh flew a modified Ryan monoplane and navigated with a compass and sextant. He is expected to claim the $25,000 prize for being the first person ever to fly nonstop across the Atlantic.

This paragraph primarily communicates facts. But most of the paragraphs you write will go beyond stating facts in order to explain, analyze, or interpret them. Such paragraphs are usually most effective when unified by a controlling idea.

A controlling idea, sometimes called a topic sentence, helps you to separate what is relevant from what is irrelevant. If your controlling idea is that Lindbergh succeeded because of his knowledge, experience, thoroughness, and luck, you will probably see at once that some of your collected notes are irrelevant and should be discarded. For example, the fact that Lindbergh had no radio and that he took along five sandwiches is not clearly connected to the reasons for his success. In the same way, the fact that the flight took 33 hours, that it began in Long Island and ended at Orly Airport, or that it won Lindbergh $25,000 is not directly related to knowledge, experience, thoroughness, and luck. By omitting such irrelevant material and by including only details that develop the controlling idea, you can construct a unified and effective paragraph:

> **Lindbergh was successful in flying nonstop across the Atlantic because of his knowledge, his experience, his thoroughness, and his luck.** He knew airplanes both as a pilot and navigator. He had gained extensive flying experience from mail runs and the barnstorming circuit. He carefully

selected his own plane and thoroughly modified it for the arduous flight by extending its wingspan, installing stronger landing gear, and increasing its fuel capacity. And, as popular songs like "Lucky Lindy" made clear, he had plenty of luck.

Aside from providing a principle for selecting ideas and details, the controlling idea often suggests a principle of organization as well. Here the controlling idea has four parts—knowledge, experience, thoroughness, and luck—and each of the four sentences that follow the controlling idea illustrates one of its four parts.

From the same controlling idea, many different paragraphs can be constructed, depending again on your selection and organization of ideas and supporting details. One useful option is to begin your paragraph with a question that the remainder of the paragraph answers. In such a paragraph your controlling idea may be positioned not at the beginning but at the end:

Why did Charles Lindbergh succeed in flying nonstop across the Atlantic when others before him had failed? For one thing, he knew airplanes both as a pilot and navigator. For another, he had gained extensive flying experience from mail runs and the barnstorming circuit. Perhaps most importantly, he carefully selected his own plane and thoroughly modified it for the arduous flight by extending its wingspan, installing stronger landing gear, and increasing its fuel capacity. Finally, as popular songs like "Lucky Lindy" make clear, he had plenty of luck. **Lindbergh succeeded because of his knowledge, experience, thoroughness, and luck.**

Whenever you have difficulty finding a controlling idea, it's helpful to start asking questions about the information you've gathered. For example, one of your notes says that Lindbergh was "made a hero" after his flight. A question you might ask yourself and then try to answer is whether Lindbergh really deserved to be made into a hero. The question itself indicates the topic of a potential paragraph or essay, and your answer to it helps define a controlling idea. If you answer that "Lindbergh deserved his status as a hero" and choose that statement as your controlling idea, the next step is to select from your notes those details that are relevant and to discard those that are not. The most relevant details for establishing Lindbergh's heroism relate to the length and difficulty of his journey, to his primitive flight instruments, and to the uniqueness of his achievement. Those details might be organized into a paragraph like this:

> Charles Lindbergh was hailed as a hero when he landed safely in Paris because, by flying nonstop across the Atlantic, he had done what had never been done before. And he did it under almost impossible conditions. He piloted a single-engine Ryan monoplane capable of no more than 130 miles per hour. He flew alone for 33 hours, without a radio and with only a sextant and magnetic compass for navigational help. He often cruised but ten feet above the ocean waves in order to estimate wind speed and wind direction. Because his was truly a heroic feat, **Lindbergh deserved to be a hero.**

Details in the earlier paragraph explaining why Lindbergh succeeded were deliberately omitted from this paragraph because they were no longer relevant. The details about Lindbergh's knowledge, experience, thoroughness, and luck did not directly support the controlling idea that "Lindbergh deserved to be a hero." As always, it is your controlling idea that determines which details are relevant and which are not.

If you had asked how Lindbergh modified his plane instead of why he succeeded or whether he deserved to be a hero, still another paragraph with a different controlling idea could have grown out of your notes. From the details that Lindbergh changed the plane's original wingspan, landing gear, engine, fuel capacity, and seat, you might have written a paragraph developing the idea that after Lindbergh modified his plane, even its manufacturers couldn't recognize it:

> The plane Charles Lindbergh flew nonstop across the Atlantic only began as a Ryan monoplane. That was before Lindbergh started modifying it. First, he extended the wingspan by 10 feet and added stronger landing gear. Then he increased its fuel capacity from 50 to 450 gallons and installed a 200-horse-

power Wright Whirlwind engine. Before he was through, he even replaced the original seat with a lightweight cane chair. When he was done, **the original builders probably wouldn't have recognized their own creation.**

Once again, the controlling idea governed your selection and exclusion of details. Because the details of Lindbergh's difficult flight and primitive instruments did not help develop a controlling idea about plane modifications, you carefully excluded such details from your paragraph.

Sometimes your controlling idea and even the purpose of your paragraph become clear to you only after you have begun writing. Just as often, what you have written may give you new ideas for developing the paragraph. Here is a paragraph you might have written to support the controlling idea that Lindbergh was a skillful planner, pilot, and navigator:

When 25-year-old Charles Lindbergh took off from Long Island to claim the $25,000 prize for flying nonstop to Paris, most of the onlookers thought he was just another exbarnstormer doomed to failure. They didn't know that **"Lucky Lindy" was a skillful planner, pilot, and navigator.** He had carefully chosen the Ryan monoplane and supervised its modifications. He had installed a 200-horsepower radial air-cooled engine that gave him a top speed of 130 miles per hour. He had the wingspan extended by ten feet for more lift. And he had the normal 50-gallon fuel tank increased to 450 gallons. He was an excellent navigator and pilot who kept track of wind direction and wind speed by flying ten feet above the ocean. When he sighted land, it was precisely where he expected—in Ireland.

But after completing such a paragraph, you might begin to see a new idea emerging—the contrast between the nickname "Lucky Lindy" and the facts indicating that Lindbergh had prepared for his flight with great care and skill. To develop this contrast as the controlling idea of a revised version of your paragraph, you would first want to return to your notes for additional supporting information.

There you would find two further details to illustrate Lindbergh's careful preparation—his experience as a pilot of barnstormers and mail planes and his carrying enough fuel for a 300-mile navigational error. By incorporating these details and excluding others, by revising and rearranging sentences, but especially by emphasizing in both your first and last sentences the contrast between luck on the one hand, and care and skill on the other, you are now able to construct a new and highly effective paragraph:

> **Though the world called him "Lucky Lindy"** after he became the first person to fly nonstop across the Atlantic, the 25-year-old **Charles Lindbergh had actually depended on skill and careful preparation** for the flight. He was an expert pilot and navigator with years of experience flying barnstormers and mail planes. He carefully selected the Ryan monoplane from among the available aircraft as the best suited for his difficult task. And he personally supervised its modification, which included extending its wingspan by ten feet and increasing its fuel capacity by 400 gallons so as to allow for a 300-mile navigational error. When "Lucky Lindy" touched down in Paris 33 hours after leaving Long Island, it was because he had left little to luck.

*　　*　　*

Your major options in constructing paragraphs and essays include defining your controlling idea, carefully selecting your supporting details, and then arranging both idea and supporting details into an effective whole.

PHYSICAL FITNESS

Select from the list below all the notes that support the controlling idea that "catering to physical fitness has become a multimillion-dollar business." Then organize those notes into an explanatory paragraph unified by the controlling idea.

1. More than $200 million worth of tennis clothes are sold annually.
2. Fitness enthusiasts gain a renewed sense of vitality, of a goal conquered, and of confidence in coping with life.
3. Sex and age are no barrier to physical training.
4. Tennis players and racquetball enthusiasts suffer tennis elbow, the inflammation of the tendon that joins the forearm muscles to the elbow.
5. There are more than 1300 books on fitness in print now.
6. *Runner's World* magazine increased from 35,000 circulation in 1975 to over 200,000 circulation by 1978.
7. Middle-aged joggers in poor condition may be setting off heart attacks if they begin without proper advice.
8. A recent Gallup poll indicates that 47 percent of Americans take part in some form of physical fitness daily.
9. Jogging is one of the best cures for depression, report many psychologists.
10. Exercise can become an addiction, and those who exercise become evangelists, recruiting others.
11. The United States now has over 500 racquetball clubs.
12. Some joggers report a feeling of euphoria—not unlike a drug-induced high—from runs of more than 3 miles.
13. Fitness buffs are rejecting sports like golf and bowling for jogging, bicycling, tennis, swimming, and racquetball.
14. Some people jog in $150 jogging suits—with stripes down the sides—and $100 shoes.
15. Jogging helps protect against two causes of heart attacks—inactivity and tension.
16. There are over 8 million joggers in the country, over 29 million tennis players.

17. There are now over 3000 health clubs and spas around the nation with millions of total members.
18. YMCA membership has increased by 16 percent in the past decade.
19. Addidas alone sells over 200 styles of athletic shoes.
20. Over $2 billion worth of sports equipment is sold every year.

GAME SHOWS

Construct a unified and ordered paragraph by picking one of the three statements below to serve as a controlling idea and then choosing appropriate supporting details from the notes.

A. Game show prizes aren't always as good a deal as they seem to be.

B. Game shows use gaudy sets, sex, and gimmicks to create excitement.

C. Game shows thrive on placing contestants in humiliating situations.

1. Game show hosts are usually young and attractive.
2. They dress in the latest fashions.
3. Game show sets are alive with flashing lights and gaudy colors.
4. Women assistants on shows like "The Price Is Right," "Let's Make a Deal," and "Treasure Hunt" are dressed in sexy outfits.
5. On "The Price Is Right" contestants called down from the audience are told to run from their seats to the stage.
6. They often exhibit no regard for others sitting in their area.
7. Contestants on all the shows are encouraged to use cutthroat tactics to eliminate their competition.
8. Prizes like cars, boats, and furs are displayed in the flashiest way possible to make them appear more exciting.
9. Contestants display their greed when they consider the value of their prizes or decide which door to choose.

10. Most shows don't allow winners to substitute cash value for the prizes.
11. When prizes do arrive, they are often defective, the wrong model, or the wrong color.
12. People from certain areas of the country have no use for sailboats, scuba gear, or snowmobiles—common game show prizes.
13. Since taxes on prizes are high, many winners are forced to sell their prizes for money to pay the taxes.
14. Winners frequently report having to wait for months before getting their prizes.
15. Some people have strong moral objections to fur coats—common prizes.
16. Certain prizes require expensive upkeep.
17. Many of the game shows are gimmicky.
18. They are geared to creating a false sense of suspense.
19. Contestants often act like children in order to amuse the host or audience.
20. When contestants win prizes, they often become hysterical and cry.
21. Hosts take advantage of contestants' peculiarities to make them look ridiculous.
22. The "Newlywed Game" exposes intimate personal information about couples and encourages family arguments on stage.
23. "Let's Make a Deal" forces people to dress up in ridiculous costumes.
24. All the shows encourage contestants to go for the most expensive items displayed.

THE WRITING ON THE WALL

Suppose your next writing assignment is a 300–400 word paper on graffiti. After examining the following list of graffiti, decide on the controlling idea you want to develop. You may wish to define graffiti, or compare/contrast different types of graffiti, or analyze the reasons for graffiti. In any case, select items from this list—and, if you wish, include examples of your own—to illustrate your central idea.

1. Sisters unite
2. You've come a long way, baby
3. Get a divorce today, a lover tomorrow
4. Dismember rapists
5. Kilroy was here
6. Sex kills—come here and live forever
7. Flaming Skulls rule
8. Incest begins at home
9. Forest fires prevent bears
10. Hitler is alive and running a Dairy Queen in Kansas
11. Joan of Arc is alive and medium well in Argentina
12. Coffee, tea, or Cuba?
13. Should a gentleman offer a lady a joint?
14. Repeal inhibition
15. Never trust anyone under 12
16. Keep grandma off the streets—legalize bingo
17. Help stamp out graffiti—abolish desks
18. Join male chauvinism
19. Free the Indianapolis 500
20. Help, I'm slowly being bored to death
21. Hire the morally handicapped
22. If you feel far from God, guess who moved?
23. You're never alone with a split personality
24. A watched boy will never pot
25. Find help fast in the Bible pages
26. Sin now—pay later
27. Look homeward, pregnant angel
28. A woman's work is never done—or recognized, or paid for, or honored, or commended
29. Love thy neighbor. But don't get caught
30. In memory of those who died waiting for this class to end
31. Due to lack of interest, nobody is paying attention in class
32. Due to lack of originality, this desk is cancelled
33. Due to circumstances beyond my control this class will meet Friday—(signed) God
34. Familiarity breeds contempt—and children
35. Abortion: pick on someone your own size
36. Rome wasn't built in a day—the pizza parlors alone took several days

37. To err is human—but ain't it divine?
38. I'm afraid of Virginia Woolf
39. Is there sex after death?
40. The early bird gets the worm—the early worm gets the shaft
41. Money does talk—it says goodbye
42. God is not dead. He just doesn't want to get involved
43. Ban the H-bomb; save the world for conventional warfare

unit *18*
USING DETAILS

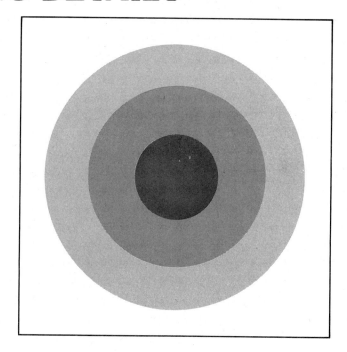

Using Details To Create Vividness

To make your writing interesting and engaging, you must be able to use details that create vivid experiences for your readers. Simply stated, writing comes alive with details that evoke the sights, sounds, smells, tastes, and textures of the real world.

Here are two papers by beginning college writers, both about moving into a dorm for the first time. Which do you think better recreates the experience?

Meeting My Roommate

I was more anxious about meeting my roommate than about almost anything else when I first came to college. The last night of vacation was awful. I hardly slept. I worried about school and about my future roommate and what she was going to be like. After all, I'd have to live with her for the next nine months.

That morning I got up bright and early and got ready to go to Pearson College. The butterflies were fluttering around in my stomach more than ever. My family and I arrived at Pearson about 3:30 P.M. I went to Shriver Hall, registered, received my keys to the room and dorm, and then took all my clothes and things up to my room. I found that my room was empty, and there was no sign of my roommate. That eased things a bit, although I would have liked to have met her and gotten it over with!

Then I made another trip from my room down to the car to get some more clothes and things, but this time when I got to my room, there was another family! I knew it had to be her—my roommate. Actually meeting each other wasn't bad after all. We introduced ourselves and our families, said a few more words, and that was it! My first impression wasn't too bad.

After our families left for home, my roommate and I had a better chance to get to know each other and found out that we had a lot in common. It was great! I knew then that this year was going to be a good one, and all the worrying had been for nothing.

A Friendly Face

I climbed the stairs exhausted, carrying a suitcase in one hand, a lampshade in the other, my father following with two more suitcases. By the time I got to the third floor of Avis Hall, I'd had it. I was tired, frustrated—frankly lonely and a bit scared. To top it all off, Dad tripped on the landing and sent my new American Tourister suitcases flying down the hall, bumping into walls like in some mad commercial about the durability of luggage. "Damn," he screamed, the veins in his forehead pulsing quickly. I knew trouble was ahead. Whenever Dad's veins pulse, look out!

How would I ever get him to finish unloading the car without screaming at me, making a scene in front of the girls in the dorm, the girls I would have to spend the rest of the year with?

Doors were already opening and heads peering out of cracks. My first year of college would be a disaster just because of a torn piece of carpet and those suitcases still bouncing off walls.

"Find the room quickly," I thought. "Get him into a chair and calmed down." But then again, would there even be a chair in 316? Or would it be an empty room? I'd find out soon enough, for the number 316 glared at me as if it were a gawdy, blinking neon sign beckoning just ahead.

Hesitantly, I turned the key in the lock and pushed the door open, with Dad still muttering about a bruised knee or something. I put my head into the space between the door and the jamb, expecting the worst. But to my surprise, the room wasn't empty at all! It was furnished and decorated, with posters of Aspen and Daytona Beach on the walls, beige curtains, and an area rug. It looked like a page from *Seventeen*'s "All American Dorm Rooms."

And there on a well-made bed sat Alice, my new roomy, dressed in starched khaki shorts and a dark blue knit blouse. "Hi, you must be Sally," she said in a soft Southern drawl. Then she turned down the stereo and looked over at Dad. "And of course you're Mr. Franklin," she remarked, smiling at Dad, a bright blue-eyed smile. "Would you like a glass of iced tea?" Dad's vein shrank slightly and turned decidedly less red before he could utter a subdued "yes."

I knew then that Alice and I would be friends, and my first year of college would be a success.

If you think that "A Friendly Face" is the better paper, we agree. It's alive with vivid images. "Meeting My Roommate," though it is correctly written, lacks the specific details that would bring it to life for the audience. It tells us how the writer felt and what she did: we find out that she was worried, that she went to the dorm, that she took her clothes up to her room, and that she met her roommate and her roommate's family. But these generalizations are never made specific, and the paper is weak because of what it leaves out. Because we don't see, or hear, or feel what the writer saw, or heard, or felt, we are left unsatisfied, not really knowing what went on.

In "A Friendly Face," on the other hand, the details are forceful and energetic. Here are Sally and her father exhausted after climbing three flights of stairs carrying furnishings and suitcases. There is Mr. Franklin shouting, "Damn." Then we can see the suitcases "flying down the hall, bumping into walls like in some mad commercial. . . ." We can hear Sally's mind racing, "Get him into a chair and calmed down." When Mr. Franklin begins to calm down, the veins on his forehead shrink and turn "decidedly less red before he could utter a subdued 'yes.'" The writer gives us enough details about Alice and the room to suggest what kind of person Alice is. She's blue-eyed, Southern, organized, tasteful, and not easily rattled. She certainly knows how to defuse a tense situation, by staying cool and offering Mr. Franklin a glass of iced tea. "A Friendly Face" succeeds because the writer makes the characters and situations come alive with details that appeal to our senses and to our imagination.

Show Don't Tell

As you can see by contrasting the two papers, it's generally better to show than to tell. The writer of "A Friendly Face" doesn't tell us that Alice is neat and "preppy." She shows us Alice's "starched khaki shorts and dark blue knit blouse." She doesn't have to say that the girls in the dorm may have been watching. She shows us "doors were opening and heads peering out of cracks."

You can use the same technique. Do you want your readers to know that a character is nervous? Don't say that he is nervous. Show that his hand is wet and clammy when you shake it. Does the professor in your story smoke too much? Don't tell the readers. Show that his clothes stink from tobacco and that his fingers are discolored by nicotine. Were you uncomfortable sitting in the gym? Show that the bleachers were so rough they left ridges on your rear. Did the judge at traffic court irritate you? Show that her voice sounded like chalk squeaking on a blackboard, sending shivers down your spine.

Adding Details to Sentences

When you describe scenes, you want to sharpen and focus impressions for your readers. You can do so by adding details to main clauses in the form of grammatical structures like participles, appositives, absolutes, and subordinate clauses. Notice the difference between the next two sentences:

What I first noticed when Henry walked in the door was his suit.

What I first noticed when Henry walked in the door was his suit, **rumpled and slightly frayed.**

The first sentence tells that the writer noticed Henry's suit, but we do not know what about the suit caught the writer's eye. In the second sentence, the words **rumpled** and **frayed** furnish that information by giving characteristics of the suit. While some details give characteristics, others distinguish parts. In the next sentence, the writer first tells us that the tennis player's movements are arrogant, then narrows the focus to what in his movements made her come to that conclusion—the way he holds his shoulders and focuses his eyes:

There was a touch of arrogance in the way Jimmy Connors moved around the tennis court—his shoulders hunched, his eyes focused on himself.

Sally uses this technique of adding focusing details to sentences several times in "A Friendly Face." In the opening sentence, for instance, we find out she is exhausted climbing the stairs. Then we are shown the details of the scene in the modifiers that are added to the main clause:

I climbed the stairs exhausted, **carrying a suitcase in one hand, a lampshade in the other, my father following with two more suitcases.**

Sometimes the details you add to your sentences can sharpen the focus by showing that one thing is like something else. Usually you make such comparisons with phrases that begin with **like** or **as**:

The children scampered onto the playground, **like** playful puppies out for a romp.

The breakdancer spun on his shoulder blades, **as** still in motion **as** a top.

Sally says that her suitcases flew down the hall "like in some mad commercial about the durability of luggage," and remarks that the room number glared at her "as if it were a gaudy, blinking neon sign beckoning just ahead." In brief, you can sharpen and focus impressions in your writing by adding details that (a) show accompanying circumstances (b) distinguish parts, or (c) make comparisons, as in the following three sentences:

(a) Down the slope came Peter, **intent on keeping his balance.**

(b) Down the slope came Peter, **his hands tightly clutching the ski poles.**

(c) Down the slope came Peter, **as awkward as a newborn colt trying to walk for the first time.**

You can often add more than one detail to a sentence, as in the next examples:

The math class anxiously waited for the teacher to distribute the exams, some students fidgeting in their seats, like fathers-to-be in a hospital waiting room.

With the full tray on his fingertips, the waiter moved gingerly through the crowded dining room as a tightrope walker might cross a highwire, cautious yet daring.

Remember, though, that you don't have to add details to all your sentences. Sometimes a short, unmodified sentence is just right. In "A Friendly Face," for instance, the brief "I knew trouble was ahead" nicely emphasizes Sally's discomfort at that point by changing the pace from the two longer sentences preceding it. In the best prose, sentences will vary from simple to elaborate, becoming smaller or larger in relation to their meaning and purpose.

Changing Telling Statements into Showing Statements

It's not always enough to add a detail to a sentence in order to make it more vivid and appealing. Sometimes you have to rewrite a telling statement in order to make it a showing statement. For example, the sentence "Larry Byrd is unusually tall" becomes more memorable if you change it into "Larry Byrd ducks his head whenever he comes through a door." The young woman who wrote "Meeting My Roommate" missed an opportunity to stimulate the reader's imagination in her first paragraph when she wrote "I hardly slept." How much more of an image she would have created for the reader if she had written instead, "All night I tossed and turned uncomfortably, twisting my sheets and covers into a tangled mess." Sally, on the other hand, doesn't miss many opportunities to write showing sentences in "A Friendly Face." Notice that she does not say, "Dad got angry," after her father tripped and dropped the suitcases. She shows you how he reacted and what she thought at the time and lets you conclude that he got angry:

> "Damn," he screamed, the veins in his forehead pulsing quickly. I knew trouble was ahead. Whenever Dad's veins pulse, look out!

It's that sort of writing that makes "A Friendly Face" so lively.

What if you were writing about a trip that you and your mother had recently taken and you wanted to indicate that the bellhop who carried your bags in a New York hotel was stiffly courteous? You could make a telling statement to that effect, leaving readers to wonder what it was about the bellhop that made you think he was stiffly courteous:

> A stiffly courteous bellhop carried our bags to the room.

Or you could show what the bellhop did, letting the readers see the bellhop's actions and even hear him speak:

> "May I take your bags, Sir?" the bellhop snapped, picking up my duffel in one hand and—turning precisely, like a drill sergeant —reaching for Mom's suitcase with the other. At the same time, he said, "I'll bring that to your room, Ma'am. Please leave it right there."

Notice that, since the readers can see and hear the bellhop being stiff and courteous in the second version, they don't need to be told how he acted: they can draw the conclusion themselves.

*   *   *

Whether you're writing narrative, explanatory, or persuasive prose, you'll find plenty of opportunities for showing rather than telling. Look for places to add details in order to sharpen images, and be especially careful to change telling statements into showing statements whenever you want your reader to experience rather than merely understand what you are saying.

ADDING DETAILS I

In order to sharpen the focus of the following sentences, add details that give characteristics, that distinguish parts, or that make comparisons. Write at least two versions of each sentence, one with a single modifier, the other with several modifiers.

Example

> The coach demonstrated the reverse layup.
>
> ↓
>
> The coach demonstrated the reverse layup **by driving under the basket and banking the ball off the backboard.**
>
> OR
>
> The coach demonstrated the reverse layup, **balancing the ball on his fingertips, his upper body stretching toward the backboard as gracefully as a ballet dancer doing leaps.**

A. The boys trashed the yard.

B. Jonathan couldn't finish the marathon.

C. The janitor wore mismatched clothes.

D. A helicopter hovers over the brightly lit scene.

E. The fat woman questioned Phil Donahue's guest expert.

SNOWBOY

Combine the following sentences into a narrative essay about a boy who wants to stay out in the snow while his mother wants him to come in for dinner. Add details of your own that will enhance the contrast between Ricky's boyhood dreams and his mother's adult reality.

1. Ricky heard his mother.
2. She was calling him in.
3. Her voice sounded colder than the winter wind.

4. He turned reluctantly from the frozen white walls.
5. He had made the walls.
6. He looked hopefully to the back door.
7. His cheeks were red from hours of play.
8. His nylon snowsuit was a shade darker from the melted snow.

9. No reprieve came.
10. He waved to his day-long companion.
11. His companion was the snowman.
12. He began the trek to his house.
13. The distance was 50 feet.
14. He prolonged every step.
15. He took last glimpses of his empire.

16. He dragged his black golashes through the snow.
17. The dragging was heavy.
18. He thought only of the day's fun.
19. He thought of the snowballs thrown.
20. He thought of the new territories conquered.

21. The warm dinner seemed less inviting than the many mouthfuls of snow.
22. His mother would insist the warm dinner was good for him.
23. He had swallowed snow while crawling.
24. He crawled through his network of tunnels.

25. His only comfort was one last wild plunge.
26. He plunged over the snowy yard.
27. He plunged through an enemy fort.
28. The walls of the fort were already weak.
29. The weakness was from his earlier barrage of iceballs.

30. Ricky's day was ending.

31. It had seemed to go on forever.
32. Now the games were gone.

33. The friends were gone.
34. The runny noses were gone.

35. Ricky lingered awhile on the porch.
36. He stomped his boots clean.
37. He clapped his mittens free of the snow.
38. Snow was frozen in every crease.
39. He wished to return to his real home.
40. The yard was his real home.

41. His mother finally hurried him into the house.
42. She was growing impatient.
43. The house swallowed him for the evening.

MAKING SHOWING STATEMENTS

Change the following telling statements into showing statements. Make the showing statements so vivid that readers can sense the actions and ideas.

Example

The senator spoke defiantly.

↓

The senator shouted, "baloney," to the reporter, punctuating his remark by sharply bashing his fist on the podium.

A. The radio blared.

B. VCRs are popping up all over.

C. The kitten was playful.

D. The teddy bear needed repairs.

E. Mary was depressed.

F. The artist labored over the drawing.

G. The professor lectured quietly.

H. Jennifer was nosy.

I. MTV assaults our senses.

J. Susan tried to look cool and at ease.

TRY AEROBICS

Combine the sentences into a letter from a college freshman to an old friend whom she's trying to interest in an exercise program. Add details from your own experience whenever you can make the letter more interesting and engaging.

Dear Amy,

1. I am glad to see this.
2. You are trying to slim down.

3. You know this.
4. I tried for a long time.
5. I was unsuccessful.

6. But I have slimmed down a lot.
7. And I have felt better, too.
8. This has been during the last month or so.
9. This has been through aerobics.

10. You might try aerobics.

11. Aerobics is great exercise.
12. And it isn't boring.

13. You know this.
14. I could never keep up running.
15. I could never keep up biking.

16. But I have been able to keep up aerobics.
17. And I even like aerobics.

18. I thought I would die.
19. This happened the first time I went to class.

20. Jane dragged me down to the gym.
21. Jane is my roommate.
22. I was protesting all the way.

23. I never liked exercise class in high school.
24. And I thought aerobics class would be like that.

25. It was not like aerobics class.

26. The woman is a dance instructor.
27. She runs our class.
28. She is a slim lady.
29. She is a gorgeous lady.
30. She is a 35-year-old lady.
31. She can bend and stretch in ways.
32. You wouldn't believe the ways.

33. She played a series of rock records.
34. She had taped the records at home.
35. This was for the first class.

36. We did leg stretches and kneebends to Billy Joel.
37. We did leg stretches and kneebends to Michael Jackson.

38. She called out, "one, two, three, four."
39. She called out, "bend, stretch, bend, stretch."

40. I bent all right.
41. I stretched.
42. I pulled.

43. I felt awful the next morning.
44. I felt sore and achy.

45. But I bought some new leotards.
46. I bought some new leg warmers.
47. I went to every session this month.

48. I love it.

49. I can stretch better.
50. I never stretched well before.
51. I can bend farther.
52. I never bent far before.

53. I can touch the floor!
54. I don't have to bend my knees!

55. I feel great now.
56. This happens when I wake up in the morning.

57. The soreness is gone.
58. I've lost five pounds.

59. Do you remember those Calvin Klein jeans?
60. I bought them before I left home.

61. Well, I had not been able to get into them in a couple of months.
62. I had had too many pizzas on weekends.
63. I had had too much beer on weekends.

64. You know this.
65. Weight always goes to my thighs.
66. Weight always goes to my rear end.

67. This morning something happened.
68. I could get into them again.

69. I slid right in!

70. Oh, I was pleased.

71. I'm telling this, Amy.
72. Aerobics is great.

73. It makes you feel good.

74. The doctors say this.
75. It's good for your heart.

76. And it helps you lose weight, too.

77. Why don't you try it?

Love,
Janet

ADDING DETAILS II

In order to sharpen the focus of the following sentences, add details that give characteristics, that distinguish parts, or that make comparisons. Write at least two versions of each sentence, one with a single modifier, the other with several modifiers.

Example

The satellite went out of control.

The satellite went out of control, pirouetting like a weightless dancer marking infinite time.

OR

The satellite went out of control, rising, dipping, and looping haphazardly until it re-entered the atmosphere in a fiery flash.

A. Mick Jagger prances around the stage.

B. The protesters stood at the entrance to the waste dump.

C. Mr. Rogers zipped up his cardigan.

D. The '55 Chevy sits rusting in the yard.

E. The crowd watched the break dancers.

BITTERSWEET

Combine the following sentences into an essay that expresses a young man's personal view of what it's like to live with diabetes, how it makes you different from others. Add details or rephrase sentences when you think there is not enough vividness to make the ideas lifelike and engaging for the reader.

1. My sister yelled this from the kitchen.
2. "Does anyone want this last doughnut?"

3. Mom said, "no."

4. My little brother hollered this.
5. "Go ahead and eat it."
6. He didn't lift his head from his homework.

7. My sister didn't wait for my reply.

8. She knew I would say no.
9. Or maybe I wouldn't answer at all.

10. You see this.
11. I'm diabetic.
12. And so I can't touch sugar.

13. I have to watch my diet carefully.
14. I have to count my calorie intake.
15. I have to keep track of the food that I eat.

16. And, of course, I have to do this.
17. I give myself a shot of insulin every day.
18. I do this for a reason.
19. My pancreas doesn't produce enough insulin.
20. Insulin properly metabolizes blood sugar.
21. Insulin is a hormone.

22. The scene in the kitchen happens to me often for a reason.
23. I have to watch my diet so carefully.

24. I turn down more food than I take.

25. Mothers of my friends frequently ask this.
26. "Would you like some cake?"

27. I have to reply this.
28. "No thank you."

29. One of the guys in the dorm asked this the other night.
30. "Would you like to go out for a pizza?"

31. I said this.
32. "No, I can't."
33. "You see, I'm diabetic."

34. He replied, "oh."
35. His expression changed.

36. He recoiled a bit.
37. It was as if I were a freak or something.

38. The kids knew not to ask.
39. This was in elementary school.

40. The teachers told them.
41. This happened when I was out of the room, of course.

42. And the teachers had orders to keep candy away from me.
43. They had orders to keep other sugared goodies away from me.
44. This was during parties.

45. I would sit there.
46. I would wear a hat like the other kids.
47. But I had a diet soda.
48. I had crackers.
49. My mother knew to send crackers and diet soda to every party.

50. And I sit here now.
51. I am munching a carrot stick.
52. At this time the other guys are pigging out on pizza.

53. The television ads for the Diabetes Association show this.
54. Parents are with children.
55. The children have to take awful shots.

56. The ads imply this.
57. The worst part of diabetes is this.
58. You have to stick a small needle into your skin once a day.

59. That isn't the worst.

60. You get used to needles.

61. You never get used to this.
62. You are different.
63. You have to separate yourself from others at meals.
64. You have to separate yourself from others at parties.
65. You have to separate yourself when others snack to their heart's content.

unit *19*
REVISION

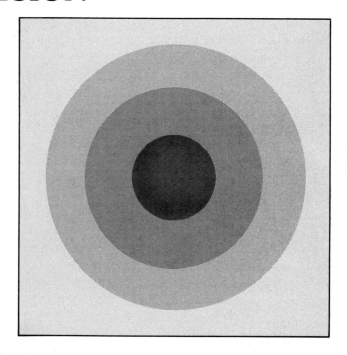

Revision literally means "seeing it again." But in the context of writing, "revision" means more than just "seeing." It means rethinking, reworking, improving what the writer has already written. It means going back through the last sentence or paragraph, or the entire essay; it means sounding out the language, weighing again the choice of words and sentence patterns, pondering the meaning, the direction, the overall effect of the text. Revision is the writer's "flight correction"—a series of checks and adjustments in response to the questions, "Am I on course?" "Am I going where I want to be going?" Pilots must monitor and adjust the plane's altitude, speed, and direction to stay on course; writers must repeatedly measure the looks, the sound, the flow, the sense, the structure of their evolving draft against the tastes and expectations of their intended readers. Revision is, ultimately, a way of making sure that readers understand what the writer has to say.

In a way, this whole book is a series of exercises in revision. By working with the writer's many options for expressing ideas, by learning to change and improve original wordings and syntactic choices for the sake of clarity or effect, you have in fact been practicing revision. This concluding unit tries to put into focus some of the *reasons* why revision is desirable and useful. These reasons all boil down to one overriding need: writers revise in order *to accommodate their readers.*

You can accommodate readers by (1) getting their attention, (2) gaining their confidence, and (3) maintaining their interest.

Getting the Reader's Attention

In an age of intense competition for people's time and attention, a piece of writing that does not create interest *up front* is likely to go unread. Your first revision task is to assure that the title and especially the first sentence of your paper catch the reader's attention. Your options for an introductory sentence include both direct openers and indirect openers such as fronting, a question, a story or example, and partial information that creates suspense.

Direct Openers. Your opening sentence may be a general statement expressing the controlling idea—a pattern characteristic of direct paragraphs. Such a statement should be clear and concise. The following revision eliminates the awkward repetition of the word "different" and moves the key phrase "liquor advertisements" to the front of the sentence, where it is immediately noticed:

> Looking at different types of liquor advertisements, one can see that different advertisers use different methods to get the consumer to buy their products.

> ↓

> Liquor advertisements are designed to appeal to a variety of potential customers.

Indirect Openers. A common option to such a direct but general opening sentence is the use of specific and concrete language to establish rapport with the reader and then lead to the controlling idea. Your many options for an indirect opener include sentences that begin with some "fronted" key words appealing to the reader's senses or establishing some pleasant associations; that ask a thought-provoking question; that cite an unusual example or story; or that give just enough information to create suspense.

Fronting. To create more interest, you might rewrite the opening sentence about the liquor ads as follows:

> Romance, glamour, exotic travel—whatever your secret fantasies, liquor ads skillfully combine a subtle promise of their fulfillment with an inviting message about the advertised products.

Here the fronted words "Romance, glamour, exotic travel" immediately evoke the image of something desirable but perhaps beyond reach—an image which many readers will find inviting.

Opening Question. Questions tend to stimulate thinking about answers, especially when the answer is not obvious. By opening your essay with a question, you can immediately engage the reader's interest:

> Recent research has shown evidence of "body type bias" among school superintendents in hiring high school principals. It seems that tall and slim applicants have a much better chance of being hired than short and chubby ones. These results may suggest society's image of an ideal leader.

↓

> Are you short? Overweight? Or both? If so, forget about becoming a high school principal. Recent research has shown that school superintendents rate tall and slim applicants much higher than short and chubby ones. Perhaps these results say something about society's ideal image of a leader.

Story or Example. People are naturally interested in others, and a "live" opener such as a story or concrete example—instead of a general statement—can help stimulate that interest:

Some companies use handwriting analysis to evaluate applicants for demanding positions. Such analysis is used to measure emotional responses, mental processes, and capacities to achieve—criteria that the companies consider important.

↓

The more your handwriting leans to the right the more passionate you are. If it leans left, you are emotionally inhibited. Do you round the top of your letter "m"? Then your thinking pattern is slow and methodical. A V-shaped M-top shows you to be an investigative thinker, while a needle-point M-top reveals a fast, comprehensive pattern of thinking. If you apply for an important position in some companies, your handwriting may be subjected to such an analysis to determine your suitability for the job.

Creating Suspense. You can often get the reader to read on by implying but withholding some vital information. You can create such suspense—and thus kindle the reader's curiosity—by using a word (commonly a pronoun) for which there is no preceding context or referent. For example, the opening sentence "It happened quickly, without a warning." will invite your reader to wonder "What? What happened?" and hence to read on to find out. Here is another example:

Noise is becoming an important environmental problem in our society.

↓

From everywhere it assaults us. It gets ahead of us; we take vacations to escape from it, but it waits for us at our destinations when we arrive. It pollutes the environment, jostles our psyches, rattles our nerves, and erodes the tiny delicate hairs in our ears that transport sound to our brains. It is the brutal invader of inner space—noise.

Gaining the Reader's Confidence

An effective opening sentence will engage your readers' interest. But to gain their confidence, your paper needs a clear focus, a proper

sense of the writer's presence, and a tone consistent with your purpose.

Focusing the Reader's Attention

Before going too far into a paper, most readers want a sense of the
paper's direction and of the writer's purpose. The next paragraph,
though it begins with an intriguing foreign expression, does not
focus on any clear idea:

> *Hablar o no hablar.* To speak or not to speak—a foreign lan-
> guage, that is. Many college students wonder whether to take
> foreign language courses or spend their time on other subjects.
> It's easy to learn a language as a child, but oh boy, Spanish 101
> is a different story. Many colleges require a foreign language,
> though. Apparently the study of foreign languages is becoming
> more popular in the States. Wouldn't it be nice to be a kid again
> and start learning a foreign language from scratch?

In this paragraph the initial issue—that "college students wonder
whether to take foreign language courses"—is never resolved. The
following revised version focuses the reader's attention by introducing a clear controlling idea: that if you want to learn a foreign
language well, the best time to start is while you are a child:

> *Hablar o no hablar.* To speak or not to speak—a foreign lan-
> guage, that is. For many college students the dilemma is
> whether to take courses in a foreign language or in other
> subjects instead. If you have never moved your tongue and lips
> in strange ways before, Spanish 101 can be rough indeed! The
> culprit is not the course nor the language—it's your age. You
> only wish you were a child again when your tongue and lips
> moved freely and Spanish 101 would have been a cinch.

Controlling the Writer's Presence

Some people are important enough so that what they think or how
they feel about certain matters, including themselves, can be worth-

while information for a broad audience. Most of us are not in that category. By calling attention to ourselves as writers, unless for good reason, we divert attention away from the topic of our paper. By doing so we erode the readers' confidence that the text serves *their* interests.

Here is an example of writer-centered prose, one that is characteristic of unskilled writing:

> From my childhood I conceived that I possessed undeniable moral convictions which governed the daily origin of my beliefs. I rarely dwelled on their origin until recently. I always assumed that my parents were the origin of my beliefs. However, my English class discussion of Horatio Alger led me to a fantastic discovery. I have concluded that my moral views could stem from a popular nineteenth-century ideology which is often nicknamed "Algerism."

Such "I-centered" writing may be appropriate when you are asked to give a personal testimony, opinion, or experience. But to most readers, this paragraph will be interesting only insofar as it suggests a more general truth: young people sometimes discover that their moral convictions are shaped by a literary or cultural heritage rather than their parents' influence. Accordingly, a revised version would focus on that truth and play down the writer's own process of discovering it:

> You believe in honesty, industry, and frugality. You value education. You don't smoke or drink. You obviously have strong moral convictions, a commitment to traditional values. Where did these values come from? How did you acquire them? You learned them from your parents, of course—right? Wrong— maybe. Sometimes young people discover, as I did, that their moral convictions may have been shaped by a literary or cultural heritage rather than their parents' influence. One such heritage is the popular nineteenth-century ideology often nicknamed "Algerism."

Note that even the revised version includes an instance of "I"; there is nothing wrong with that pronoun if it is not overused.

Finding the Right Tone

The tone we choose in communicating with others follows from our personal relationships. Whether we talk "up" or "down" to our audience, choose our words carefully or with abandon, tease and become "personal" or remain distant and formal—all this is normally determined by the speaker's sense of how well we know each other or how good (or bad) we want that relationship to be. The tone of your paper may be understood as its message; if you lose control of your tone, you may end up getting the wrong message across.

The next three paragraphs are versions of a note you might write to your landlord about a broken furnace. How would you describe the tone of each?

Mr. Berry, did you know we in Apt. 234 are not Eskimos? Frankly, we're tired of camping out in an igloo, especially for $285 a month. You've known over a week that our furnace was out. Should we present our next reminder on a silver tray?

↓

Dear Mr. Berry, this is another reminder that the furnace unit in Apt. 234 is still out and we feel like we're living in an igloo. Mr. Beery, it's *cold* up here and we would rather not build a fire in the middle of the living room, though we have considered it. We need the furnace repaired right away. Please do something.

↓

Dear Mr. Berry, we hope you haven't forgotten about us poor souls with shivering bodies but warm hearts in Apt. 234. As you know, the furnace konked out on us over a week ago, and we have been wondering when it might be fixed. We know you have had other things to worry about lately, and if you want us to, perhaps we can call the furnace repair man on your behalf. We'll be glad to help.

These revisions from one version to another did not change the purpose of your note to Mr. Berry, they changed only the tone. But as the tone changed, so did the message—from "you don't care about your tenants and we don't respect you" to "come on, you are a reasonable guy, get on this case" to "you're slow but you mean well and we basically like you."

Maintaining the Reader's Interest

Good writing has energy and life. You can enhance your paper's vitality—and your reader's continued interest—by varying the length of your sentences; by putting vivid, interesting details *in* and by taking empty, dead words *out* of your paper; and by constructing smooth, readable paragraphs.

Sentence Length

In reading over your draft you may discover that many of your sentences are either too short, or too long, or too uniform in length. If so, you may wish to revise.

Too Short: Putting It Together. If your paper contains too many short, overly simple sentences, it may create the impression of being simple-minded in content. Such sentences may seem easy to read, but by breaking up ideas that are closely related, they can in fact make for choppy, disjointed reading:

> The Beatles' tune "All You Need Is Love" became the theme song for young people in the Sixties. It first appeared in their "Yellow Submarine" album in 1967. It was written by John Lennon and Paul McCartney. The song was a great success on the Beatles' "Magical Mystery Tour." It has a pleasant tune and lyrics. They are easy to remember and sing along: "All you need is love; All you need is love; All you need is love, love; Love is all you need."

Now compare the revised version in which some of the sentences are combined. In what respects might this version be an improvement?

> "All You Need Is Love. . . ." This tune became a theme song for young people in the Sixties. Written by John Lennon and Paul McCartney, the song first appeared in the Beatles' "Yellow

Submarine" album in 1967 and became a great success on their "Magical Mystery Tour." It has a pleasing tune and lyrics that are easy to remember and sing along: "All you need is love; All you need is love; All you need is love, love; Love is all you need."

Too Long: Taking It Apart. Longer sentences are not necessarily better. A long sentence needs revision especially when it is too complex for easy reading:

> In view of recent reports on the decline and devaluation of the college degree because of the widespread "anything goes" curriculum and because professors are more interested in research than in teaching in order to get tenured and promoted, with the curricula succumbing to a marketplace philosophy where, as one report points out, students are shoppers and professors are merchants of learning, the basic question is how this mentality can be changed and some rhyme or reason to requirements for the undergraduate degree introduced.

↓

> According to recent reports, the value of the college degree has declined. Experts blame this decline on the widespread "anything goes" curriculum and on professors' preoccupation with research at the expense of teaching to assure their tenure and promotion. Some critics claim that the curricula have given way to a marketplace philosophy "where students are shoppers and professors are merchants of learning." One wonders how this mentality can be changed and some rhyme or reason to requirements for the undergraduate degree introduced.

Too Uniform: Mixing Short and Long. Too many sentences of approximately the same length and structure tend to create a lulling, monotonous effect. In the following example the revision helps perk up the prose by introducing some sentence variety without changing the content:

> Anteaters are animals with long snouts that are common to tropical America and Africa and feed on termites or white ants. The

ant bear, the three-toed anteater, and the silky anteater are common types that have small mouths but long tongues which can be extended to catch insects. Anteaters have claws that are long and hooked for digging into insect nests, and strong and sharp for self-defense. The anteater is a nocturnal animal that sleeps during the day and curls her tail around her for protection against the elements.

↓

Anteaters are mammals common to tropical America and Africa. With their long snouts they feed on white ants—termites. The common types of anteaters—the ant bear, the three-toad anteater, and the silky anteater—have small mouths, long tongues that can be extended to catch insects, and claws that are both long and hooked for digging into insect nests, as well as strong and sharp for self-defense. Like other nocturnal animals, the anteater sleeps during the day, her tail curled around her for protection against the elements.

Putting Details In

Revision in the next example changes an empty, vague paragraph into one that—through its concrete language—dramatically puts the message across:

Traveling is an important part of one's general education. By traveling one can experience other cultures firsthand and thus come to understand one's own better. This is especially true when one has a chance to speak to people in a foreign country.

↓

Traveling through other countries can be a profound education. I had hitch-hiked to this one border crossing at the desert town of Shola, and while waiting for the gate to open I struck up a conversation with an elderly man, a native of the area, who had been at the border since dawn. In his accented but fluent English he spoke of the hardships of his people, of their daily humiliations under the present government. He pointed his trembling finger toward the city, where he was born and where he now worked but which he had to leave every day by sundown for reasons of government "security." Then the border gate opened and I waited for my turn. Instead, the guard ushered me and the other foreigners through, past the old man and his folks. Puzzled and embarrassed, I could only mumble "I'm sorry" as I went by him; with his head high and a grateful smile on his sun-worn face, he said "thank you." I never saw him again. He may never know how much he has contributed to my education.

Taking Empty Words Out

Words that are used only for "padding" are likely to take the punch out of your writing. Good writing wastes no words. By removing empty words and combining the remaining sentence parts, you can increase the energy of your sentences:

> Although not everyone may agree, I think it is true that each of us is made up of several different personalities. Those different personalities cause us to behave differently with different groups of people and in different situations. There are actually quite a few reasons for people to change their behavior. These reasons include the following: we want to be accepted into a peer group, to please our parents, or to achieve personal goals.

↓

> It seems that each of us has several different personalities which cause us to change our behavior from one situation to another —whether our purpose is to be accepted into a peer group, to please our parents, or to achieve personal goals.

Revising for Readability

Good writing is free from distractions that may divert the reader's attention from the content. One type of distraction is "eyesores" on a page—visual blemishes ranging from torn edges, spots, and cross-outs to typos or misspellings, wrong capitalization or punctuation. Other distractions include errors in grammar or word choice. Re-reading your paper to eliminate such flaws—commonly called *proof-reading*—will help you produce a clean text, one which is visually and mechanically readable. But in this unit—and throughout this book—we are more concerned with revision that will enhance the effectiveness and readability of sentences and paragraphs.

Coherence. A piece of prose is readable if it minimizes the reading effort for the reader. In particular, good writing helps the reader to make mental connections from sentence to sentence and thus to understand without undue effort the progression and development of the writer's ideas.

The following paragraph lacks coherence and is difficult to follow because the connections are unclear or missing. The revision creates a more readable paragraph by improving those connections:

Whether the four years in school might not be better spent on a job is often questioned by college students. It will return an average of 9 to 14 percent increased earning power over a lifetime. Recent research on the benefits of higher education indicates this. College graduates enjoy their jobs more than those without a degree. Stronger family bonds and smaller, healthier families are on the horizon.

↓

College students often wonder whether their four years in college might not be better spent on a job. They need not be concerned. Recent research on the benefits of higher education indicates that a college degree will return an average of 9 to 14 percent increased earning power over a lifetime. Furthermore, college graduates will enjoy their jobs more than those without a degree, and have stronger family bonds and smaller, healthier families. Apparently college is worth it.

Proportion and Balance. "Readable" can also mean that the flow of your sentences gives the reader pleasure or creates excitement. One revising option to help make your writing forceful and perhaps elegant is the use of repetition:

The parking situation on campus is intolerable. It cannot be solved by more ticketing. Raising the cost of parking permits won't work either. Why do we need more resolutions by the

Student Senate and by Faculty Council? The president has appointed a committee to study the problem, but it has not come up with a solution. There is only one possible solution: build more parking lots.

↓

The intolerable parking situation on campus will be solved by neither more ticketing nor increased parking permit fees, neither more resolutions nor more committee studies. It will be solved only by building more parking lots.

* * *

Revision gives you a chance to have second thoughts about what you have already written and to improve your draft for the reader's benefit. The following exercises provide practice in getting the reader's attention, gaining the reader's confidence, and maintaining the reader's interest.

GETTING THE READER'S ATTENTION

Revise each of the following paragraphs by using an indirect opener such as fronting, a question, a story or example, or partial information to create suspense. In each case, also consider revising the title. Make any other changes that will help get the reader's attention.

Example

Hemingway

> Ernest Miller Hemingway was born in 1898 and committed suicide in 1961. He wrote of people living dangerous lives, and he lived—and died—in the manner of his heroes. His theme was stoic courage, expressed in tales of resolute soldiers, bum-luck athletes, aged fishermen, and above all bullfighters. He once said that he liked to write "commencing with the simplest things, and one of the simplest things and most fundamental is violent death."

↓

The Simplest Thing

> He wrote of people living dangerous lives. His theme was stoic courage, expressed in tales of resolute soldiers, bum-luck athletes, aged fishermen, and—above all—bullfighters. He once said that he liked to write "commencing with the simplest things, and one of the simplest things and most fundamental is violent death." Ernest Miller Hemingway lived—and died—by the code of his heroes. Born in 1898, he committed suicide in 1961.

Hospitals

> Hospitals no longer point to the training and qualifications of their doctors, their good track record in surgery, and the professionalism of their nursing staff as the only reasons for their

good reputation. Now they find that diplomas on the wall are not enough to fill their beds. The competition for patients—guests!—has created a new buzzword: hospitality.

Invention

The U.S. Patent Office estimates that there are some 2.5 million Americans out there working on their inventions—not just in high-tech labs but in garages or down the basement, trying to come up with a better wrench or hairpin. Invention seems to be the last frontier where individuals can still make a fortune with their own ideas.

Mickey Mouse

Disney characters and other memorabilia are among the most valued collectible items the world over. Mickey Mouse leads the parade, with old Mickey Mouse watches and wind-up toys, playing cards, and storybooks constantly rising in value. To many collectors Mickey may still be what one journalist called him in the 1930s: "the best-known and most popular international figure of the day."

GAINING THE READER'S CONFIDENCE I

Revise each paragraph below by sharpening the focus on a single controlling idea. Make any other changes that will help gain the reader's confidence.

Example

Americans have a very intimate relationship with their automobiles. The car provides the operator with an escape from almost anything that troubles him. If he is to escape, it might as well be to an exotic place. Monte Carlo is such a place, and Monte Carlo is a luxury car with a plush interior and a wide range of options. Through elegant design and a name suggesting an exotic place, the manufacturers have implied that their vehicle offers a temporary escape to a place like Monte Carlo.

↓

The fancy name for your late model car was not picked out of a hat. It was selected after extensive and expensive market research on the values held by targeted customers. For example, many Americans seem to yearn for exotic places where they can escape from their mundane todays and tomorrows. So why not sell them luxury cars with exotic names that will make them *think* they are escaping? Monte Carlo! Elegant design, plush interior, all those extras, and it's all at your fingertip. The exciting casinos, romantic alleys, and warm beaches of the real place are just around the corner.

A. The U.S. government has a "crisis relocation" plan designed to evacuate 80 percent of urban residents from about 400 high-risk areas in case of an imminent nuclear attack. Presumably 20 percent couldn't be moved or would refuse. Some of the 3000 host sites would be in rural areas up to 300 miles away. The 20 percent estimated dead translates into more than 40 million people—20 times the number of Americans killed in all previous wars. And after the attack, epidemics unlike any since the Middle Ages can be expected. There will be immense social chaos. Nuclear weapons kill not only directly but also indirectly, by breaking down the man-made and natural systems on which individual lives collectively depend.

B. Humans today have a longer life span than ever before, and coupled with our gift of life comes a complex society and the problems of being a member of it. You look at the decisions you must make every day and compare them to the decisions of your parents and grandparents, and you find the right answers much harder to discover. But how *do* you discover them? It's nice to find the time to escape from the pressures that tax your brain. We were given a natural gift to deal with this frightening world we live in—the gift of the imagination.

C. Very few men in history can claim the great esteem and admiration paid to this nation's sixteenth president, Abraham Lincoln. Though much of the Lincoln image is based on a romanticized version of the man, certainly his varied activities and interests helped create the image. The conception of Lincoln as "the common, familiar-as-an-old-shoe, average citizen" endeared him to the public. He acquired America's trust. He was renowned for pursuing his goals, through all hardships, if he felt that their realization would benefit mankind.

GAINING THE READER'S CONFIDENCE II

Revise each of the following paragraphs either by de-emphasizing the writer's presence or by finding the right tone, as indicated in parentheses. Make any other changes that will help gain the reader's confidence.

Example

Thanksgiving, huh? What a farce. You had better know that nobody gives thanks and no one feasts on Thanksgiving Day in the tepees of an Indian cultural and spiritual encampment in the Black Hills. They have nothing to be thankful for. The next time you munch on your turkey breast or savor mother's cornbread filling to commemorate that successful harvest in 1621, just think of how Thanksgiving really started, according to some documents recently found: as a celebration of a successful massacre of Wampanoag Indians. So much for Thanksgiving. (Make the tone less hostile and more objective.)

Not everyone celebrates Thanksgiving by feasting and giving thanks. While most Americans believe that Thanksgiving Day commemorates the first successful colonial harvest in 1621, some Native Americans discount this tradition and claim—based on some documents recently found—that the colonists' first true Thanksgiving was a celebration of a massacre of Wampanoag Indians. It is understandable if in some tepees in the Black Hills, no turkey is served at candlelight on the fourth Thursday of November.

A. Did you know that it is commonly thought that left-handedness is an inherited trait, like blue eyes or blond hair? Well, it is. But doctors—when they are not playing golf—are now beginning to investigate the possibility that left-handedness is caused by stressful births, which reduce the supply of good old oxygen to the left side of the noggin, the side that controls language functions and right-handedness. In other words, the attending doc goofs up the delivery and you end up with your wrong paw the right one! The incidence of stressful births is twice as high among southpaws than righties, and dullards with language disorders have a higher incidence of left-handedness than the normal population. It may be that left-handedness is the most common and harmless effect of birth stress. But then again, what do doctors know, anyway—besides playing golf? (Make the tone consistent and more respectful of doctors.)

B. Many people think commuting from home to a college is the worst thing they can do. But I live near a college, and my experience is different. For example, contrary to the belief that commuters do not have much of a social life I have found the exact opposite. I belong to the OCS (Organization of Commuting Students) which plans many activities, and I belong to a sorority which sponsors activities also. I go downtown with my friends on the weekends and I also participate in many campus-sponsored activities. But commuting can also save you money and inconvenience. I not only save the cost of room and board, I don't have to worry about getting home for holidays! One of my friends has to take a bus for 6 hours to get home, and another has to ride to the airport and then fly three planes (and back), just for a day and a half at home. Commuters never have such problems. (De-emphasize the writer's presence and focus on the advantages of commuting in general.)

C. When we think of the "Wild West," a picture comes to mind of crowded, music-filled saloons, rugged men usually equipped with a cowboy hat and a holster, and inevitably, petite, daintily dressed women. Some people think this picture—especially of the women—is over-romanticized because it suggests that (heaven forbid!) all women looked and acted like women. There were also in that Wild West, they say, women with a "great impact on frontier life," women who skinned mules and drove the stagecoach and worked on the railroad—like Calamity Jane. Calamity Jane!? Are today's women supposed to take pride in ruthless, uncultured forerunners like Jane Hickok (alias Calamity Jane), an outlaw with a raging temper who could "stand up to men" only by bullying them with an untamed gun? Surely, women can do better than that. (Make the tone less sexist and more understanding toward Calamity Jane.)

MAINTAINING THE READER'S INTEREST I

Revise each of the following paragraphs using the strategy indicated in parentheses: by supplying concrete details or by making changes in sentence length. Make any other changes that will help maintain the reader's interest.

Example

Did you ever reserve a room in a foreign hotel? They often don't have the luxuries Americans have come to expect. But we didn't always expect such luxuries. In fact, until the 1850s no American hotel offered private baths. Until the 1830s none even offered private rooms. Guests slept "spoon fashion." And there weren't even separate accommodations for men and women. (Supply concrete details.)

↓

Did you ever reserve a room in a foreign hotel **only to discover that you had to share a bathroom with everyone on your floor? That you had to open the windows and hope for a breeze? Or that you had to sleep in under-size beds?** Americans have come to expect such luxuries as **individual bathrooms, air conditioning, and double beds.** But we didn't always. In fact, until the 1850s no American hotel offered private baths, and until the 1830s none even offered private rooms. Guests slept "spoon fasion," **often sharing beds with strangers, as Ishmael did with Queequeg in Melville's *Moby Dick*.** And there weren't even separate accommodations for men and women.

A. In creating the endearing "Peanuts" comic strip over 30 years ago, Charles M. Schultz has provided hours of pleasure for generations of Americans. Through the antics of a group of cartoon characters, he has vividly represented the joy and embarrassment, the fun and friendship of childhood years. The "Peanuts Gang" and the world that surrounds them appeal to us all— perhaps because each of the characters represents a different facet of the human personality. (Supply concrete details.)

B. Americans seem to like their history fictionalized and their fiction laced with history, which explains the success of novels like *Ragtime* and *The Confessions of Nat Turner* and also provides a clue to the success of the television phenomenon called "docudrama," that is, history and biography spiced with enough exaggeration or fabrication to make it fresh and titillating, with docudramas like "Roots" and "Shogun" being popular because they have both the excitement of fiction and the easy identification of history—and although the critics complain of historical inaccuracies in such TV fare, the public seems more concerned with a good story than with historically accurate details. (Break up the sentence into several shorter sentences as you deem appropriate.)

C. Ray Kroc opened his first restaurant in 1955. He was a milkshake machine salesman. He gambled his life savings by investing in this restaurant. He did so in the belief that Americans would rather wolf down a meal than linger over it, as Europeans do. His gamble paid off. In 1978 Kroc opened the 5000th store in his chain. Stores in the chain continue to multiply all over the world. They are multiplying in Europe, too, changing the eating habits of young people. The golden arches have become a symbol of American culinary culture. Kroc had revolutionized the world's food industry with a new concept of food. It is hygienic, copious, and quick. It is the Big Mac. (Combine some of the sentences as you deem appropriate.)

MAINTAINING THE READER'S INTEREST II

Revise each of the paragraphs below following the strategy indicated in parentheses: by eliminating wordiness, by improving the coherence, or by creating sentence proportion and balance. Make any other changes that will help maintain the reader's interest.

Example

Earlier in this century, during the late twenties and early thirties, there was an attempt made by the U.S. government to outlaw the use of alcohol. Although it was formed with good intentions and with the best interests of the country in mind, prohibition backfired and was one of the biggest flops of the century. In retrospect, it was naive to suppose that people would stop drinking and would obey the law. They didn't. So what happened was that the government lost millions of dollars in taxable revenues yearly—something that it could ill afford—while at the same time moonshiners thrived and smugglers flourished. Clearly, this is not what the government had in mind. But the end result was the same: by "drying up" the United States, prohibition sent millions of rural citizens sprawling to the backwoods to make highly potent but impure and dangerous alcohol. Prohibition had another unforeseen effect, equally undesirable: the emergence of "boot-leggers," organized criminals who boosted their profits at the expense of the American government—well, actually more like at the expense of the taxpayer. (Make the paragraph more concise by eliminating wordiness.)

↓

During the twenties and early thirties, the U.S. government attempted to outlaw the use of alcohol. But Prohibition backfired. While the government lost millions in tax revenues, illegal booze produced by moonshiners or smuggled into the country by rum runners kept the country as "wet" as it had ever been. Obviously, the people never intended to stop drinking, and so they refused to obey the law. The continued demand for alcohol served to boost the profits of organized crime at the government's expense and turn the Mafia into a big-time business.

A. As news reports inform us from time to time, elected politicians and unelected entrepreneurs can get into an awful lot of trouble with the federal government for "laundering" money through Caribbean bank accounts. Now doing your wash is of course not illegal, but that is *not* what politicians and entrepreneurs do with their money in the Caribbean banks. Where, then, does the word "laundering" money come from? You will be surprised to know that in the early 1900s the U.S. Treasury actually did *wash* money. It had a machine that washed, rinsed, and dried old bills. Workers then ironed the bills, which were put back in circulation. But after 1921 the Treasury Department began to destroy old money rather than launder it. Did it run out of soap? The truth is, they realized that laundered money feels different and is easier to counterfeit. (Make the paragraph more concise by eliminating wordiness.)

B. Most people think of archeological expeditions as fascinating treasure hunts to uncover the glories of the past. The strange and magnificent artifacts in King Tut's tomb were discovered in the 1920s, and the Dead Sea Scrolls contained important religious documents. Most expeditions are tedious to anyone but the dedicated scholar interested in the mundane, everyday existence of ancient peoples. Insects, poor food, bad weather, primitive accommodations, and meddling by local officials wear out the archeologist's patience on the site. Glittering monuments of civilizations are hoped for. The archeologist has to be satisfied with pottery shards from ancient trash heaps, more often than not. (Improve the coherence.)

C. The image of the movie hero has changed in recent years. No longer does he have to be tall, strong, and firm like Clark Gable. Now he can be short, fragile, and sensitive like Woody Allen. He doesn't have to be like Cary Grant any more—cool, detached, and well groomed. Like Dustin Hoffman, he can be neurotic, involved, and unkempt now. Like Hoffman, he can even wear a skirt and still be a hero. (Heroine??) (Create sentence proportion or balance.)

SUGGESTIONS FOR WRITING

Narrative Topics

In narrative writing, you try to tell a story so that your readers experience what is happening. Your aim is less to explain or to inform than to share an experience. For this reason you will probably want to use specific, concrete, and (probably) personal details. Although most good stories do not have an obvious moral or lesson, they often have a point or a theme: they do try to say something about the human experience. Above all, a good story is interesting to read.

1. Tell a story about being afraid.
2. Tell a story about the last time you cried (or felt like crying but didn't).
3. Tell a story about a time you apologized to someone and really meant it (or should have apologized but didn't).
4. You just received a letter from this year's editor of your high school yearbook. She is asking you and several others to write a story titled either "A Great Day in High School" or "A Sad Day in High School" for possible inclusion in this year's yearbook. Write a story about a great day or a sad day that you remember from high school.
5. Tell a story about discovering that you—or someone else—had more guts than you had thought.
6. Tell a story about doing something you knew you shouldn't have done (or about almost doing it).
7. Tell a story about discovering prejudice or bigotry in yourself or someone else.
8. Tell a story about an argument or quarrel—yours or someone else's.
9. Tell a story about one of the funniest things that's ever happened to you.
10. Tell a story about getting or being lost.
11. According to a popular song, breaking up is hard to do. Tell a story that illustrates this point.
12. In order to qualify for a scholarship, you are asked by a local

civic organization to show your love for either God or country. Tell a story that demonstrates either your religious values or your patriotism.

13. Tell a story about being rejected (by another person or by a group) or about rejecting someone else.
14. Tell a story about the last time you hit someone or someone hit you.
15. A prospective employer specifies as part of the job application that each candidate write a story of 500 words illustrating his or her honesty and sense of responsibility. Write the story so that you will get the job.
16. Tell a story about a time when you disliked yourself.
17. Tell a story about a time when it felt great to be alive.
18. Tell a story about the beginning of a love or friendship.
19. Think back to your years in elementary school, and quickly list (in no more than five minutes) whatever events and happenings you remember from those. Then choose the one you remember most fully, and write a story about it that you will later share with your family during Thanksgiving or Christmas vacation.
20. Write a story on a topic of your choice.

Descriptive Topics

In descriptive writing, you describe an object, a place, a person or group of people, an activity, or an event so as to make your readers feel what you felt, sense what you sensed, and experience what you experienced. Good description often relies on showing rather than on telling, and in order to show, you will probably want to use specific and concrete details and illustrations. Because description and narration overlap, you might want to consider writing a descriptive paper on one of the narrative topics.

1. Visit a local nursery school or kindergarten and write a description of the children at play that will appear in the school's advertising brochure.
2. Describe your reactions to a work of art—a painting or a piece of sculpture—that you especially like or dislike.
3. Describe an exciting event—like a football game, circus, rock concert, or panty raid—in order to communicate its excitement to your readers.

4. Describe a place that is special for you—a roller rink or amusement park, an athletic field or playground, a cabin on a lake or a bench under a tree, a farm, bar, or pizza parlor—in order to make your readers sense its specialness.
5. Describe someone that you either love or hate in order to make your readers feel what you feel.
6. Describe a college party so that someone who's never been to one gets a feeling of what it's like.
7. Describe what it's like downtown after the football team has won a big game.
8. Describe what goes on at a fraternity or sorority rush party so that your friend who will attend one next week knows what to expect.
9. Describe what it was like to do something special for the first time—like driving, drinking, flying, making love, waterskiing, hang gliding, or traveling abroad.
10. That special person you met this spring in Fort Lauderdale has written to ask, "Is the person I met on the beach the real you?" Answer the question in a letter that describes "the real you."
11. Describe a trip that you took by yourself or with others—to a city, to the ocean, to a national park, to a college, or to some other place.
12. Your kid brother is thinking about trying out for the wrestling team (track squad, school play, newspaper staff), but he isn't sure whether he'll like it or not. Describe a typical practice session to give him a sense of what it's like and whether he'll find it enjoyable.
13. Describe how you felt when you were forced to spend some time with someone you didn't like—say on a blind date.
14. Describe the meeting of two people—friends, relatives, or lovers —who haven't seen each other for a long time.
15. The psychiatrist you have an appointment to see next month wants you to write "an honest description of your inner self." Do it.
16. In order to get along better with your parents (or sister or friend), describe for them an aspect of yourself that they've never really recognized or understood.
17. Describe a city you've visited—or a foreign country—so that others would want to visit it, too.
18. Take an object or set of objects that you once cared deeply about—perhaps a bike, a car, a set of electric trains, a doll, a pair

of roller skates, a teddy bear, a set of baseball cards, a tree hut, a hat—and describe it to a friend so that he or she comes to feel how emotionally important it was to you.

19. Describe what happens on a holiday at your home in order to give an outsider a sense of the relationships among the members of your family.

20. Write on a topic of your choice that makes use of description.

Explanatory Topics

In explanatory writing, you try to explain to your readers something they do not already know. When they have read what you've written, you want them to say, "Wow, I never understood that before" or "Now I see things much more clearly." But a good explanatory paper is interesting as well as informative. To create interest, remember to be concrete and specific, and try at least occasionally to use narration and description whenever they can help clarify, develop, or illustrate the central idea of your paper.

1. Explain why so many people watch television soap operas (or television game shows).

2. Explain the appeal of any single television program— "M*A*S*H," "Dallas," "Hill Street Blues," "60 Minutes," or any other.

3. Explain the effectiveness of any magazine advertisement that makes you want to run out and buy the advertised product. (Submit the magazine ad along with your paper.)

4. Explain what you can learn about college students from their graffiti.

5. Write a paper explaining to yourself some question you really want to answer—like (a) why weren't you as popular in high school as you wanted to be? (b) why are you no longer close to someone who was once your best friend? (c) why do you feel differently about your parents than you used to? (d) why do you like certain kinds of music and not other kinds? or (e) why do you both like and dislike some of your friends?

6. Explain why your favorite college or professional sports team will (or will not) win the league championship next season.

7. Write a unified summary of your intellectual interests and achievements for the scholarship committee of your college.
8. Explain the reasons for the success of any musical group, single performer, album, or single song.
9. Explain how you have overcome a prejudice (racial, ethnic, religious, class, or sexual).
10. Explain in a letter to your high school principal (or teacher or coach) why (or why not) your high school experience adequately prepared you for college.
11. Explain what the toys children buy tell us about the adult world.
12. Explain why people swear (or explain what we can learn about ourselves from the kind of words we consider "dirty" or "obscene").
13. Explain in a letter to a close friend why you believe that sleeping around is immoral (or not immoral).
14. Explain to your classmates how you go about completing a writing assignment. What, exactly, do you do between the moment an assignment is announced and the moment you submit your completed paper? Be as honest as you can in analyzing your own activities.
15. Explain why so many men are male chauvinists.
16. Explain in a letter to your priest, minister, or rabbi why you pray —or why you do not.
17. Decide what is your favorite book of all time—or your favorite movie. Then explain to a close friend why the book or movie means so much to you.
18. Explain why people go to demolition derbies (or amusement parks, rock concerts, stock car races, or any other event).
19. Explain why a large number of Americans do not vote (or do not belong to either major political party).
20. Explain what you can learn about college students from the kinds of parties they throw.
21. Explain in a letter to your parents why you are going to change your major (or why you want to transfer to another school).
22. Explain the major reasons why you and your friends become embarrassed.
23. Explain in a letter to your parents why God has recently become more (or less) important to you.
24. Explain how a recent rule change has affected the way a sport is played.

25. Explain the emotional and psychological reasons for joining a sorority or a fraternity.
26. Explain why any television program, movie, or comic strip is funny.
27. Explain to someone with a record of failure how you go about meeting and getting to know members of the opposite sex on a college campus.
28. A good friend is planning to visit a city (or other geographical area) that you know well, but he or she can only spend a day there. Explain to your friend how best to spend his or her limited time.
29. Explain in a humorous essay how *not* to do something—how not to go on a diet, how not to study for a final examination, how not to prepare for spring break at Daytona Beach, how not to choose a major, how not to exercise, how not to win the affection of the person who sits just in front of you in Sociology 101.
30. Write an explanatory paper on a topic of your choice.

Argument and Persuasion Topics

In argument, you try to convince your readers to believe what you want them to believe. In persuasion, you try to convince them to do what you want them to do. So both argument and persuasion depend for their success on moving readers from one position to another. You should assume, in other words, that your readers begin in opposition to your own position: your job is to bring them around. To do so, you usually have to accomplish two tasks: (1) you have to refute—or at least weaken—support for their position; and (2) you have to establish support for your own position.

1. Write a letter to convince your parents that you are sincere and serious in holding a moral, political, or religious belief that differs substantially from theirs.
2. By a 6–3 vote, the U.S. Supreme Court ruled in 1985 that police officers do not have the right to shoot an alleged criminal fleeing from the scene of a crime—unless the lives of the officers or others are in danger. Write an editorial for your school newspaper—or a letter to the editor of your city newspaper—supporting or condemning the court's decision.

3. Persuade a close friend to donate blood as part of a drive that your campus organization is sponsoring.

4. Argue for or against the assertion that the abolition of the grading system at American colleges and universities would bring about an increase in learning.

5. Write a letter persuading a high school teacher (or coach) to change in some fundamental way the methods she uses to teach her class (or to coach her sport).

6. Argue for or against the proposition that sex education (or driver education, physical education, freshman composition) should be a required course in high school (or college).

7. Write a letter persuading your parents to help finance a year of study abroad (or your Christmas vacation in the Bahamas or the Riviera).

8. Argue for or against a state law that would require that all drivers wear a seat belt and that would punish violators with a small fine.

9. Write a letter persuading a friend to try something your friend has never done before: jogging, organic gardening, transcendental meditation, scuba diving, or any other activity.

10. Argue for or against legislation that would legalize prostitution (or gambling) in your home state.

11. Your parents are strongly considering a divorce, but their decision will be greatly influenced by your feelings. Write a persuasive letter to them.

12. Argue for or against the proposition that public schools should set aside time for prayer.

13. Write a letter persuading a roommate or close friend to drop out of school (or not to) or to change majors (or not to).

14. Argue for or against the proposition that the National League should follow the American League in using a designated hitter.

15. One of your best friends back home has been admitted to the school you are now attending as well as to a couple of other schools. Write a letter persuading your friend to attend (or not to attend) your school.

16. Argue for or against federal legislation that outlaws strip mining (or any other piece of legislation that relates either to energy or the environment).

17. You just talked to your kid brother on the phone. Some of his friends want him to start smoking pot with them, but he's not sure. Write him a persuasive letter.

18. Argue for or against the proposition that the United States must stay ahead of the Soviet Union in the arms race. Or choose another proposition that relates to American foreign policy.
19. You just got an unusually frank letter from your kid sister. Some of her closest friends are sleeping with their boyfriends, and she wants your advice whether to follow their example. The tone of her letter makes it clear that she will be strongly influenced by what you say. Write a persuasive letter to her.
20. Argue for or against the proposition that American presidential (or congressional) elections should be publicly financed.
21. Write a letter persuading a pregnant, unmarried friend to have (or not to have) a *legal* abortion.
22. Argue for or against the raising (or lowering) of the drinking (or driving) age in your state.
23. Write a letter persuading a high school friend to live (or not to live) in a coed dormitory during the freshman year of college.
24. Argue for or against school busing as an appropriate means of achieving racial integration.
25. Write a letter persuading your parents to allow you to attend school, instead of working, this coming summer.
26. Argue for or against legislation that permits substantial amounts of state revenue to be used by private and parochial schools.
27. Write a letter persuading the editor of a newspaper (or the director of a television news program) that there is a serious local problem that needs to be publicized.
28. Argue for or against the abolition of any rule or regulation currently operating at your school.
29. Write a letter persuading a prospective employer that you should be hired.
30. Write an argument or persuasion paper on a topic of your choice.

INDEX

Page numbers in italics refer to the major discussion of the term.